Autism and Inclusive Education

This handbook provides educators and school practitioners with a practical resource to successfully support speaking and non-speaking autistic students in K–12 school settings.

Each chapter discusses an approach founded on current research on the self-reported school priorities of autistic students, which historically have been overlooked in research and education. Incorporating the views and experiences of autistic students promotes the use of human-rights-centred pedagogies and ensures that evidence-based practices are both ethical and effective in supporting the learning and well-being success of autistic students. The informative content challenges assumptions of normative ability and highlights opportunities where evidence-based practices to support autistic students can be used alongside inclusive best practices to improve the educational experiences of all students.

This handbook's flexible and easy-to-use design can be used in its entirety or as a reference tool for school practitioners, teachers, and parents.

Chandra Lebenhagen is a lecturer at several Canadian universities, where she teaches graduate courses in inclusive education, autism, and evidence-based practices to support students with disabilities in K–12 settings. Her research focuses on ethics, critical disability, inclusive education, and evidence-based practices.

Autism and Inclusive Education

A Guide for Teachers, Practitioners, and Parents

Chandra Lebenhagen

Routledge
Taylor & Francis Group

NEW YORK AND LONDON

Designed cover image: © Getty

First published 2025
by Routledge
605 Third Avenue, New York, NY 10158

and by Routledge
4 Park Square, Milton Park, Abingdon, Oxon, OX14 4RN

Routledge is an imprint of the Taylor & Francis Group, an informa business

ISBN: 9781032687964 (hbk)
ISBN: 9781032598819 (pbk)
ISBN: 9781032687926 (ebk)

DOI: 10.4324/9781032687926

Typeset in Gill Sans
by Newgen Publishing UK

Contents

Acknowledgements

Many thanks to the participants in my original research conducted as part of my doctoral degree at the University of Calgary. Seventy-two students completed the online survey, and ten students completed an online interview. Their eagerness and honesty to share what does and does not work in education is enlightening, and their genuine appreciation for their views to be included is inspiring.

Contributors

Teachers, Practitioners and Parents

There are 15 contributors to this guide, including teachers, specialists, a coun-selor, a speech-language therapist, an occupational therapist, a physical therapist, and parents. Each of these people graciously and enthusiastically volunteered their time to share a personally meaningful experience in the form of a vignette. Some of the contributors are autistic, identify as being neurodivergent, or are a parent of an autistic child, thus offering critical insider perspectives on discussed themes. In no order, the following people agreed to be publicly acknowledged for their contributions: Shaylene Penner, Mitch Loverin, Lorraine Lower, Rachel Tipper, Katie Reed, Megan Dobchuk-Land, Elaine McGreevy, Kevin Van Es, and Sheija Abraham. While not all contributors wished to be named, all are appreci-ated for their time and commitment to improving the inclusive education experi-ences of autistic students.

Autistic Students

Most importantly, there were several autistic children and youth who, with the support of teachers, practitioners, and parents, agreed to share their views on their school experiences. These viewpoints are ethically and critically important, for we would be directionless without them. Pseudonyms have been used in all vignettes and quotes from research participants.

Chapter 1

Introduction

Who Are Autistic People?

Introductions to autism and autism-related topics usually begin by answering the question, *what is autism?* Rather than a more human-centred approach, *who are autistic people?* Words express our conscious and unconscious beliefs; and when we act on our words, we make our beliefs visible (Bargh, 2008). Relatedly, our views on autism and about autistic children are found in our language and actions (or inactions) in classrooms. Research exploring the relationship between beliefs and actions finds that a person's beliefs on the etiology or causes of autism affect parent-child bonding (Yu et al., 2020), and professional views are linked to the selection and use of certain interventions in clinical and education settings (Chen et al., 2021). When asked, autistic people also share that autism is difficult to define and describe (Wood, 2019), which should prompt all those seeking new knowledge on conceptualisations of autism always are, and always should be, evolving based on the first-hand accounts of autistic people.

Broadening and deepening discourse to include the personhood of autism does not mean that research and discussion on the neurobiology of autism are not essential—it is, especially as it is used to remove barriers and improve the

DOI: 10.4324/9781032687926-1

quality of lives of autistic people across the lifespan. However, continually hyper-focusing on the biological and behavioural characteristics of neurodivergence has led to the over-pathologising and dehumanisation of autistic people and, sub-sequently, unappreciation for their unique and often challenging lived experi-ences (Ashby & Causton-Theoharis, 2009; Cage et al., 2019). Similar to other marginalized groups who experience discrimination because of their age, race, ethnicity, and gender, disabled people have been devalued for centuries (Paterson & Hughes, 1999) and continue to do so despite increased awareness through advocacy and diversity, equity, and inclusion initiatives. For instance, as a result of Eurocentric deficit-based medical models of disability, Indigenous communities in Canada continue to be dishonoured and discriminated against, resulting in an over-diagnosis of fetal alcohol spectrum disorder in place of autism diagnoses, consequently leading to underdevelopment of early intervention and parent sup-port programs and overrepresentation in child welfare systems (Gerlach et al., 2022; Ineese-Nash, 2020; Inman, 2019; Shochet et al., 2020).

When We Know Better, We Do Better

While there have been significant improvements in research on disability-related topics and evidence-based practices to support inclusion, it has required people to hold space for uncomfortable and disruptive cycles of unlearning and re-learning. This process is based on ongoing reflection of our unconscious and con-scious biases that typically uphold outdated, ineffective, and oppressive systems. As you spend time reading about the self-reported school experiences of autistic students, understanding that there are few universal truths about autism (Murray, 2012), the simple adage—*when we know better, we do better*—may be helpful. As previously mentioned, challenging the status quo is indeed challenging. It requires recursive cycles of de-constructing and re-constructing our core beliefs and values (Simbardo & Leippe, 1991), which will undoubtedly include periods of disruption, tension, and even feelings of anxiousness, fear, and regret by some. While uncom-fortable and inconvenient, these are positive indicators of growth. To assist readers in engaging in the process of self-reflection, a section titled Notes & Reflections is included at the end of each chapter. It is an invited space for you to record your thoughts, ideas, and questions in personally relevant and meaningful ways.

Section Highlights

- Individual and collective views on disability are represented in language, policy, practice, and architecture.
- Learning about autistic people and their lived experiences through a human-centred lens helps minimise and replace deficit views of ability.
- Knowing better leads to doing better, which involves reflective inquiry and periods of unlearning and re-learning.

The Purpose of This Guide

This guide has two primary purposes. The first is to elevate the voices of speaking and non-speaking autistic students to increase awareness of their self-identified school priorities, and the second is to introduce practical inclusionary frameworks teachers, practitioners, and parents can use to help bridge the research-to-practice gap commonly found in classrooms.

A Novel Approach

The discussion of autistic students' self-reported[1] school priorities is presented alongside the perspectives of parents, teachers, and practitioners in semi-fictional vignettes. Using vignettes to elevate the voices and experiences of autistic students is unique in autism-related literature, as most centre on the perspective of researchers, educators, practitioners, and parents. Therefore, by elevating the voices of autistic people, we not only position ourselves to co-construct knowledge based on the lived experiences of actually autistic people, but we also re-position traditional authoritative stances on what works best for autistic students. Furthermore, when the discussion of evidenced-based interventions is done alongside the perspectives of key stakeholders, including parents, contextual factors affecting the implementation and sustainability of interventions can be carefully considered, enabling the ***actioning*** of research in classrooms. In education, action research is a form of investigation that focuses on problem-solving in context, where factors related to cognition, well-being, instruction, and assessment are accounted for to inform which pedagogical practice educators use (Manfra, 2019; Roberts & Webster, 2020). While thorough investigations and critical discussions of theories on inclusive education, interventions, and strategies to support autistic students are essential, if they are not considered in the context of autistic students' real-world experiences, inclusive of families, peers, curriculum, and classrooms, they are at risk of becoming rhetoric resulting in undesired outcomes, including underachievement for students, inappropriate use of resources, and frustration for those involved.

Alongside the discussion of evidenced-based interventions, principles of Universal Design for Learning are also discussed (see Chapter 3 for further explanation) and integrated into responsive frameworks introduced in each chapter; they are also applied throughout this guide to improve accessibility for readers. This means that scholarly jargon and acronyms are minimized wherever possible, headings and sub-headings follow a similar sequence, and bulleted summaries are included at the end of lengthy or detailed sections. To promote clarity and organisation, tables and frameworks use alternating shades of white and grey, evidenced-based practices are bolded, and, as previously mentioned, space is provided at the end of each chapter to record reflections, questions, and notes.

The Structure of This Guide

Following this Introduction, Chapter 2 summarises research on the self-reported school priorities of autistic students (published from 2008–2023). Chapter 3 synthesizes research on evidence-based interventions and briefly discusses their use in the context of inclusive classrooms. Chapters 4 through 8 integrate student priorities and evidenced-based interventions alongside teacher, practitioner, and parent perspectives. To help stakeholders bridge the gap between theory and action, a responsive framework is provided following each vignette and discussion of research. More specifically, the purpose of each framework is to a) provide a practical tool for educators, practitioners, and parents to enhance the inclusionary and learning success of autistic students, b) highlight the flexible implementation of evidence-based practices, c) assist stakeholders in identifying strengths and gaps in existing processes used to support autistic students, and d) draw attention to fundamental aspects of inclusive best practice that are needed to enhance the effectiveness of evidence-based practices to support autistic students. Following the presentation of autistic students' perspectives and discussion of evidence-based practices, Chapter 9 creates provocations for readers to re-consider ideas related to problem behaviour. Lastly, Chapter 10 offers provocations on the future of inclusive education for autistic students.

The Advantages of Vignettes

Vignettes are a form of storytelling that captures a specific moment of a personal experience. Since they are narrated from the perspectives of those directly involved, they prompt reflection and learning from outsiders because they a) help us consider multiple perspectives of a situation or event, b) assist in identifying relevant context factors affecting people and behaviour, and c) encourage reflection on responsive and responsible actions that consider people in context. While the primary audience of this guide is teachers, practitioners, and parents, autistic students may connect with the stories and experiences of other neurodivergent students and feel encouraged to use or modify responsive frameworks to express their views and assist them in advocating for equity in education.

A Note on the Organisation of Chapter 4 through Chapter 9

To promote organisation and predictability, Chapters 4 through 9 follow the same repetitive organisation, which includes two main sections. Section One of each chapter introduces one of five school themes identified by autistic students in research and then presents a) Vignettes, b) Research Connections,

c) A Responsive Framework, and d) Learning and Inclusionary Benefits. Each vignette describes a situation from the perspectives of a student and then either a teacher, practitioner, or parent perspective. Section Two of each chapter includes the following parts: a) Framework Template, b) Reflective Questions, c) Additional Readings and Resources[2], d) Chapter Summary, and e) Notes and Reflections. An example of the chapter outline is as follows.

SECTION ONE:

1. Student Priority #1 | Communication
2. Vignette 1: Student Voice

    a. Research Connections
    b. Responsive Framework
    c. Learning and Inclusionary Benefits

3. Vignette 2: Disclosure

    a. Research Connections
    b. Responsive Framework
    c. Learning and Inclusionary Benefits

4. Vignette 3: Augmentative and Alternative Communication
    a. Research Connections
    b. Responsive Framework
    c. Learning and Inclusionary Benefits

SECTION TWO:

1. Responsive Framework Template
2. Reflective Questions for Teachers, Practitioners, and Parents
3. Additional Reading and Resources
4. Chapter Summary
5. Notes and Reflections

Section Highlights

- The main purpose of this guide is to increase awareness of the school priorities of autistic students and to use this insider knowledge to prompt change in inclusive practice and policy.
- Examples of inclusionary frameworks are provided after each vignette to help stakeholders bridge the gap between autistic students' school priorities and evidence-based practices.

A Shared Understanding of Terms

While academic and education-related jargon is minimally used throughout this guide, a few terms are worth defining to promote understanding of discussed themes and research. Specifically, the terms autism, neurodiversity, neurodivergence, neurotypical, ableism, and identity-first language are briefly defined below.

Autism

According to medicalized definitions, Autism Spectrum Disorder is a lifelong neurological disorder caused by complex interactions between environmental and genetic factors (Lord et al., 2020). The current Diagnostic and Statistical Manual of Mental Disorders, Fifth Edition (DSM-5) specifies that people diagnosed as autistic have impairments in (a) social communication and social interaction across multiple contexts; (b) restricted, repetitive patterns of behaviour, interests, or activities; (c) symptoms must be present in early childhood but usually do not fully manifest until social demands exceed limited capacities; (d) symptoms together limit and impair everyday functioning; and (e) these limitations are not explained by an intellectual disability or global developmental delay (American Psychological Association, 2013). In addition to diagnostic characteristics, many autistic people experience co-occurring medical conditions, including gastrointestinal issues, sleep disturbances, seizures, attention deficit and hyperactivity disorder, anxiety, and depression (Bougeard et al., 2021). Estimates of the worldwide prevalence of autism are variable, with some research showing 60/10,000 children having a diagnosis of autism (Salari et al., 2022) and other research showing 100/10,000 children have a diagnosis of autism (Zeiden et al., 2022). Explanations for the disparity in worldwide estimations include variations in study design, geographical regions, country, and country income (Talantseva et al., 2023). For instance, the prevalence of autism in the United States is estimated to be 1/36 (CDC, 2023), 1/34 in the United Kingdom (O'Nions et al., 2023), 1/50 in Canada (Public Health Agency of Canada, 2023), and 1/100 in Australia (Australian Bureau of Statistics, 2018). Despite the variability, there are several explanations for the growing prevalence of autism worldwide, which include increased awareness, broader inclusion criteria, and actual increases in prevalence (Zablotsky et al., 2019). Understanding the prevalence of autism is important because this information is used to improve medical, social, and educational services to support autistic people and their families, and encourage advancement in professional and public knowledge.

Neurodiversity, Neurodivergence, and Neurotypical

In 1998 Judy Singer, a sociologist and disability activist, coined the term neurodiversity (Chapman, 2020). Neurodiversity opposes binary categories of normal and abnormal brain functioning, suggesting variation exists in all human brains

(Armstrong, 2015). Activists from the neurodiversity movement have challenged difference as deficit-type thinking and advocate for the improvement of vocabularies so that autistic people learn to understand themselves in positive ways (Chapman, 2020). Autistic self-activist Kassiane Asasumasu developed the term neurodivergent, which refers to a person's specific divergence(s) from what is traditionally considered a "typical" brain, which may include attention deficit and hyperactive disorder autism, dyspraxia, dyscalculia, dyslexia, Tourette Syndrome, autism, and others (Astle & Fletcher-Watson, 2020). Lastly, the term neurotypical refers to people whose brain functions similarly to peers in the general population. To help illustrate the difference in terms, it might be helpful to imagine that within neurodiverse groups (i.e., all colours of the rainbow), there are people with neurotypical brains (i.e., primary colours), which are the largest sub-group of neurodiversity and people with neurodivergent brains (i.e., secondary colours), which make up neuro minorities within neurodiverse groups. Therefore, a person is neurodivergent (individual), and a group, such as a classroom of children, is neurodiverse.

Ableism

Ableism is the unconscious bias towards "normal," "typical," and "standard" human abilities, which leads to the devaluation of disability (Hehir, 2002). The influences of ableism are found in medical and educational practices that seek to cure or reduce the visibility of a person's disability (Timberlake, 2020), which then perpetuates beliefs that having a disability is a tragedy or results in living a less meaningful life (Abrams & Adkins, 2022). There are many examples of ableism in education; however, like sexism and racism, they are deeply entrenched and customary, even within some of the most progressive diversity, equity, and inclusion initiatives (Timberlake, 2020). A common ableist practice found in education is policies and practices that limit participation based on a student's ability to demonstrate eligibility, such as verbal ability (Graham et al., 2020). While not an exhaustive list, below are a few additional examples of ways ableism presents in schools.

Environmental Ableism:

- Physically inaccessible school spaces and playgrounds
- Loud and crowded learning spaces.
- Restrictive seating arrangements, including desk pods that place four or more students together in one learning space.

Instructional Ableism:

- Restricting access or separating students based on the characteristics of their disability, including adaptive functioning (i.e., eating and toileting skills) and/or cognitive functioning (i.e., intelligence scores).

- Presenting class material in single modalities (i.e., in-person, verbal presentation without visual supports or lesson summaries).
- Not providing support (i.e., technology) and accommodations (i.e., extra time to complete tests) to students who demonstrate their learning in non-standard ways.
- Providing supports that are embarrassing and/or stigmatising to students (i.e., large colourful visual schedules in high school settings).

Social-Communication Ableism:

- Assuming that a minimally or non-speaking student's communication abilities are an indication of their comprehension and cognitive abilities.
- Spontaneously asking students with anxiety or communication difficulties a question in front of their classmates.
- Speaking on behalf of students without first seeking their perspective on the matter.

Identity First Language

In addition to shaping beliefs and guiding actions, language is instrumental in identity formation (St. Pierre, 2015). Autistic advocate Lydia Brown (2011) encourages neurotypical people to reflect on the connection between language and acceptance from the perspective of autistic people and refrain from using terms that make autistic people feel ashamed of their autistic identity. Autobiographical accounts of autistic students highlight the numerous implicit and explicit messages they receive through language used by others, expecting them to be more normal, which often leads to feelings of anxiousness, depression, and self-rejection (Humphrey & Lewis, 2008).

In the United Kingdom, over 500 autistic students were surveyed on their preference for using identity-first or person-first language. Most students shared that they preferred identity-first language because, to them, their autism is a positive aspect of their identity (Kenney et al., 2016).

Thus, deficit-based language that accentuates a person's differences affects not only autistic people's feelings of acceptance and belonging but also their ability to accept themselves as unbroken, valuable members of society—which is easy to understand why some parents and autistic children struggle with decisions around disclosure because of fears around stigmatisation, unequal treatment, and reduced opportunity (Cohen et al., 2022).

Chapter Summary

Before learning about the school experiences and priorities of autistic students, it is beneficial to pause and consider the impacts of ableism in education, including terminology that focuses on diagnostic deficiencies, educational programming that aims to remediate, and environments that encourage assimilation. A simple and just action to promote understanding and acceptance is to broaden inquiry from *What is autism?* to a more human-centred approach: *Who are autistic people?* This chapter also describes the purpose and structure of this guide to help readers become familiar with the organisation of content and to encourage active reflection and participation in ways that are relevant and meaningful to the individual, the context they are working in, and the outcomes they desire.

Notes & Reflections

Notes

1 All vignettes are semi-fictional accounts written by named contributors for the sole purpose of this guide.
2 Most of the listed resources are authored by neurodivergent people and are provided to promote accessible neuro-affirming learning for children, parents, and professionals.

References

Abrams, T., & Adkins, B. (2022). Tragic affirmation: Disability beyond optimism and pessimism. *The Journal of Medical Humanities, 43*(1), 117–128. https://doi.org/10.1007/s10912-020-09612-y

American Psychiatric Association. (2013). American Psychiatric Association: Diagnostic and statistical manual of mental disorders (5th ed.). Washington, DC: American Psychological Association.

Armstrong, T. (2015). The myth of the normal brain: Embracing neurodiversity. *AMA Journal of Ethics, 17*(4), 348–352.

Ashby, C., & Causton-Theoharis, J. (2009). Disqualified by the human race: A close reading of the autobiographies of individuals identified as autistic. *International Journal of Inclusive Education,13*(5), 501–516.https://doi.org/10.1080/13603110801886673

Astle, D. E., & Fletcher-Watson, S. (2020). Beyond the core-deficit hypothesis in developmental disorders. *Current Directions in Psychological Science, 29*(5), 431–437. https://doi.org/10.1177/0963721420925518

Australian Bureau of Statistics. (2018). *Disability, ageing and carers, Australia: Summary of findings*. ABS. https://www.abs.gov.au/statistics/health/disability/disability-ageing-and-carers-australia-summary-findings/latest-release.

Bargh, J. A., & Morsella, E. (2008). The unconscious mind. *Perspectives on Psychological Science: A Journal of the Association for Psychological Science, 3*(1), 73–79. https://doi.org/10.1111/j.1745-6916.2008.00064.x

Bougeard, C., Picarel-Blanchot, F., Schmid, R., Campbell, R., & Buitelaar, J. (2021). Prevalence of autism spectrum disorder and co-morbidities in children and adolescents: A systematic literature review. *Frontiers in Psychiatry, 12*, 744–709. https://doi.org/10.3389/fpsyt.2021.744709

Brown, L. (2011). The significance of semantics: Person first language: Why it matters. *Autistic Hoya*. https://www.autistichoya.com/2011/08/significance-of-semantics-person-first.html

Cage, E., Di Monaco, J., & Newell, V. (2019). Understanding, attitudes and dehumanisation towards autistic people. *Autism: The International Journal of Research and Practice, 23*(6), 1373–1383. https://doi.org/10.1177/1362361318811290

Chapman, R. (2020). *Neurodiversity Studies: A New Critical Paradigm.* In H. Rosqvist, N. Chown, & A. Stenning (Eds.; 1st ed.). Routledge.

Chen, W. J., Zhang, Z., Wang, H., Tseng, T. S., Ma, P., & Chen, L. S. (2021). Perceptions of autism spectrum disorder (ASD) etiology among parents of children with ASD. *International Journal of Environmental Research and Public Health, 18*(13), 6774. https://doi.org/10.3390/ijerph18136774

Cohen, S. R., Joseph, K., Levinson, S., Blacher, J., & Eisenhower, A. (2022). "My autism is my own": Autistic identity and intersectionality in the school context. *Autism in Adulthood*, *4*(4), 315–327.

Gerlach, A., Matthiesen, A., Moola, F., & Watts, J. (2022). Autism and autism services with Indigenous families and children in the settler-colonial context of Canada: A critical scoping review. *Canadian Journal of Disability Studies, 11*, 1–39. 10.15353/cjds.v11i2.886.

Hehir, T. (2002). Eliminating ableism in education. *Harvard Educational Review, 72(1)*, 1–32.

Higashida, N. (2016). *The reason I jump: The inner voice of a thirteen-year-old boy with autism*. Random House Trade Paperbacks.

Humphrey, N., & Lewis, S. (2008). "Make me normal": The views and experiences of pupils on the autistic spectrum in mainstream secondary schools. *Autism, 12*(1), 23–46. https://doi.org/10.1177/1362361307085267

Ineese-Nash, N. (2020). Disability as a colonial construct: The missing discourse of culture in conceptualizations of disabled Indigenous children. *Canadian Journal of Disability Studies, 9*(3), 28–51. https://doi.org/10.15353/cjds.v9i3.645

Inman, C. E. (2019). Absence and epidemic: Autism and fetal alcohol spectrum disorder in Indigenous populations in Canada. *Canadian Journal of Disability Studies, 8*(4), 227–261.

Kenny, L., Hattersley, C., Molins, B., Buckley, C., Povey, C., & Pellicano, E. (2016). Which terms should be used to describe autism? Perspectives from the UK autism community. *Autism: The International Journal of Research and Practice, 20*(4), 442–462. https://doi.org/10.1177/1362361315588200

Lord, C., Brugha, T. S., Charman, T., Cusack, J., Dumas, G., Frazier, T., & Veenstra-VanderWeele, J. (2020). Autism spectrum disorder. *Nature Reviews Disease Primers, 6*(1), 5. https://doi.org/10.1038/s41572-019-0138-4

Manfra, M. M. (2019). Action research and systematic, intentional change in teaching practice. *Review of Research in Education, 43*(1), 163–196. https://doi.org/10.3102/0091732X18821132

Murray, S. (2012). *Autism*. Routledge.

O'Nions, E., Petersen, I., Buckman, J. E. J., Charlton, R., Cooper, C., Corbett, A.... & Stott, J. (2023). Autism in England: Assessing underdiagnosis in a population-based cohort study of prospectively collected primary care data. *The Lancet Regional Health. Europe, 29*, 100626. https://doi.org/10.1016/j.lanepe.2023.100626

Paterson, K., & Hughes, B. (1999). Disability studies and phenomenology: The carnal politics of everyday life. *Disability & Society, 14*(5), 597–610.https://doi.org/10.1080/09687599925966

Pierre, J. (2015). Cripping communication: Speech, disability, and exclusion in liberal humanist and posthumanist discourse. *Communication Theory, 25*(3), 330–348. https://doi.org/10.1111/comt.12054

Public Health Agency of Canada. (2023, April). Message from the Minister of Health-World Autism Awareness Day. https://www.canada.ca/en/public-health/news/2023/03/message-from-the-minister-of-health--world-autism-awareness-day.html

Salari, N., Rasoulpoor, S., Rasoulpoor, S., Shohaimi, S., Jafarpour, S., Abdoli, N.... & Mohammadi, M. (2022). The global prevalence of autism spectrum disorder: A comprehensive systematic review and meta-analysis. *Italian Journal of Pediatrics, 48*(1), 112. https://doi.org/10.1186/s13052-022-01310-wSt.

Shochet, I. M., Orr, J. A., Kelly, R. L., Wurfl, A. M., Saggers, B. R., & Carrington, S. B. (2020). Psychosocial resources developed and trialled for Indigenous people with autism spectrum disorder and their caregivers: A systematic review and catalogue. *International Journal for Equity in Health, 19*(1), 134. https://doi.org/10.1186/s12939-020-01247-8.

Talantseva, O. I., Romanova, R. S., Shurdova, E. M., Dolgorukova, T. A., Sologub, P. S., Titova, O. S.... & Grigorenko, E. L. (2023). The global prevalence of autism spectrum disorder: A three-level meta-analysis. *Frontiers in Psychiatry, 14*, 1071181. https://doi.org/10.3389/fpsyt.2023.1071181

Timberlake, M. (2020). Recognizing ableism in educational initiatives: Reading between the lines. *Research in Education Policy and Management, 2*(1), 84–100. https://doi.org/10.46303/repam.02.01.5

Wood, R. (2019). *Inclusive education for autistic children: Helping children and young people to learn and flourish in the classroom.* Jessica Kingsley Publishers.

Yu, L. D., Stronach S., & Harrison A. J. (2020). Public knowledge and stigma of autism spectrum disorder: Comparing China with the United States. *Autism. 24*,1531–1545. https://doi.org/10.1177/1362361319900839

Zablotsky, B., Black, L. I., Maenner, M. J., Schieve, L. A., Danielson, M. L., Bitsko, R. H.... & Boyle, C. A. (2019). Prevalence and trends of developmental disabilities among children in the United States: 2009–2017. *Pediatrics, 144*(4), e20190811. https://doi.org/10.1542/peds.2019-0811

Zimbardo, P.G., & Leippe, M. R. (1991). *The psychology of change and social influence.* McGraw-Hill Book Company.

Chapter 2

The Self-Reported School Priorities of Autistic Students

CHAPTER OVERVIEW

1. A Brief History of Autism and Inclusive Policy
2. Speaking, Minimally Speaking, and Non-Speaking Autistic Students
3. School Priorities of Autistic Students: A Review of the Research
4. The 5 Cs of Meaningful Inclusion: Communication, Connection, Classroom Environment, Curriculum, and Collaboration
5. Priorities of Teachers, Practitioners, and Parents
6. Chapter Summary

A Brief History of Autism and Inclusive Policy

The path toward inclusion in education has been and continues to be challenging for most autistic students. To better appreciate historical and present-day obstacles and to encourage continued progress for fair and equitable opportunities, it is worthwhile to re-visit early conceptualisations of autism and the ensuing treatment of autistic people.

Classification and Institutionalisation

In 1911, Swiss psychiatrist Eugen Blueler (1857–1939) extended Freud's theories on infantile hallucinations and used the Greek word "autos" (meaning self) to describe the autistic child as having a "predominance of the inner life" and a "detachment from reality" (Blueler translated by Zinken, 1950, p. 64). Blueler considered autism as one of the most severe expressions of schizophrenia (Evans, 2014; Verhoeff, 2013). Either unknown or overlooked, female Russian psychiatrist Grunya Sukhareva was the first person to publish a clinical

DOI: 10.4324/9781032687926-2

description of autism in 1925, which has similarities to current diagnostic criteria outlined in the Diagnostic and Statistical Manual, 5th Edition (APA, 2013; Sher & Gibson, 2023; Zeldovich, 2018). Traditionally thought of as the father of autism, Austrian psychiatrist and pediatrician Hans Asperger (1906–1980) first coined the term autistic psychopathy (Frith, 1991), describing autistic children as lacking empathy, disinterested in friendships, hyper-focused on special interests, and clumsy (Attwood,1997). Over time, Asperger Syndrome became synonymous with high-functioning autism, a term no longer supported by the autism community because of its discriminatory beliefs that erroneously assume that autistic people of a specific cognitive, behavioural, and communicative profile do not require additional support (Alvares et al., 2020). In 1943, an Austrian-American psychiatrist and physician, Leo Kanner (1894–1981), introduced the classification of Early Infantile Autism (Verhoeff, 2013). Kanner did not support Bleuler's theories of autism as a feature of schizophrenia and instead considered autism a disorder with biological, psychological, and social origins, including abnormal maternal influence (Eisenberg & Kanner, 1956; Kotsopoulos, 2014). In 1967, Austrian-born psychologist Bruce Bettleheim (1903–1990) published an article titled Infantile Autism: The Birth of Self (Bettleheim, 1967), which includes descriptions of autistic children behaving like robots in response to cold parenting from their refrigerator mothers (Zager et al., 2012). Bettleheim's theories were an extension of Asperger and Kanner's work, and they reflected the dominant ideologies of Nazi Germany, including an intense preoccupation with assessing, sorting, and ranking children based on their abilities and economic usefulness (Davis et al., 2020; Donavan & Zucker, 2016). Up until the 1960s, autistic children were considered to have a type of mental illness and were generally considered defective and ineducable and thus were removed from their homes for institutionalised care and treatment (Davis et al., 2020; Donavan & Zucker, 2016; Evans, 2014; Lüddeckens, 2021).

Advocacy, Human Rights, and Education

During the 1960s and into the early 1970s, alongside other parents of disabled children, parents of autistic children advocated for equal access to community-based schooling so that their children could receive an education alongside their siblings and peers (Donvan & Zucker, 2016; Silverman, 2011; van IJzendoorn et al., 2020; Graham et al., 2020). However, like other calls for reform, including addressing racism and sexism in schools, inclusive policy lagged behind disability rights. For example, until the late 1970s, school administrators could refuse a disabled student placement in a mainstream classroom if it was believed that the school had insufficient resources to support the child or if the child was determined to be ineducable (Donavan & Zucker, 2016; Graham, 2020). Civil rights movements throughout the 1960s and 1970s demanded equal and fair participation in community and education for children with disabilities, and in 1960, the *Convention Against Discrimination in Education* was adopted (UNESCO, 1960). In 1975, the United Nations adopted the *Declaration on the Rights of Disabled Persons* (United Nations General Assembly, 1975) to prevent discrimination against disabled people. In 1989, the *Convention on the Rights of the Child* was approved and currently serves as an international human rights treaty that protects children's rights, including a child's rights to free and compulsory education, equal opportunity in education, including individual programming to help a child reach their fullest potential (Article 29).

In response to international human rights policy and increasing enrollment of students with disabilities, teacher-preparation programs expanded their disability-related courses (Hanushek & Raymond, 2003). However, in most instances, unless a pre-service teaching degree focused on special education, compulsory completion of disability-related courses was not required, resulting in teachers lacking the knowledge and skills to support students with disabilities in areas of programming, assessment, and classroom management (Allan et al., 2013; Ashby, 2012). The inclusive education movement continued to progress throughout the 1990s and early 2000s. In 1994, following the World Conference on Special Needs, the *Salamanca Statement and Framework for Action on Special Needs Education* (UNESCO, 1994) was developed, which meant that the educational inclusion of all students with disabilities would become a global standard. More than ten years later, in 2006, the *Convention on the Rights of the Person with a Disability* (United Nations, 2006) replaced the 1975 *Convention on the Rights of Disabled Persons* and was the first internationally developed treaty co-developed with the voices and perspectives of disabled people (Kayess, 2019). There are many critical aspects of the *Convention on the Rights of the Person with a Disability* (United Nations, 2006) that are unfamiliar to educational stakeholders, including a clear understanding of the evolving concept of disability as a result of changes in social attitudes and increased awareness of environmental factors that create barriers for persons with disabilities (Preamble No. 5). Also, for students who are non- or minimally speaking, they have a right to access multiple forms of technology to freely express their opinions and seek and receive information in timely ways that do not place additional costs on the student (Article 21). Communication technologies include tools such as Braille, large print, augmentative and alternative communication, and sign language.

To address persistent challenges observed in the implementation of articles in the *Convention on the Rights of Persons with Disabilities,* in 2016, the United Nations drafted *General Comment No. 4*, which is the first legally binding document to ensure that disabled people have the right to quality inclusive education (CRPD, GC4). *General Comment No. 4* stresses that transforming culture, policy, and practice is a precursor to the authentic and meaningful inclusion of students with disabilities. This means that opportunity and access to inclusion do not rely on the disabled person's capability to fit into existing educational structures and processes. Instead, it is the responsibility of the education system to adapt and provide equitable opportunities for meaningful inclusion based on the abilities and priorities of disabled people. This shift in perspective and responsibility meant that teacher preparation programs were expected to prepare *all* teachers to teach *all* students (Graham, 2020). However, despite additional guidance and resources from international experts, school-based definitions of inclusion and what it meant to be included varied among policymakers, teachers, practitioners, parents, and students (Göransson & Nilholm, 2014; Loreman, 2014). This discrepancy has led to inconsistent policy development and ineffective implementation of pedagogical practices to support students, including autistic students (Graham et al., 2020; Haug, 2017; Roberts & Simpson, 2016). In 2000, teachers, academics, policymakers, and politicians from 164 countries met at the World Education Forum and adopted the *Education for All framework*, encompassing six broad education goals to be achieved by 2015 (UNESCO, 2000). However, the 2015 *Global Education Monitoring Report* found that only one-third of countries achieved all *Education for All* goals set in 2000 (UNESCO, 2015). Following these results, world leaders have committed to the goals set in the newer *Education 2030 Sustainable Development Agenda* to ensure inclusive and equitable education for all students by 2030 (UNESCO, 2015).

While tracing the history of international human rights and inclusive policy in education is somewhat of an arduous endeavour, it's time well spent because it reminds us of our collective responsibility to provide fair and equitable opportunities for autistic students and to create processes that make way for equitable participation in all aspects of education. To help build clarity regarding international policy on disability and inclusion, Table 1 provides a timeline summary.

Section Highlights

* Understanding the historical views of autism and the treatment of autistic people is beneficial for the continued improvement of outdated practices.

Table 1 Summary of International Policy on Disability and Inclusion

Year	International Policy
1975	Declaration on the Rights of Disabled Persons (DRDP)
1989	Convention on the Rights of the Child (CRC)
1994	Salamanca Statement and Framework for Action on Special Needs Education
2006	Convention on the Rights of the Person with a Disability (CRPD)
2015	Education for All by 2030—SDG4
2016	General Comment No. 4 on Article 24—Right to Inclusive Education

- As a result of parent advocacy, civil rights movements, and international human rights policy, equal access to inclusive education for students with disabilities began to improve in the 1970s.
- All students with disabilities have the right to inclusive education, and schools are responsible for providing quality education and appropriate support and accommodations.

Speaking, Minimally Speaking, and Non-Speaking Autistic Students

While most autistic students speak to communicate, approximately one-third of autistic students are minimally speaking or non-speaking and rely on Augmentative and Alternative Communication methods to communicate (Jaswal et al., 2020; Tager-Flusberg & Kasari, 2013). For autistic students who speak to communicate, the success of spoken communication can be unreliable and is often impacted by sensory stimuli, social pressures, and emotional states (Sparrow, 2017; Zisk & Dalton, 2019). Speech errors are more prevalent in autistic children than non-autistic children due to reduced oral neuromuscular coordination, motor planning, and sensory-motor synchronisation (Chaware et al., 2021). Awareness of the complex integration and coordination between internal and external factors required for autistic students to produce desired messages is critically important when assessing their language and communication skills.

A possible reason to explain why autistic students experience more academic and social exclusion than any other disability group (Brede et al., 2017) is that their speaking ability is often used as a deciding factor for mainstream or specialised placement (Woodfield & Ashby, 2016). Exclusionary practices based on verbal performance are rooted in ableist biases that presume a person's speaking ability reflects their intellectual ability (Ashby & Causton-Theoharis, 2009; Humphrey & Lewis, 2008). Further complicating the neurotypical biases is when autistic students rely on the support of a communication partner to produce their messages, which is referred to as facilitated communication. Facilitated communication involves a combination of frequent and intermittent physical support from a communication partner that may include hand-over-hand, wrist, forearm, elbow, or shoulder prompting (Faure et al., 2021; Hemsley et al., 2018). While understanding and acceptance of communication partners are greater when used to support people with physical disabilities, including those with vision impairments, awareness, and acceptance of communication partners to support minimally and non-speaking autistic students in schools is less common (Denney et al., 2022; Woodfield & Ashby, 2016). For instance, some researchers defend that physical support from the communication partner precedes the pointing finger of the autistic person; therefore, spelling or typing is not independently produced by the autistic person (Hemsley et al., 2018). However, with advancements in technology, researchers challenge this position, defending that through the use of advanced eye-gaze technology, autistic participants consistently show evidence of looking at the letter before pointing to it (Jaswel et al., 2020) therefore, demonstrating independent authorship of their messages (Faure et al., 2021). Relatedly, to promote communication ability and independence, non-speaking autistic individuals and researchers are co-exploring the benefits of virtual reality communication devices where autistic people wear a transparent visor to type their messages on a holographic letter board, while at the same time being able to see their surroundings, such as their teacher and classroom environment (Krishnamurthy et al., 2022). This advanced technology promotes the development of language, communication, and motor skills in real-world environments and encourages equitable participation of non-speaking autistic people in age-appropriate curricula.

The debate on the legitimacy and autonomy of message production for those using facilitated communication began in the 1990s and continues today, although very few replication studies have been published since the original presentation of arguments against its authenticity (Heyworth et al., 2022; Jaswal et al., 2020). Not so ironically, autistic scholars and advocates call on researchers for their voices and perspectives to be included in the debate. They call on 25-year-old research to be repeated using current ethical standards and improved design, including co-production and analysis with speaking and non-speaking people (Heyworth et al., 2022).

In education, the systemic preference for spoken communication over non-speaking communication is also evident, where non-speaking autistic students are repeatedly expected to conform to ableist preferences for speaking communication (Donaldson et al., 2023), and even in doing so, are burdened with the responsibility of providing frequent evidence of authorship. Providing opportunities for speaking and non-speaking autistic students to have autonomy (Woodfield & Ashby, 2016) in their communication preferences aligns with international policy and appeals from the autistic community that access to self-preferred modes of communication is a human right.

Section Highlights

- Approximately one-third of autistic students are minimally or non-speaking.
- Intellectual ability should not be presumed based on autistic speaking ability or preference.
- Access to communication supports improves autistic students' engagement in learning and reduces feelings of frustration and anxiety.
- Access to communication support is a human right backed by international law.

School Priorities of Autistic Students: A Review of the Research

Despite significant advancements in autism-related research in the last few decades, research on the self-reported school priorities of autistic students is scarce (Horgan et al., 2022; Roberts & Simpson, 2016; Zanuttini et al., 2023). The main reason for the lack of research is because of the ableist influences that restrict the authentic participation of speaking and non-speaking autistic people, leading to inaccurate interpretations of experience and deficit-based views of autistic ability (Lebenhagen, 2020; Ollson & Niholm, 2023; Yeung et al., 2023). For instance, research designs that do not use universal design principles to support multi-modal communication restrict participant eligibility to those who speak to communicate (Lebenhagen, 2020; Zanuttini et al., 2023). Over time, these exclusionary biases have established a literature base that centres on neurotypical interpretations of autistic ability and experience (Goodall, 2018; Hummerstone & Parsons, 2021). In education, this means that most of our understanding and knowledge of autistic students' school experiences is based on outsider perspectives and the development of practices that focus on remediation rather than recognition. Additionally problematic is the limited research on the self-described experiences of autistic students mostly represents males with low support needs who speak to communicate and who reside in high-income countries (Williams et al., 2019; Zanuttini et al., 2023). Current meta-reviews on the school experiences of autistic students were conducted by Zanuttini et al. (2023) who focus on methods used to elicit autistic students' perspectives in research, and Horgan et al. (2022), who focus on synthesizing qualitative data on the experiences and perspectives of autistic students in mainstream post-primary and secondary education.

Researchers Zanuttini et al. (2023) found that 34 studies met inclusion criteria, with the majority grounded in medical models of disability, which meant they focused on the core features of autism and the efficacy of interventions to remediate autistic traits. Substantiating the pervasiveness of deficit-based views in autism-related research, Olson & Niholm (2023) found that of the 80 most cited reviews from 2001 to 2016, 98% focused on remedial aspects of teaching autistic students, and only 4% explicitly focused on factors promoting or inhibiting inclusive education for autistic students. Similar to appeals by the autistic community for improvements in research design to enable the authentic inclusion of minimally speaking and non-speaking autistic participants, researchers using a critical disability lens suggest that more quality research on the school inclusion of autistic students is needed to help bridge the research-to-practice gap to improve the practical use of evidence-based practices to support autistic students in schools (Lebenhagen, 2022; Olsson & Niholm, 2023; Robers & Simpson, 2016; Zanuttini et al., 2023).

Therefore, as you proceed to the synthesis of research on the self-reported school experiences and priorities of autistic students, it is important to recognise that limitations exist in the identified themes because a) they are based on a limited number of studies, b) the methodological design of included studies mainly focus on finding ways to reduce autistic traits as a way to improve school outcomes, and c) most data represents the experiences and perspectives of a narrowly defined demographic (i.e., male students who speak to communicate). However, despite these limitations, the benefits of available research are that it is novel and offers first-of-its-kind insider perspectives on autistic students' school experiences and priorities, which is useful for improving strength-based pedagogies in education and methodological design in future autism research.

The 5 Cs of Meaningful Inclusion: Communication, Connection, Classroom Environment, Curriculum, and Collaboration

A synthesis of three meta-analyses finds that there are five main school priorities of autistic students: 1) communication, 2) connection, 3) classroom environment, 4) curriculum, and 5) collaboration, hereafter called the 5Cs of Meaningful Inclusion. While each of the 5 Cs of Meaningful Inclusion is named and discussed separately, they are highly interconnected and interdependent, where the strength of one impacts the success of another and vice versa. A point of interest is that autistic students do not identify behaviour support as a school priority. This omission and the ensuing discussion of behaviour supports are discussed in more detail in Chapter 9, titled Re-Conceptualising Student Behaviour.

Communication

- *For me, specifically, it [typing] helps me bring my thoughts out much quicker, with ease and more organized than writing or even speaking. (Shaun)*
- *I like to think about my answer first and be able to type it out and change it if I want to. In-person or talking can be stressful sometimes if I do not know how to answer the question or what I want to say. (Frankie)*

Most autistic students report feeling misunderstood by school staff and peers, leading to feelings of frustration, anxiousness, rejection, and hurt (Hummerstone & Parsons, 2021; Lebenhagen, 2022). Breakdowns in social communication with peers are likely to increase autistic students' feelings of isolation, loneliness, and susceptibility to bullying (Humphrey & Lewis, 2008; Lebenhagen, 2022; Skafle et al., 2020). When autistic students can convey their messages predictably and clearly, they are assigned higher-quality learning goals by teachers and receive more individualised effective supports and accommodations that fit with their abilities and needs (Humphrey & Lewis, 2008). Additionally, when parents perceive strong communication between their children and school staff, their views on school inclusion are more positive (Simon et al., 2022). Fluctuating states of sensory-related regulation strongly impact autistic students' ability to communicate successfully, and students report that the unpredictability of learning environments and peer interactions creates additional stressors impacting their feelings of calmness, therefore, their ability to successfully communicate with others (Hummerstone & Parsons, 2021). In support of successful communication, autistic students appreciate when teachers establish predictable communication routines, including frequent teacher check-ins to receive feedback and additional time to ask questions after class (Humphrey & Lewis, 2008; Lebenhagen, 2022).

Connection

- *Unfortunately, other than my friends I did not really feel appreciated or respected by my other peers, though I did not feel disrespected either. This was mainly due to my lack of interaction with them due to my shy and quiet nature at the time. (Kerri)*
- *One of the other kids in that group was teasing me about my shirt. I don't like to be teased (who does). But the nice girl stepped in and told the other girl to stop it and that I looked nice. I have had more respect for her since then. (Kai)*
- *When a teacher wants me in their class, things are good, but most teachers think I am a burden. They see me as extra work. (Andrea)*

Autistic students report stronger school connections with teachers and peers when they feel welcome, understood, and accepted (Goodall, 2020; Hummerstone & Parsons, 2021; Lebenhagen, 2022; Saggers, 2015). Unfortunately, many autistic students expend significant energy trying to fit in and act normal (Humphrey & Lewis, 2008). In their attempts to feel accepted, many autistic students employ unconscious and conscious strategies to conceal aspects of their autism, commonly referred to as camouflaging or masking (Cook et al., 2021; Sedgewick et al., 2021). Similar to their neurotypical peers, autistic students desire friendships based on shared interests but often are unsure of how to initiate and maintain friendships and attribute their weirdness and awkwardness as barriers preventing the development and maintenance of friendships (Cook et al., 2022; Humphrey & Lewis, 2008; Lebenhagen, 2022). Bullying, either in-school or online, is another concern of autistic students (Carrington et al., 2017; Saggers, 2015), however, students tend only to report such incidences when they have strong relationships with teachers and school staff (Saggers, 2015). Compared to their neurotypical peers, autistic students feel more socially disconnected despite wanting friendships (Cresswell & Cage, 2019; Hebron, 2018), and a lack of school belonging increases autistic students' feelings of stress, overwhelm, anxiousness, and depression (Cook et al., 2021; Goodall, 2018; Humphrey & Lewis, 2008). However, like their non-autistic peers, autistic students feel more school connectedness and a greater sense of belonging when school staff are fun, fair, patient, flexible, understanding, and good listeners (Goodall, 2018, 2020; Hummerstone & Parsons, 2021; Roberts & Simpson; 2020; Lebenhagen, 2022; Saggers, 2015).

Classroom Environment

- *Information received. Gathering information. Loading answer.*

  There are certain spaces I avoid because they are kinda dark and secluded, making it hard or awkward to kinda chat because it feels weird. Like any dark and secluded or narrow place makes me want to leave the room or place. Another point is how the classroom is organized. I prefer a classroom with symmetry and desks all facing the same way. Classrooms with desks in random or weird orientations would distract me or make me anxious. (Alex)

- *Places people are eating. Cafeterias, public spaces around mealtimes. Many people chew with their mouths open or eat messily or talk with food in their mouths, and no matter how much I like those people, the sensory experience of being near them is very off-putting. This does not just apply at school—I have had this problem with my own family at the dinner table too. I used to leave because it was too much and then maybe not eat, but now I eat separately from them. (Charlie)*

One of the most significant factors affecting autistic students' physical and psychological well-being, therefore, school experiences, is the classroom environment (Horgan et al., 2022; Roberts & Webster, 2020; Zanuttini et al., 2023). Time and again, autistic students share that classroom environments positively or negatively affect their mood, sense of well-being, and ability to concentrate and communicate (Lebenhagen, 2022; Saggers, 2015; Woodfield & Ashby, 2016). Classrooms that are loud, unpredictable, and disorganised make it difficult for autistic students to maintain concentration and the ideal regulatory states required for learning (Goodall, 2018, 2020; Lebenhagen, 2022; Saggers et al., 2011; Woodfield & Ashby, 2016; Skafle et al., 2020). Autistic students also report that hectic schedules requiring frequent transitions between learning environments and people are stressful and tiring (Horgan et al., 2022). However, when autistic students are offered a choice in accessing a variety of learning spaces, including preferential seating and quiet spaces with fewer students, they feel less anxious and overwhelmed and are better able to meet curricular demands and successfully communicate with others (Goodall, 2018; Lebenhagen, 2022; Makin et al., 2017; Saggers et al., 2011).

Curriculum

- *I felt welcomed and trusted by teachers. For example, I was not capable of doing public presentations. Some of my teachers offered alternative ways for me to do the assignment as soon as I spoke to them about the problem. While others asked me to provide doctor's and parent's notes, which cost a lot of extra time and money. (Randy)*
- *There was one high school teacher that I can remember; he was my grade 11 and grade 12 chemistry teacher. In the middle of the semester, I was already doing poorly. I was close to failing my first quiz and midterm. He asked me to stay late after class every day and spent an hour teaching it step by step to me. He even used small chemistry experiments to show me how those chemicals react. I loved it. He even let me borrow his chemistry model set to play with at home so I could understand the concepts. (Aarav)*

Keeping up with the curriculum demands, including the pace of instruction and fear of failure as a result, are other factors autistic students report as negatively impacting their school experiences, which is a bigger problem as students advance into higher grades (Dillon et al., 2016; Horgan et al., 2022; Poon et al., 2014). Managing fast-paced lessons, increased workloads, and shorter deadlines are common stressors (Aubineau & Blicharska, 2020; Goodall, 2018; Magiati et al., 2014; Neal & Frederickson, 2016; Poon et al., 2014; Saggers et al., 2011; Saggers, 2015), and over time repeated experiences of falling short of curricular expectations increases students' feelings of exhaustion, frustration, and failure (Goodall, 2018; Lebenhagen, 2022; Saggers et al., 2011; Saggers, 2015). Autistic students report that access to technology support and fewer expectations to handwrite improves their ability to keep up with curriculum demands (Aubineau & Blicharska, 2020). Additionally, allowing students to work in groups or individually helps improve their motivation to engage in class activities and complete assignments because they can more easily navigate unpredictable sensory stimuli associated with unstructured and unpredictable environments (Lebenhagen, 2022). Autistic students report more optimism in high school because of increased opportunities to explore a diverse range of curricular topics that are personally interesting (Bond & Hebron, 2016).

Collaboration

- *A great feature many of my teachers seem to share, which I absolutely appreciate, is that they support whatever makes you succeed, regardless of how dumb it is. They are also very insistent on making sure you do your best and looking out for your mental state, whereas in other schools I've been to I've been given zero chance to succeed and often looked down on by teachers and often forced*

to pass—making me a problem for someone else to deal with. I also appreciate how accommodating they are and the lengths they would go to help you succeed or reach your goal. (Aisha)
- *School was a horrible experience. It was not until I was 18 that they discovered I was autistic. Teachers called my parents every evening to complain about my behaviour. (Taylor)*

A repeated theme throughout the literature is that autistic students generally feel misunderstood by school staff (Brede et al., 2017; Goodall, 2018, 2020; Humphrey & Lewis, 2008; Lebenhagen, 2022; Roberts & Simpson, 2016) and believe that professionals need to have a better understanding of autism and the unique factors impacting their participation and achievement in school (Roberts & Simpson, 2016; Roberts & Webster, 2020). To help bridge this gap, autistic students want more autonomy (i.e., voice and choice) in matters affecting their schooling and increased opportunities to share their ideas on what works best for them (Hummerstone & Parsons, 2021; Ollson & Niholm, 2023; Zanuttini, 2023). Relationships between autistic students and teachers are less close and more defined with conflict than teacher relationships with neurotypical students (Blacher et al., 2014). When teachers establish collaborative relationships with autistic students, student engagement and achievement improve, supports are more responsive to students' individual needs, and students feel a greater sense of school belonging and connectedness to their school community (Caplan et al., 2016; Howell et al., 2022; Losh et al., 2022; Noble & McGrath, 2012).

Section Highlights

- Research on the self-reported school priorities of autistic students is limited, mainly representing the perspectives of those who speak to communicate and who are males living in high-income countries.
- A synthesis of current research shows that autistic students' school priorities are communication, connection, classroom environment, curriculum, and collaboration, named the 5Cs of Meaningful Inclusion.

Priorities of Teachers, Practitioners, and Parents

While elevating the voices of autistic students is a critical step in improving the school experiences and outcomes for autistic students, innovation and change requires input from diverse perspectives, including those represented by teachers, practitioners, and parents. Research on the school priorities of educational partners is presented below to provide alternative insights into factors preventing and enabling the successful inclusion of autistic students.

Teacher Priorities

Primarily because of the type of training teachers receive in teacher preparation programs and professional in-servicing, identified priorities for their autistic students tend to focus on remediating atypical skill development related to cognition, communication, social interactions, challenging behaviour, emotional well-being, independence, and academic skills (Brock et al., 2020; Howell, 2022; McDougal et al., 2020). Similar to autistic students, teachers express concern with organisational processes and structures affecting student success, such as timetabling, transitions, class sizes, and availability of resources (Hummerstone & Parsons, 2021; McDougal et al., 2020). Most teachers are aware that they require additional knowledge and training to better respond to the unique needs of autistic students (Gómez-Marí et al., 2022); however, they are unsure of which sources are trustworthy and will provide practical solutions to support student anxiety sensory needs and positive behaviour (McDougal et al., 2020: Brock et al., 2020). Teachers also recognize the benefits of developing positive relationships with their autistic students, and that getting to know them on a personal level is an important first step in academic goal-setting and providing effective support (Brock et al., 2020; Hummerstone & Parsons, 2021; McDougal et al., 2020; Ravet, 2018; Villegas et al., 2022). When teachers feel that they or their autistic students are struggling, they attribute insufficient time, difficulty collecting and interpreting data, and reduced collaboration between team members as the main barriers preventing success (Brock et al., 2020; Esqueda Villegas et al., 2022).

Practitioner Priorities

In most instances, the priorities of practitioners, inclusive of school psychologists, occupational therapists, and speech-language therapists, are based on results from specialized assessments and tend to focus on cognition, communication, socialisation, and behaviour (Astle & Fletcher-Watson, 2020; Brock et al., 2020; Roberts & Simpson, 2016). School-based practitioners work as part of an integrated service delivery team and consult with teachers and parents to co-identify learning goals, assessment priorities, and effective interventions to increase autistic students' functional independence, academic achievement, and social success. Research finds up to 90% of speech-language therapists' school-based caseloads include autistic students (Benigno, 2020). However, similar to teachers, improvements in practitioner knowledge of autism and confidence in implementing evidenced-based interventions in school settings are needed as they are generally found to be minimally adequate (Paynter et al., 2018). To better prepare them for the complex realities of inclusive classrooms, practitioners feel they would benefit from more hands-on clinical experience before graduation (Harris et al., 2020; Benigno, 2020). Also, like teachers, many practitioners share that school organisation and culture and the coordination of services amongst team members are significant barriers affecting their support of autistic students (Malik et al., 2022; Paynter et al., 2018; Woodcock & Woolfson, 2019).

Parent Priorities

Parents are most concerned about their child's physical safety and social-emotional well-being at school (Ashburner et al., 2019; Roberts & Simpson, 2016; Webster et al., 2017) and are most worried about the impacts of school and cyberbullying on their child's school attendance, self-esteem, and mental health (Ashburner et al., 2019). Parents are keen to receive timely information from school staff on social and behavioural supports for their child and are interested in learning about strategies to promote skill development in these areas and to ensure positive relationships develop between their child and their teachers and peers, and so that their child's academic achievement is not negatively affected (Clark & Adams, 2020; Roberts & Simpson, 2016). Home-school communication is another priority for parents; however, parents are reluctant to ask teachers for additional times to meet because they appreciate teachers' busy schedules and daily obligations to respond to complex demands (Azad et al., 2018). As long-term advocates, parents also express feeling frustrated and burned out (Adib et al., 2019; Weitlauf et al., 2022) with the year-over-year responsibility of sharing information about their child with new teachers and often worry about teacher knowledge of autism and the availability of support (Clark & Adams, 2020).

Section Highlights

- Teacher priorities for autistic students relate to academic, communication, social, and behavioural skill development.
- Practitioner priorities for autistic students are primarily based on assessment outcomes and co-identification of learning goals with teachers and parents.
- Parent priorities for their autistic children include social-emotional and physical safety and well-being, followed by communication and behavioural skill development.

Chapter Summary

Research on the self-reported school experiences of autistic students is limited; however, available research provides important foundation information to improve stakeholder knowledge and strengthen inclusive practice. Backed by parent advocacy and international rights policy that states all students with disabilities have the right to an education in inclusive settings with reasonable access to support autistic students' school placements have advanced from institutionalisation to inclusion. Research on the self-reported school priorities of autistic students finds that autistic students are most concerned with communication, connection, classroom environments, curriculum, and collaboration, which have been named the 5Cs of Meaningful Inclusion. Although connections can be found with student-identified, the priorities of teachers, practitioners, and parents more closely align with skill development and remediation related to the diagnostic characteristics of autism, including communication skills, social skills, and behaviour skills.

Notes & Reflections

References

Adib, N. A. N., Ibrahim, M. I., Rahman, A. A., Bakar, R. S., Yahaya, N. A., Hussin, S., & Wan Mansor, W. N. A. (2019). Perceived stress among caregivers of children with autism spectrum disorder: A state-wide study. *International Journal of Environmental Research and Public Health*, *16*(8). https://doi.org/10.3390/ijerph16081468

Allday, R. A., Neilsen-Gatti, S., & Hudson, T. M. (2013). Preparation for inclusion in teacher education pre-service curricula. *Teacher Education and Special Education*. https://doi.org/10.1177/0888406413497485

Alvares, G. A., Bebbington, K., Cleary, D., Evans, K., Glasson, E. J., Maybery, M. T.... & Whitehouse, A. J. (2020). The misnomer of 'high functioning autism': Intelligence is an imprecise predictor of functional abilities at diagnosis. *Autism: The International Journal of Research and Practice*, *24*(1), 221–232. https://doi.org/10.1177/1362361319852831

American Psychiatric Association. (2013). *Diagnostic and statistical manual of mental disorders* (5th ed.). American Psychiatric.

Ashburner, J., Saggers, B., Campbell, M. A., Dillon-Wallace, J. A., Hwang, S., Carrington, S., & Bobir, N. (2019). How are students on the autism spectrum affected by bullying? Perspectives of students and parents. *Journal of Research in Special Educational Needs*, *19*(1), 27–44. https://doi.org/10.1111/1471-3802.12421

Ashby, C. (2012). Disability studies and inclusive teacher preparation: A socially just path for teacher education. *Research and Practice for Persons with Severe Disabilities*, 37(2), 89–99. https://doi.org/10.1177/154079691203700204

Ashby, C., & Causton-Theoharis, J. (2009). Disqualified by the human race: A close reading of the autobiographies of individuals identified as autistic. *International Journal of Inclusive Education,13*(5), 501–516. https://doi.org/10.1080/13603110801886673

Attwood, T. (1997). *Asperger's syndrome: A guide for parents and professionals*. Jessica Kinsley Publishers.

Aubineau, M., & Blicharska, T. (2020). High-functioning autistic students speak about their experience of inclusion in mainstream secondary schools. *School Mental Health*, *12*(3). https://doi.org/10.1007/s12310-020-09364-z

Azad, G., Wolk, C. B., & Mandell, D. S. (2018). Ideal interactions: Perspectives of parents and teachers of children with autism spectrum disorder. *School Community Journal*, *28*(2).

Benigno, J. P.; McCarthy, J. W.; Taylor, S. O.; Hamm, H.; & Gornichec W. B. (2020). Training university students about autism spectrum disorder through outreach to school-based speech-language pathologists, *Teaching and Learning in Communication Sciences & Disorders*, *4*(1). DOI: https://doi.org/10.30707/TLCSD4.1/ZNRR1070

Bettleheim, B. (1967). *The empty fortress: Infantile autism and the birth of the self*. The Free Press.

Bleuler, E. (1950). *Dementia praecox or the group of schizophrenias,* trans. Joseph Zinkin. New York: International Universities Press (pp. 63–68).

Bond, C., & Hebron, J. (2016). Developing mainstream resource provision for pupils with autism spectrum disorder: Staff perceptions and satisfaction. *European Journal of Special Needs Education*, *31*(2). https://doi.org/10.1080/08856257.2016.1141543

Brede, J., Remington, A., Kenny, L., Warren, K., & Pellicano, E. (2017). Excluded from school: Autistic students' experiences of school exclusion and subsequent re-integration into school. *Autism & Developmental Language Impairments*, 2. https://doi.org/10.1177/2396941517737511

Brock, M. E., Dynia, J. M., Dueker, S. A., & Barczak, M. A. (2020). Teacher-reported priorities and practices for students with autism: Characterizing the research-to-practice gap. *Focus on Autism and Other Developmental Disabilities, 35*(2), 67–78. https://doi.org/10.1177/1088357619881217

Carrington, S., Campbell, M., Saggers, B., Ashburner, J., Vicig, F., Dillon-Wallace, J. & Hwang, Y-S. (2017) Recommendations of school students with autism spectrum disorder and their parents in regard to bullying and cyberbullying prevention and intervention, *International Journal of Inclusive Education, 21*(10), 1045–1064. https://doi.org/10.1080/13603116.2017.1331381

Chaware, S. H., Dubey, S. G., Kakatkar, V., Jankar, A., Pustake, S., & Darekar, A. (2021). The systematic review and meta-analysis of oral sensory challenges in children and adolescents with autism spectrum disorder. *Journal of International Society of Preventive & Community Dentistry, 11*(5), 469–480. https://doi.org/10.4103/jispcd.JISPCD_135_21

Clark, M., & Adams, D. (2020). Listening to parents to understand their priorities for autism research. *PLoS ONE, 15*. https://doi.org/10.1371/journal.pone.0237376

Cook, J., Crane, L., Hull, L., Bourne, L., & Mandy, W. (2022). Self-reported camouflaging behaviours used by autistic adults during everyday social interactions. *Autism, 26*(2), 406–421. https://doi.org/10.1177/13623613211026754

Cook, J., Hull, L., Crane, L., & Mandy, W. (2021). Camouflaging in autism: A systematic review. *Clinical Psychology Review, 89*. https://doi.org/10.1016/j.cpr.2021.102080

Cresswell, L., & Cage, E. (2019). 'Who am I?': An exploratory study of the relationships between identity, acculturation and mental health in autistic adolescents. *Journal of Autism and Developmental Disorders, 49*(7). https://doi.org/10.1007/s10803-019-04016-x

Davis, J., Gillett-Swan, J., Graham, J., & Malaquias (2020). Inclusive education as a human right. In Graham, L. (Ed), *Inclusive education for the 21st century: Theory, policy and practice* (pp.79–99). Routledge.

Denney, K. E., Anderson, K. L., & Watson, J. M. (2022). Exploring the communication needs and challenges of adults with autism spectrum disorders: Communication partners' perspectives. *International Journal of Speech-Language Pathology, 24*(6), 607–615. https://doi.org/10.1080/17549507.2022.2027520

Dillon, G. V., Underwood, J. D. M., & Freemantle, L. J. (2016). Autism and the U.K. secondary school experience. *Focus on Autism and Other Developmental Disabilities, 31*(3), 221–230. https://doi.org/10.1177/1088357614539833

Donaldson, A. L., Corbin, E., Zisk, A. H., & Eddy, B. (2023). Promotion of communication access, choice, and agency for Autistic Students. *Language, speech, and hearing services in schools, 54*(1), 140–155. https://doi.org/10.1044/2022_LSHSS-22-00031

Donvan, J., & Zucker, C. (2016). *In a different key: The story of autism.* Broadway Books.

Eisenberg, L., & Kanner, L. (1956). Childhood schizophrenia: Symposium, 1955:6. Early infantile autism, 1943-1955. *The American Journal of Orthopsychiatry, 26*(3), 556–566. https://doi.org/10.1111/j.1939-0025.1956.tb06202.x

Esqueda Villegas, F., van der Steen, S., & Minnaert, A. (2022). Interactions between teachers and students with autism spectrum disorder in mainstream secondary education: Fundamental, yet under-researched. *Journal of Autism and Developmental Disorders.* https://doi.org/10.1007/s40489-022-00346-2

Evans B. (2014). The foundations of autism: The law concerning psychotic, schizophrenic, and autistic children in 1950s and 1960s Britain. *Bulletin of the History of Medicine, 88*(2), 253–285. https://doi.org/10.1353/bhm.2014.0033

Faure, P., Legou, T., & Gepner, B. (2021). Evidence of authorship on messages in Facilitated Communication: A case report using accelerometry. *Frontiers in Psychiatry, 11*, 543385. https://doi.org/10.3389/fpsyt.2020.543385

Frith, U. (1991). Autistic psychopathy in childhood. *Autism and Asperger Syndrome*, 37–92. https://doi.org/10.1017/CBO9780511526770.002

Gómez-Marí, I., Sanz-Cervera, P., & Tárraga-Mínguez, R. (2022). Teachers' attitudes toward autism spectrum disorder: A systematic review. *Education Sciences, 12*(2), 138. https://doi.org/10.3390/educsci12020138

Goodall, C. (2018). 'I felt closed in and like I couldn't breathe': A qualitative study exploring the mainstream educational experiences of autistic young people. *Autism and Developmental Language Impairments, 3.* https://doi.org/10.1177/2396941518804407

Goodall, C. (2020). Inclusion is a feeling, not a place: A qualitative study exploring autistic young people's conceptualisations of inclusion. *International Journal of Inclusive Education, 24*(12), 1285–1310. https://doi.org/10.1080/13603116.2018.1523475

Göransson, K., & Nilholm, C. (2014). Conceptual diversities and empirical shortcomings - A critical analysis of research on inclusive education. *European Journal of Special Needs Education, 29*(3). https://doi.org/10.1080/08856257.2014.933545

Graham, L. (2020). *Inclusive education for the 21st century: Theory, policy and practice.* Routledge

Hanushek, E. A., & Raymond, M. E. (2003). Improving educational quality: How best to evaluate our schools? In Y. Kodrzycki (Ed.), *Education in the 21st century: Meeting the challenges of a changing world* (pp. 193–224). Boston, MA: Federal Reserve Bank of Boston.

Harris, B., McClain, M. B., Schwartz, S., & Haverkamp, C. R. (2020). Knowledge of autism spectrum disorder among school psychology graduate students. *Contemporary School Psychology, 24*(2), 239–247. https://doi.org/10.1007/s40688-019-00266-9

Haug, P. (2017). Understanding inclusive education: Ideals and reality. *Scandinavian Journal of Disability Research, 19*(3), 206–217. https://doi.org/10.1080/15017419.2016.1224778

Hebron, J. S. (2018). School connectedness and the primary to secondary school transition for young people with autism spectrum conditions. *British Journal of Educational Psychology, 88*(3), 396–409. https://doi.org/10.1111/bjep.12190

Hemsley, B., Bryant, L., Schlosser, R. W., Shane, H. C., Lang, R., Paul, D.... & Ireland, M. (2018). Systematic review of facilitated communication 2014–2018 finds no new evidence that messages delivered using facilitated communication are authored by the person with disability. *Autism & Developmental Language Impairments, 3.* https://doi.org/10.1177/2396941518821570

Heyworth, M., Chan, T., & Lawson, W. (2022). Perspective: Presuming autistic communication competence and reframing facilitated communication. *Frontiers in Psychology, 13*, 864–991. https://doi.org/10.3389/fpsyg.2022.864991

Horgan, F., Kenny, N., & Flynn, P. (2022). A systematic review of the experiences of autistic young people enrolled in mainstream second-level (post-primary) schools. *Autism.* https://doi.org/10.1177/13623613221105089

Howell, M., Bradshaw, J., & Langdon, P. E. (2022). 'There isn't a checklist in the world that's got that on it': Special needs teachers' opinions on the assessment and teaching priorities of pupils on the autism spectrum. *Journal of Intellectual Disabilities, 26*(1), 211–226. https://doi.org/10.1177/1744629520972901

Hummerstone, H., & Parsons, S. (2021). What makes a good teacher? Comparing the perspectives of students on the autism spectrum and staff. *European Journal of Special Needs Education, 36*(4). https://doi.org/10.1080/08856257.2020.1783800

Humphrey, N., & Lewis, S. (2008). "Make me normal": The views and experiences of pupils on the autistic spectrum in mainstream secondary schools. *Autism, 12*(1), 23–46. https://doi.org/10.1177/1362361307085267

Jaswal, V. K., Wayne, A., & Golino, H. (2020). Eye-tracking reveals agency in assisted autistic communication. *Scientific Reports, 10*(1). https://doi.org/10.1038/s41 598-020-64553-9

Kayess, R. (2019). Drafting Article 24 of the Convention on the Rights of Persons with Disabilities. In G. de Beco, S. Quinlivan, & J. E. Lored (Eds.). *The right to inclusive education in international human rights law.* Cambridge: Cambridge University Press, (pp. 122–140).

Kotsopoulos, S. (2014). The parents of the child with autism. *Encephalos, 51*(1943), 23–27.

Krishnamurthy, D., Jaswal, V., Nazari, A., Shahidi, A, Subbaraman, P., & Wong, M. (2022). HoloType-CR: Cross reality communication training for minimally verbal autistic persons. *2022 IEEE International Symposium on Mixed and Augmented Reality Adjunct (ISMAR-Adjunct).* 10.1109/ISMAR-Adjunct 57072.2022.00042. 978-1-6654-5365-3. (187–190)

Lebenhagen, C. (2020). Including speaking and nonspeaking autistic voice in research. *Autism in Adulthood, 2*(2), 128–131. http://doi.org/10.1089/aut.2019.0002

Lebenhagen, C. (2022). Autistic students' views on meaningful inclusion: A Canadian perspective. *Journal of Education.* https://doi.org/10.1177/00220574221101378

Loreman, T. (2014). Measuring inclusive education outcomes in Alberta, Canada. *International Journal of Inclusive Education, 18*(5), 459–483. https://doi.org/10.1080/ 13603116.2013.788223

Lüddeckens, J. (2021). Approaches to inclusion and social participation in school for adolescents with Autism Spectrum Conditions (ASC)—a systematic research review. *Review Journal of Autism and Developmental Disorders, 8*, 37–50. https://doi.org/10.1007/ s40489-020-00209-8

Makin, C., Hill, V., & Pellicano, E. (2016). The primary-to-secondary school transition for children on the autism spectrum: A multi-informant mixed-methods study. *Autism & Developmental Language Impairments.* https://doi.org/10.1177/2396941516684834

Malik, J. H., Rehman, A. U., Qamar, R., Imtaiz, R., Muhammad, A. S., & Bari, S. (2022). Barriers in collaborative practice among SLP/Ts and special educationists working in special education settings. *Journal of Pakistan Society of Internal Medicine, 3*(1), 20–26

McDougal, E., Riby, D. M., & Hanley, M. (2020). Profiles of academic achievement and attention in children with and without autism spectrum disorder. *Research in Developmental Disabilities, 106.* https://doi.org/10.1016/j.ridd.2020.103749

Musso, M. (2021). How the letter board changed my life. *The Art of Autism: Empowering Through the Arts.* https://the-art-of-autism.com/how-the-letterboard-chan ged-my-life/

Olsson, I., & Nilholm, C. (2023) Inclusion of pupils with autism: A research overview. *European Journal of Special Needs Education, 38*(1), 126–140. https://doi:10.1080/08856 257.2022.2037823

Paynter, J., Sulek, R., Luskin-Saxby, S., Trembath, D., & Keen, D. (2018). Allied health professionals' knowledge and use of ASD intervention practices. *Journal of Autism and Developmental Disorders, 48*, 2335–2349. https://doi.org/10.1007/s10803-018-3505-1

Poon, K. K., Soon, S., Wong, M. E., Kaur, S., Khaw, J., Ng, Z., & Tan, C. S. (2014, October 3). What is school like? Perspectives of Singaporean youth with high-functioning autism spectrum disorders. *International Journal of Inclusive Education*. Routledge. https://doi.org/10.1080/13603116.2012.693401

Ravet, J. (2018). 'But how do I teach them?': Autism & Initial Teacher Education (ITE), *International Journal of Inclusive Education, 22*(7), 714–733, DOI: 10.1080/13603116.2017.1412505

Roberts, J., & Simpson, K. (2016). A review of research into stakeholder perspectives on inclusion of students with autism in mainstream schools. *International Journal of Inclusive Education, 20*(10), 1084–1096. https://doi.org/10.1080/13603116.2016.1145267

Roberts, J., & Webster, A. (2022) Including students with autism in schools: A whole school approach to improve outcomes for students with autism. *International Journal of Inclusive Education, 26*(7), 701–718. DOI: 10.1080/13603116.2020.1712622

Saggers, B. (2015). Student perceptions: Improving the educational experiences of high school students on the autism spectrum. *Improving Schools*. https://doi.org/10.1177/1365480214566213

Saggers, B., Hwang, Y. S., & Mercer, K. L. (2011). Your voice counts: Listening to the voice of high school students with autism spectrum disorder. *Australasian Journal of Special Education, 35*(2), 173–190.https://doi.org/10.1375/ajse.35.2.173

Sedgewick, F., Hull, L., & Ellis, H. (2021). *Autism and Masking: How and Why People Do It and the Impact It Can Have*. The University of Bristol.

Sher, D. A., & Gibson, J. L. (2023). Pioneering, prodigious and perspicacious: Grunya Efimovna Sukhareva's life and contribution to conceptualising autism and schizophrenia. *European Child & Adolescent Psychiatry, 32*, 475–490 (2023). https://doi.org/10.1007/s00787-021-01875-7

Silverman, C. (2011). *Understanding autism: Parents, doctors and the history of disorder*. Princeton University Press.

Simón, C., Martínez-Rico, G., McWilliam, R. A., & Cañadas, M. (2022). Attitudes toward inclusion and benefits perceived by families in schools with students with autism spectrum disorders. *Journal of Autism and Developmental Disorders*. https://doi.org/10.1007/s10803-022-05491-5

Skafle, I., Nordahl-Hansen, A., & Øien, R. A. (2020). Short report: Social perception of high school students with ASD in Norway. *Journal of Autism and Developmental Disorders, 50*(2), 670–675. https://doi.org/10.1007/s10803-019-04281-w

Sparrow, M. (2017, November 13). Coping with a crisis when you have un-reliable or intermittent speech. *Thinking Persons Guide to Autism*. http://www.thinkingautismguide.com/2017/11/coping-with-crisis-when-you-have.html

Tager-Flusberg, H., & Kasari, C. (2013). Minimally verbal school-aged children with autism spectrum disorder: The neglected end of the spectrum. *Autism Research, 6*(6), 468–478). https://doi.org/10.1002/aur.1329

United Nations. (1975). *Declaration on the rights of disabled people*. General Assembly Resolution, 3447.

UN Committee on the Rights of Persons with Disabilities. (2016). *General comment No. 4, Article 24: Right to inclusive education*, 2 September. 2016, CRPD/C/GC/4, available at: https://www.refworld.org/docid/57c977e34.html

UNESCO. (1960). *Convention Against Discrimination in Education*. Paris: UNESCO.

UNESCO. (1994). *The Salamanca Statement and Framework for Action on Special Needs Education*. Paris: UNESCO.

UNESCO. (2015). Education for All Global Monitoring Report: Inclusion and Education, All Means. Paris: UNESCO.

UN General Assembly. (1989, 20 November). *Convention on the Rights of the Child*, United Nations, Treaty Series, vol. 1577, p. 3, available at: https://www.refworld.org/docid/3ae6b38f0.html

UN General Assembly. (2006, 13 December). *Convention on the Rights of Persons with Disabilities*, A/RES/61/106, Annex I, available at: https://www.refworld.org/docid/4680cd212.html

van IJzendoorn, M. H., Bakermans-Kranenburg, M. J., Duschinsky, R., Fox, N. A., Goldman, P. S., Gunnar, M. R.... & Sonuga-Barke, E. J. S. (2020). Institutionalisation and deinstitutionalisation of children: A systematic and integrative review of evidence regarding effects on development. *The Lancet Psychiatry, 7*(8), 703–720. https://doi.org/10.1016/S2215-0366(19)30399-2

Verhoeff, B. (2013). Autism in flux: A history of the concept from Leo Kanner to DSM-5. *History of Psychiatry, 24*(4), 442–458.https://doi.org/10.1177/0957154X13500584

Webster, A., Cumming, J., & Rowland, S. (2017). Empowering parents of children with autism spectrum disorder: Critical decision-making for quality outcomes. Springer: Singapore. https:/doi.org/10.1007/978-981-10-2084-1

Weitlauf, A. S., Broderick, N., Alacia Stainbrook, J., Slaughter, J. C., Taylor, J. L., Herrington, C. G....& Warren, Z. E. (2022). A longitudinal RCT of P-ESDM with and without parental mindfulness based stress reduction: Impact on child outcomes. *Journal of Autism and Developmental Disorders, 52*(12). https://doi.org/10.1007/s10803-021-05399-6

Williams, E. I., Gleeson, K., & Jones, B. E. (2019). How pupils on the autism spectrum make sense of themselves in the context of their experiences in a mainstream school setting: A qualitative metasynthesis. *Autism, 23*(1), 8–28. https://doi.org/10.1177/1362361317723836

Woodcock, S., & Woolfson, L. M. (2019). Are leaders leading the way with inclusion? Teachers' perceptions of systemic support and barriers towards inclusion. *International Journal of Educational Research, 93*, 232–242. https://doi.org/10.1016/j.ijer.2018.11.004

Woodfield, C., & Ashby, C. (2016). "The right path of equality": Supporting high school students with autism who type to communicate. *International Journal of Inclusive Education, 20*(4), 435–454.https://doi.org/10.1080/13603116.2015.1088581

Zager, D., Wehmeyer, M., & Simpson, R. (2012). Educating students with autism spectrum disorders: Research-based principles and practices. *Intervention in School and Clinic, 50*(4), 234–237.

Zanuttini, J. Z. (2023). Capturing the perspectives of students with autism on their educational experiences: A systematic review. *International Journal of Educational Research, 117*, 102–115. https://doi.org/10.1016/j.ijer.2022.102115

Zeldovich, L. (2018). How history forgot the women who defined autism. *Spectrum: Autism Research News*. https://www.spectrumnews.org/features/deep-dive/history-forgot-woman-defined-autism/

Zisk, A. H., & Dalton, E. (2019). Augmentative and alternative communication for speaking Autistic adults: Overview and recommendations. *Autism in Adulthood: Challenges and Management, 1*(2), 93–100.https://doi.org/10.1089/aut.2018.0007

Chapter 3

Evidence-Based Practices to Support Autistic Children and Youth

---

```
┌─────────────────────────────────────────────────────────────┐
│                                                             │
│  [map icon]  CHAPTER OVERVIEW                               │
│                                                             │
│   1. Autism and Inclusion: Research on Evidence-Based       │
│      Practices                                              │
│   2. Universal Design for Learning (UDL)                    │
│   3. A Brief Note on Autism and Intelligence                │
│   4. A Synthesis of Evidence-Based Practices to Support     │
│      Autistic Students in Inclusive School Settings         │
│   5. Chapter Summary                                        │
│                                                             │
└─────────────────────────────────────────────────────────────┘
```

Autism and Inclusion: Research on Evidence-Based Practices

Educators and practitioners use specific interventions[1] to support autistic students based on scientific evidence of effectiveness, also called evidence-based practice. While the term is commonly used in education, there is debate on what qualifies as an evidence-based practice to support skill development in autistic children and youth (Vivanti & Messinger, 2021), along with insufficient research on the generalisation and maintenance of learned skills in education (Macmillan et al., 2023). These discrepancies have been attributed to the need for a universally accepted definition of evidence-based and ambiguity in what qualifies as success among children with diverse abilities alongside co-occurring conditions (Sandbank et al., 2020; Vivanti, 2022). Furthermore, educators and practitioners may need help understanding the difference between interventions that demonstrate efficacy versus interventions that demonstrate effectiveness (Vivanti, 2022). Efficacy studies measure outcomes of interventions that are used by trained clinicians who follow strict protocols in controlled environments with

DOI: 10.4324/9781032687926-3

a homogeneous group of participants, and effectiveness studies investigate if an intervention showing efficacy produces similar outcomes in "real world" settings that consider environmental, cultural, financial, and individual factors (Vivanti, 2022). In the real world of education, teachers and practitioners must account for student characteristics, curricula, availability of resources, and their own professional experience before selecting and using evidence-based interventions (Garrad et al., 2021; Sam et al., 2020; Sulek et al., 2021). A barrier to the successful implementation and evaluation of evidence-based practices in schools is that most attention is placed on *what* strategy students should use and *how* students should use the strategy and less attention on *where* (learning environment), *when* (timing), and with *whom* (social) is most optimal for autistic students. Perhaps this oversight is because of longstanding and outdated beliefs that autistic students do not value self-determination and are unaware or unaffected by the stigma associated with certain interventions in relation to their social environments.

School ecosystems are in constant motion, ebbing and flowing in response to people, activities, even physical structures and classroom design. Every classroom includes students with unique personalities, backgrounds, abilities, likes and dislikes, and teachers are continually balancing tasks from broad jurisdictional initiatives, staffing, teaching, providing individualized student support, and parent communication. The uniquely dynamic and interdependent nature of school structures, pedagogy and student factors is not easily replicated in research settings; however, they are extremely influential and must be addressed in discussions on evidence-based practices. Henceforth, there are limitations to the proceeding discussion of research on evidence-based practices, because while empirically shown to contribute to skill development in autistic students, environmental *(where)*, timing *(when)*, and relational *(who)* factors are rarely considered in research and most cases, nor are the perspectives of autistic students—the primary recipients and users of selected interventions.

The following discussion on evidence-based practices is divided into three sections. The first section presents research on evidence-based interventions to support autistic children and youth and is considered the benchmark in professional practice. The second section focuses on research specific to autistic children and youth in inclusive education settings, and the third section focuses on evidence-based practices used in education to support students with various disabilities. The purpose of presenting research in these three areas is to a) establish a common understanding of the strengths and limitations of current research on evidence-based practices; b) draw attention to the similarities and differences between evidence-based practices and in contrast to the priorities of stakeholders (i.e., autistic students, teachers, practitioners, and parents); and c) integrate this knowledge to provide a foundation for the inclusionary frameworks used in the following chapters, which consider relevant context factors informing *what, how, when, who,* and *where* evidence-based practices should be used to support the learning, well-being, and thus the successful and ethical inclusion of autistic students.

Evidence-Based Practices to Support Autistic Children and Youth

In recent years, there has been a sharp increase in publicly available resources and programs to support autistic students; however, evidence of effectiveness is scarce to non-existent (Hume et al., 2021; Paynter, 2020). Of the available data supporting the effectiveness of interventions, most result in short-term effects on narrowly defined skills and behaviours in context-bound environments (Sandbank et al., 2021). It is worthwhile to consider that the lack of empirical support does not mean that under-researched interventions are ineffective. Instead, professionals with longstanding experience and ingenuity may develop promising practices, but they must be connected to funding sources or universities that legitimize them through research (Garrad et al., 2022). Researchers Hume et al.'s (2021) study is a third-generation review from two previous reviews (see Odom et al., 2010 and Wong et al., 2015) on evidence-based interventions to support autistic children, youth, and young adults. Of the 972 articles published from 1990–2017, 28 evidence-based practices were identified as producing positive outcomes in learning, behaviour, and social-communication in autistic children and youth and are named as follows:

1. Antecedent-Based Intervention
2. Augmentative and Alternative Communication
3. Behavioural Intervention
4. Cognitive Behavioural/ Strategies
5. Differential Reinforcement
6. Direct Instruction
7. Discrete Trail Training
8. Exercise and Movement
9. Extinction
10. Functional Behaviour Assessment
11. Functional Communication Training
12. Modeling
13. Music-Mediated Intervention
14. Naturalistic Interventions
15. Parent-Implemented Intervention
16. Peer-Based Intervention
17. Prompting

18. Reinforcement
19. Response Interruption/Redirection
20. Self-Management
21. Sensory Integration
22. Social Narratives
23. Social Skills Training
24. Task Analysis
25. Technology Aided Instruction
26. Time Delay
27. Video Modeling
28. Visual Supports

Hume et al. (2021) did not include comprehensive program models in their review because of the requirement that staff be specially trained to deliver manualized procedures that require a specified number of intervention hours for program fidelity (i.e., the Early Start Denver Model or the UCLA Young Autism Project). The omission of comprehensive program models is especially relevant to teachers and practitioners because it recognizes educators' responsibility to follow district policies to teach approved curricula and how professional obligations such as these must be considered alongside specialized programming and the availability of resources to support students. Also noteworthy, of the studies published between 2012–2017, Hume et al. (2021) found that research staff were primary implementors of interventions (52% of studies), educators and service providers implemented interventions in 20% of studies, and parents in 10% of the studies. Paying attention to the limited number of studies where interventions were delivered by teachers and education-based service providers (20%) is noteworthy and should not be overlooked when considering the effectiveness and usefulness of evidence-based practices in inclusive school settings. Also, as previously mentioned, views from the autism community on the design and use of identified interventions are lacking, resulting in autistic scholars suggesting that a reporting bias exists in research, where there is little to no reporting of adverse outcomes and an over-representation of positive outcomes in some teaching methods (Dawson & Fletcher-Wattson, 2022; Turner-Brown & Sandercock, 2020; Yeung et al., 2023).

The over-representation of non-autistic views and priorities in research perpetuates ableist preferences for "normal" skill development and behaviour, which is attributed to the issue of masking or camouflaging in autistic people (Hull et al., 2019; Ne'man, 2021; Pearson & Rose, 2021). For instance, in response to an intervention, an autistic child may reduce the frequency of a behaviour occurring (i.e., hand-flapping) and therefore appears to have developed a socially appropriate skill; however, also possible is that the student learned to hide or suppress their innate desire to use the behaviour as a beneficial regulation strategy.

Over time, repeated and harmful experiences such as these can negatively affect life outcomes for autistic people, including issues with positive identity formation, anxiety, and depression (Kapp et al., 2019; Schuck et al., 2021). To help address the problematic influences of ableism in research and adverse outcomes for autistic students, autistic scholars encourage fellow researchers, teachers, practitioners, and parents to become more aware of neurotypical biases and collaborate with the members of the autistic community to co-produce knowledge and understanding before determining what does and does not work to support autistic people (Yeung et al., 2023).

Evidence-Based Practices to Support Autistic Children and Youth in Inclusive Settings

Similar to previously discussed critiques of the research on evidence-based interventions to support autistic children, research on evidence-based practices to support autistic students in inclusive school settings is scarce, with identifiable limitations. Researchers Watkins et al. (2019) conducted a first-of-its-kind meta-analysis on the characteristics of evidence-based interventions for autistic students in inclusive settings, finding 28 studies meeting empirical research standards. The identified evidence-based practices centred on social-communication skills, self-monitoring strategies, visual supports, and function-based and peer-mediated interventions. Interestingly, while there is significant similarity between the defined interventions named in both Watkins et al.'s and Hume et al.'s (2021) reviews, none of the studies in Watkins et al.'s review was named in Hume et al.'s review. As previously discussed, this discrepancy may be due to differences in researcher definitions of evidence, leading to disparities in inclusion criteria between studies. For example, the inclusion criterion found in Watkins et al.'s review, but not Hume et al.'s review, was that the practice had to occur in an inclusive school environment and social validity factors needed to be accounted for, including cost-effectiveness, time requirements, the provision of the intervention in the natural learning environment, and implementation by a person familiar to the autistic student. Watkins et al.'s review found that all 28 studies that met inclusion criteria showed clinically significant behaviour change, were deemed socially meaningful, and occurred in the student's natural learning environment. Most teachers (75%) were satisfied with the results of the intervention, and 61% of the interventions were evaluated to be time and cost-effective; however, only 43% of the interventions appeared to be delivered by a person who was familiar with the student (Watkins et al., 2019). Each intervention type identified in Watkins et al.'s (2019) review is indicated alongside the corresponding intervention named in Hume et al.'s (2021) study in Table 1, titled *Summary of Evidence-Based Practices to Support Autistic Students in Inclusion.*

Evidence-Based Practice to Support Students with Disabilities

Research on evidence-based practices to support students with and without disabilities in school has been described by authors Mitchell and Sutherland (2020) as belonging to one of the following four categories: 1) cognitive strategies, 2) behavioural strategies, 3) social strategies, and 4) mixed strategies—which include a combination of cognitive, behavioural, and social strategies. Cognitive strategies include those that support executive functioning and memory, such as mnemonics, and self-regulated learning, such as plan-act-reflect-revise strategies. Behavioural strategies include direct instruction of desired skills, behavioural assessment approaches, and school-wide positive behaviour support to promote a positive school culture. Social strategies include social skills training, peer mentorship, and social problem solving, and mixed strategies include a combination of those mentioned above and may include the use of assistive technologies to promote social communication with peers.

Educators and practitioners commonly use broadly applicable evidence-based practices in flexible ways that consider curriculum objectives, students' abilities, and classroom environments. Similar to limitations found in autism-related research, reporting biases also exist in studies on evidence-based practices to support students with a broad range of disabilities, where data on ineffective methods are under-reported or excluded, and in some cases, conflicts of interest exist between program developers and researchers (Gorard et al., 2017; Kratochichwill & Stoiber, 2000). Despite these limitations, there have been significant improvements in practices to enable the provision of more meaningful support to students with disabilities in inclusive settings, where there is less emphasis on the physical location of students and more attention on systemic reforms, mindsets, and methods as enablers of school inclusion for students with disabilities. Including research on evidence-based practices to support students who require additional support because of a learning disability, such as dyslexia or executive functioning disability such as attention deficit hyperactive disorder, is relevant to reduce the tendency to silo students and associated interventions (i.e., autistic students do not exclusively benefit from autistic interventions). Throughout various points in their development, many autistic students benefit from graduated programming and support to ensure they reach their fullest potential over time and across environments.

Response to Intervention is a pedagogical practice that uses comprehensive assessment and data collection methods to inform the use and effectiveness of evidence-based interventions (Mitchell & Sutherland, 2020). This multi-tiered approach ensures that learner strengths and areas in need of support are jointly considered; thus, programming and the provision of support do not primarily focus on perceived deficits or current limitations experienced by the student. The first tier of the Response to Intervention framework is Universal Support, where approximately 80–85% of students' learning and behavioural needs are provided for. The second tier, Specialised Support, is where approximately 15–20% of students require specialised instruction and support in a specific learning or behavioural area. The last tier, Intensive Support, is relevant to approximately 5–10% of students who require a high degree of intensive intervention from a multi-disciplinary team to ensure their physical and psychological safety and to prevent the development of more severe issues (Mitchell & Sutherland, 2020).

Section Highlights

- There are 28 identified evidence-based interventions to support autistic children and youth, most of which have been proven to be effective in inclusive school settings.
- Limitations on research on evidence-based interventions include mostly white male participants from middle-income countries attending elementary school.
- Implementation of evidence-based interventions should take into social validity factors, including environment (*where*), when (*timing*), and social factors (*who*).
- Response to Intervention using comprehensive assessment and data collection from multiple stakeholders, including students, to inform the use of specific evidence-based interventions.

Universal Design for Learning (UDL)

Included in the *Convention on the Rights of Persons with Disabilities* (United Nations, 2016) is General Comment Number 4 (GC4), which encourages education systems to implement **Universal Design for Learning** (UDL) as an evidence-based practice to promote the inclusion of students with disabilities in education (Graham, 2020). There are three guiding principles of UDL, which focus on removing barriers to promote equitable access for all students through a) multiple means of engagement, 2) multiple means of representation, and 3) multiple means of action and expression (CAST, 2018). UDL aligns with international human rights advocacy and is a practical and effective framework professionals can use to reduce barriers to inclusion for autistic students. For instance, it can be used to address feedback from autistic students who share that noisy and crowded learning environment are one of the most significant disabling factors affecting their ability to concentrate, communicate, regulate, and socialise with others (Goodall, 2018, 2020; Horgan et al., 2022; Lebenhagen, 2022; Saggers et al., 2011). Therefore, considering principles of UDL alongside evidence-based practices is a principled and effective way to address some of the limitations found in research, specifically those that do not consider the impact of school-related factors on the efficacy and usefulness of interventions in schools. **Differentiation** or differentiated instruction is another pedagogical practice where students' voice and choice (autonomy) are intentionally sought to personalise and promote meaningful engagement in learning. Response to Instruction, UDL, and differentiated instruction are complementary pedagogies that remove barriers for students and improve equity, diversity, inclusion, and accessibility in education.

Section Highlights

- Universal Design for Learning is identified in the Convention on the Rights of Persons with Disabilities (UN, 2016) as an evidence-based practice to promote diversity, equity, inclusion, and accessibility for students in education.
- Integrating UDL principles and evidence-based practices improves learning and well-being outcomes for autistic students.

A Brief Note on Autism and Intelligence

Approximately one-third of people diagnosed with autism are also identified as having a co-occurring intellectual disability (Zeidan et al., 2022). However, researchers suggest that measured intelligence in autistic children warrants further investigation due to concerns about the validity of methods used to measure neurodivergent cognition (Billeiter & Froiland, 2022; Dawson et al., 2007; Wolff et al., 2022). For example, autistic people tend to score lower in the verbal domains of Wechsler Scales and higher on the nonverbal Raven's Matrices (Mottron, 2011). Additional factors that should be considered when determining the accuracy of intelligence scores in autistic children are the assessor's level of training and experience, sub-tests that rely on socially acquired knowledge, and restrictive time spans that do not accommodate for differences in sensory integration and motor coordination (Happe et al., 2015; Wolff et al., 2022). Similar to deficit-based medical models of autism, cultural biases also exist in tools measuring intelligence, such as overlooking Indigenous knowledge and conceptualisations of neurodiversity (Ineese-Nash, 2020).

Continually investigating the validity of assessments used to measure autistic intelligence will not only help professionals presume competency in autistic students, but it will also help clarify why, in the last 50 years, the number of autistic people diagnosed with an intellectual disability has decreased from 70% to 50% to 30% (Wolff et al., 2022). More research and education are needed to increase awareness amongst professionals of the potential limitations in assessments used to measure the intelligence of autistic students, which is especially critical when assessment information is used to inform decisions on educational placements, programming, and eligibility for support and services.

Section Highlights

- Educators, practitioners, and parents should carefully interpret tests measuring autistic intelligence as researchers note limitations to their accuracy in measuring autistic intelligence.
- Intelligence scores should not be used as gatekeepers to autistic students accessing placements in inclusive education placements or the provision of specialized supports and services.

A Synthesis of Evidence-Based Practices to Support Autistic Students in Inclusive School Settings

Research on evidence-based practices was presented in three areas: 1) autistic children and youth, 2) autistic children and youth in inclusive settings, and 3) students with disabilities. Research-identified practices in each area are combined in Table 1: Summary of Evidence-Based Practices to Support Autistic Students in Inclusion to provide a comprehensive and practical reference tool for educators, practitioners, and parents. The first two columns of the table list the name and description of each of the 28 empirically supported practices promoting skill development in autistic children and youth, as identified by Hume et al. (2021). The third column indicates evidence-based interventions with similar theoretical frameworks that have resulted in positive learning outcomes for autistic students in inclusive school settings, as presented in Watkins et al.'s (2019) review. The fourth column of the table indicates evidence-based strategies used to support students with disabilities that have the same or similar theoretical underpinnings in one of the 28 identified evidence-based practices listed in column one and is based on the work of scholars Mitchell and Sutherland (2020). The fifth and final column of the table names the corresponding chapter; each evidence-based practice is defined and **actioned** using scenario-based learning using vignettes. It is worthwhile to note that some discrepancies listed between researchers on the effectiveness of evidence-based interventions do not necessarily imply disagreement; it may mean the intervention did not meet the study inclusion criteria, for example, parent-mediated interventions in inclusive school settings.

Table 1 Summary of Evidence-Based Practices to Support Autistic Students in Inclusion

Evidence-Based Practices for Autistic Children, Youth and Young Adults (Hume et al., 2021)		Interventions to Support Autistic Students in Inclusive Settings (Watkins et al., 2019)	Evidence-Based Teaching Strategies (not autism-specific) (Mitchell & Sutherland, 2020)	Chapter
1. Antecedent-Based Intervention	Prior to the presentation of a learning activity, enabling factors are pre-arranged to increase desired learner outcomes	Yes	Yes	Chapter 9
2. Augmentative and Alternative Communication	High-tech and low-tech devices to facilitate speaking and non-speaking communication (i.e., sign language, picture symbols, text-to-speech Apps)	Yes	Yes	Chapter 4 Chapter 5
3. Behavioural Momentum Intervention	Behaviour expectations are scaffolded and reinforced to promote student engagement and success	Yes	Yes	Chapter 9
4. Cognitive Behavioural/ Instructional Strategies	Direct instruction of cognitive practises that encourage skill development in learning, behaviour, and socialisation	Yes	Yes	Chapter 7 Chapter 9
5. Differential Reinforcement of Alternative, Incompatible, or Other Behaviour	The systematic provision of different types of reinforcement to increase positive behaviour and decrease undesired behaviour	Yes	Yes	Chapter 9

6.	Direct Instruction	Sequential methods that use clear and consistent feedback for error corrections to encourage skill acquisition and generalisation	Yes	Yes	Chapter 5 Chapter 7
7.	Discrete Trail Training	Repeated teaching trials using a systematic approach of instruction-response-consequence-pause	No	No	
8.	Exercise and Movement	Movement activities to promote motor skill development to improve skills and behaviour	No	Yes	Chapter 7
9.	Extinction	Removal of reinforcing consequences of undesired behaviours	No	No	
10.	Functional Behaviour Assessment	A systematic process to determine underlying functions of behaviour to determine effective supports	Yes	Yes	Chapter 9
11.	Functional Communication Training	Teaching functional communication to replace undesired behaviours that have a communicative function	Yes	Yes	Chapter 2 Chapter 9
12.	Modeling	Demonstration of a desired skill/ behaviour that leads to skill acquisition	Yes	Yes	Chapter 5 Chapter 7
13.	Music-Mediated Intervention	Activities that use songs, melodies, rhythm, and instruments to promote learning, regulation, and wellness	Yes	No	Chapter 4

(Continued)

Table 1 (Continued)

Evidence-Based Practices for Autistic Children, Youth and Young Adults (Hume et al., 2021)	Interventions to Support Autistic Students in Inclusive Settings (Watkins et al., 2019)	Evidence-Based Teaching Strategies (not autism-specific) (Mitchell & Sutherland, 2020)	Chapter
14. Naturalistic Interventions — Strategies that naturally occur in typical activities and events the student is included in	Yes	Yes	Chapter 5 Chapter 7
15. Parent-Implemented Intervention — Parent delivered interventions to teach children, social, communication, regulation, and daily living skills	No	Yes	Chapter 7
16. Peer-Based Instruction — Peers provide modeling, coaching, and feedback to autistic children within the social context to promote skill development	Yes	Yes	Chapter 5
17. Prompting — Physical, gestural, and verbal assistance and to support skill development and independence	Yes	Yes	Chapter 7 Chapter 9
18. Reinforcement — A consequence following a student response to improve the likelihood the student will use the desired skill/behaviour in the future	Yes	Yes	Chapter 7 Chapter 9
19. Response Interruption/ Redirection — A prompt or feedback used to interrupt/redirect a student from engaging in an undesired action	No	No	

20. Self-Management	Teaching students desirable and undesirable behaviours and strategies to monitor/reward their own behaviours	Yes	Yes	Chapter 7
21. Sensory Integration	Interventions and activities that teach/support a student's ability to integrate sensory information from their body and environment in personally meaningful ways	No	Yes	Chapter 6
22. Social Narratives	Interventions and activities that explicitly describe social situations to emphasize relevant details and to provide examples of appropriate/desired responses	Yes	Yes	Chapter 5
23. Social Skills Training	Interventions and activities that clearly describe social behaviours in context to teach interpretation and desired responding	Yes	Yes	Chapter 5
24. Task Analysis	A systematic process of breaking down a macro skill into small parts to allow for the assessment and teaching of micro skills leading to macro skill acquisition	Yes	Yes	Chapter 7
25. Technology Aided Instruction	Instruction and interventions where various technologies are used to support skill development and independence	Yes	Yes	Chapter 7

(Continued)

Table 1 (Continued)

Evidence-Based Practices for Autistic Children, Youth and Young Adults (Hume et al., 2021)	Interventions to Support Autistic Students in Inclusive Settings (Watkins et al., 2019)	Evidence-Based Teaching Strategies (not autism-specific) (Mitchell & Sutherland, 2020)	Chapter
26. Time Delay — A systematic process of fading prompts used between the teacher instruction and student response, to promote independence	No	No	
27. Video Modeling — A video demonstration of desired skills/behaviour using observational learning	Yes	No	Chapter 5 Chapter 7
28. Visual Supports — The use of visuals (i.e., photographs, line drawings, symbols, words) to assist with learning, communication, organisation, independence, etc.	Yes	Yes	Chapter 7

Chapter Summary

This chapter comprehensively synthesises empirically reviewed evidence-based strategies to support autistic children and youth. The purpose of presenting research on evidence-based practices to support autistic students and students with other disabilities is to draw attention to similarities and differences and encourage stakeholders to consider their usefulness in the context of inclusive education, the 5Cs of Meaningful Inclusion: Communication, Connection, Classroom Environment, Curriculum, and Collaboration.

To address some of the barriers related to implementing evidence-based practices in inclusive classrooms, it may be worthwhile for educators and practitioners to seek ways to incorporate Response to Intervention frameworks and principles of Universal Design for Learning and differentiated instruction alongside evidenced-based practices. A table synthesising research on evidence-based practices is provided as a practical and simple tool for stakeholders to reference and serves as the foundation for inclusionary frameworks discussed in the following chapters that account for contextual factors affecting the effectiveness of evidence-based strategies to support autistic students in inclusive school settings.

Notes & Reflections

Note

1 Evidence-based interventions, evidence-based strategies, and evidence-based practices are interchangeably used throughout the guide depending on context.

References

Billeiter, K. B., & Froiland, J. M. (2022). Diversity of intelligence is the norm within the autism spectrum: Full scale intelligence scores among children with ASD. *Child Psychiatry and Human Development.* https://doi.org/10.1007/s10578-021-01300-9

Centre for Applied Special Technology. (2018). Universal design for learning guidelines, Version 2.2. http://udlguidelines.cast.org.

Dawson, M., & Fletcher-Eatson, S. (2022). When autism researchers disregard harms: A commentary. *Autism, 26,* 564–566. https://doi.org/10.1177/13623613211031403

Dawson, M., Soulières, I., Gernsbacher, M. A., & Mottron, L. (2007). The level and nature of autistic intelligence. *Psychological Science, 18*(8), 657–662. https://doi.org/10.1111/j.1467-9280.2007.01954.x

Garrad, T., Vicek, S., & Page, A. (2022). The importance of the promotion of evidence-based practice as a reasonable adjustment in mainstream education settings for students with autism spectrum disorder. *Australasian Journal of Special and Inclusive Education, 46*(1), 1010–112. https://doi.org/10.1017/jsi.2022.5

Goodall, C. (2018). 'I felt closed in and like I couldn't breathe': A qualitative study exploring the mainstream educational experiences of autistic young people. *Autism and Developmental Language Impairments, 3.* https://doi.org/10.1177/2396941518804407

Goodall, C. (2020). Inclusion is a feeling, not a place: A qualitative study exploring autistic young people's conceptualisations of inclusion. *International Journal of Inclusive Education, 24*(12), 1285–1310. https://doi.org/10.1080/13603116.2018.1523475

Gorard, S., See, B. H. & Siddiqui, N. (2017). *The Trials of Evidence-Based Education.* Routledge.

Graham, L. (2020). *Inclusive education for the 21st century: Theory, policy and practice.* Routledge.

Happe, F. (2015). Autism as a neurodevelopmental disorder of mind-reading. *Journal of the British Academy, 3.* 10.5871/jba/003.197.

Horgan, F., Kenny, N., & Flynn, P. (2022). A systematic review of the experiences of autistic young people enrolled in mainstream second-level (post-primary) schools. *Autism,* https://doi.org. 10.1177/13623613221105089

Hull, L., Mandy, W., Lai, M. C., Baron-Cohen, S., Allison, C., Smith, P., & Petrides, K. V. (2019). Development and validation of the camouflaging autistic traits questionnaire (CAT-Q). *Journal of Autism and Developmental Disorders, 49*(3), 819–833. https://doi.org/10.1007/s10803-018-3792-6

Hume, K., Steinbrenner, J. R., Odom, S. L., Morin, K. L., Nowell, S. W., Tomaszewski, B.... & Savage, M. N. (2021). Evidence-based practices for children, youth, and young adults with autism: Third generation review. *Journal of Autism and Developmental Disorders, 51*(11), 4013–4032. https://doi.org/10.1007/s10803-020-04844-2

Ineese-Nash, N. (2020). Disability as a colonial construct: The missing discourse of culture in conceptualizations of disabled Indigenous children. *Canadian Journal of Disability Studies, 9*(3), 28–51. https://doi.org/10.15353/cjds.v9i3.645

Kapp, S. K., Steward, R., Crane, L., Elliott, D., Elphick, C., Pellicano, E., & Russell, G. (2019). 'People should be allowed to do what they like': Autistic adults' views and experiences of stimming. *Autism, 23*(7), 1782–1792.

Kratochwill, T. R., & Stoiber, K. C. (2000). Empirically supported interventions and school psychology: Conceptual and practical issues: Part II. *School Psychology, Quarterly, 15*(2).

Lai, M., Anagnostou, E., Wiznitzer, M., Allison, C., & Baron-Cohen, S. (2020). Evidence-based support for autistic people across the lifespan: Maximising potential, minimising barriers, and optimizing the person–environment fit. *Lancet Neurology, 19*, 434–451. https://doi.org/10.1016/S1474-4422(20)30034-X

Lebenhagen, C. (2022). Autistic students' views on meaningful inclusion: A Canadian perspective. *Journal of Education.* https://doi.org/10.1177/00220574221101378

Lebenhagen, C. Krishnamurthy, A., Ramanath, J. & Choate, C. (2022). *Speechless dream: Narratives on autism, inclusion and hope.* Friesen Press.

Macmillan, C., Pecora, L., Ridgway, K., Hooley, M., Thomson, M., Dymond, S.... & Stokes, M. (2021). An evaluation of education-based interventions for students with autism spectrum disorders without intellectual disability: A systematic review. *Review Journal of Autism and Developmental Disorders, 10.* https://doi.org/10.1007/s40489-021-00289-0

Mitchell, D., & Sutherland, D. (2020). *What really works in special and inclusive education: Using evidence-based teaching strategies* (3rd ed.). Routledge.

Mottron L. (2011). Changing perceptions: The power of autism. *Nature, 479*(7371), 33–35. https://doi.org/10.1038/479033a

Ne'eman, A. (2021). When disability is defined by behavior, outcome measures should not promote "passing". *AMA Journal of Ethics, 23*(7), 569–575 .

Paynter, J., Luskin-Saxby, S., Keen, D., Fordyce, K., Frost, G., Immus, C., et al. (2020). Brief report: Perceived evidence and use of autism intervention strategies in early intervention providers. *Journal of Autism and Developmental Disorders, 50*(10), 1088–1094. https://doi.org/10.1007/s1080 3-019-04332-2

Pearson, A. & Rose, A. K. (2021). Conceptual analysis of autistic masking: Understanding the narrative of stigma and the illusion of choice. *Autism in Adulthood*, 52–60.http://doi.org/10.1089/aut.2020.0043

Sam, A. M., Cox, A. W., Savage, M. N., Waters, V., & Odom, S. L. (2020). Disseminating information on evidence-based practices for children and youth with autism spectrum disorder: AFIRM. *Journal of Autism and Developmental Disorders, 50*(6), 1931–1940. https://doi.org/10.1007/s10803-019-03945-x

Sandbank, M., Bottema-Beutel, K., Crowley, S., Cassidy, M., Dunham, K., Feldman, J. I.... & Woynaroski, T. G. (2020). Project AIM: Autism intervention meta-analysis for studies of young children. *Psychological Bulletin, 146*(1), 1–29. https://doi.org/10.1037/bul0000215

Schuck, R. K., Tagavi, D. M., Baiden, K. M., Dwyer, P., Williams, Z. J., Osuna, A.... & Vernon, T. W. (2021). Neurodiversity and autism intervention: Reconciling perspectives through a naturalistic developmental behavioral intervention framework. *Journal of Autism and Developmental Disorders*, 1–21. https://doi.org/10.1007/s10803-021-05316-x

Sulek, R., Trembath, D., Paynter, J., & Keen, D. (2019). Factors influencing the selection and use of strategies to support students with autism in the classroom. *International Journal of Disability, Development and Education* (68), 1–17. https://doi.org/10.1080/1034912X.2019.1695755

Tomlinson, C.A. (2017). *How to differentiate instruction in academically diverse classrooms* (3rd ed.). Alexandria, VA: Association for the Supervision and Curriculum Development

Turner-Brown, L., & Sandercock, R. (2020). Criteria to evaluate evidence in interventions for children with autism. In G. Vivanti, K. Bottema-Beutel, & L. Turner-Brown (Eds.), *Clinical guide to early interventions for children with autism* (pp. 25–39). Springer Nature. https://doi.org/10.1007/978-3-030-41160-2

UN Committee on the Rights of Persons with Disabilities. (2016, 2 September). *General comment No. 4. Article 24: Right to inclusive education*, CRPD/C/GC/4. https://www.refworld.org/docid/57c977e34.html

Vivanti G. (2022). What does it mean for an autism intervention to be evidence-based? *Autism Research: Official Journal of the International Society for Autism Research, 15*(10), 1787–1793. https://doi.org/10.1002/aur.2792

Vivanti, G., & Messinger, D. S. (2021). Theories of autism and autism treatment from the DSM III through the present and beyond: Impact on research and practice. *Journal of Autism and Developmental Disorders, 51*(12), 4309–4320. https://doi.org/10.1007/s10803-021-04887-z

Watkins, L., Ledbetter-Cho, K., O'Reilly, M., Barnard-Brak, L., & Garcia-Grau, P. (2019). Interventions for students with autism in inclusive settings: A best-evidence synthesis and meta-analysis. *Psychological Bulletin, 145*(5), 490–507. https://doi.org/10.1037/bul0000190

Wolff, N., Stroth, S., Kamp-Becker, I., Roepke, S., & Roessner, V. (2022). Autism spectrum disorder and IQ: A complex interplay. *Frontiers in Psychiatry, 13*, 856084. https://doi.org/10.3389/fpsyt.2022.856084

Wong, C., Odom, S. L., Hume, K. A., Cox, A. W., Fettig, A., Kucharczyk, S., Brock, M.... & Schultz, T. R. (2015). Evidence-based practices for children, youth, and young adults with autism spectrum disorder: A comprehensive review. *Journal of Autism and Developmental Disorders, 45*(7), 1951–1966. https://doi.org/10.1007/s10803-014-2351-z

Yeung, S. K., Warrington, K., Ramji, A., Elsherif, M., & Kapp, S., Azevedo, F.... & Shaw, J. (2023). *Bridging open scholarship with higher education and postgraduate training in autism: A primer and guide.* https://doi.org/10.31234/osf.io/duv42

Zeidan, J., Fombonne, E., Scorah, J., Ibrahim, A., Durkin, M. S., Saxena, S., Yusuf, A.... & Elsabbagh, M. (2022). Global prevalence of autism: A systematic review update. *Autism Research: Official Journal of the International Society for Autism Research, 15*(5), 778–790. https://doi.org/10.1002/aur.2696

Chapter 4

Communication

CHAPTER OVERVIEW

SECTION ONE

1. The 5Cs of Meaningful Inclusion | *Communication*
2. Vignette 1: Student Voice
3. Vignette 2: Disclosure
4. Vignette 3: Augmentative and Alternative Communication (AAC)

SECTION TWO

5. Inclusionary Framework to Support Communication and Voice
6. Reflective Questions for Teachers, Practitioners, and Parents
7. Additional Readings and Resources
8. Chapter Summary

DOI: 10.4324/9781032687926-4

SECTION ONE

The 5Cs of Inclusion | *Communication*

Review of the Research	• Autistic students often feel misunderstood by staff and peers. • Communication breakdowns with peers increase autistic students' feelings of isolation, loneliness, and bullying. • Access to predictable yet flexible communication methods improves student engagement and promotes feelings of acceptance and belonging. • Autistic students' communication and social success are impacted by learning environments, sensory processing, and motor functioning.

A central diagnostic feature of autism is the atypical development of social-communication skills, including non-verbal and reciprocal communication skills, responsiveness to spoken language or gestures, repetitive speech, and echolalia (American Psychiatric Association, 2013). Unfortunately for many autistic students, atypical social-communication is falsely associated with intelligence, resulting in misconceptions of ability resulting in fewer educational opportunities alongside same-aged peers (Woodfield & Ashby, 2016). Clinicians, including speech and occupational therapists, are important members of school teams that assist educators and parents with interpreting clinical data to inform learning, language, and communication goals and support. While receptive and expressive language difficulties do coincide with intellectual disabilities, autistic students with language delays may be unfairly disadvantaged, even on non-verbal measures, and therefore are at risk of having their cognitive abilities underestimated (Faerman et al., 2023). For instance, two factors found to affect speech and language development in autistic children are motor functioning and sensory processing (Prizant, 1996). Research finds that underdeveloped fine motor skills in toddlers strongly predict long-term language delays in autistic children, suggesting a relationship exists between motor and language development (Chenausky et al., 2019; Bal et al., 2020).

Echolalia is when children echo or repeat words they hear and is a typical stage in a child's development of speech (Schuler, 1979); however, autistic children engage in echolalia more than any sub-group, with some estimates suggesting up to 75% of younger autistic children are echolalic (van Santen et al., 2013). One explanation for this higher prevalence is that some autistic children learn language in larger chunks rather than single words, referred to as gestalt language processing (Prizant,1983). For example, when a teacher asks an autistic student if they would like to go to the gym, the student may respond with, "go to gym" rather than "yes, I'd like to go to the gym." While echolalia may appear meaningless, in most instances, it is purposeful and should be viewed as a positive adaptive response and indicator of future language development (Paltra & De Jesus, 2023).

Childhood apraxia of speech is considered by the American Speech-Language-Hearing Association (2007) as a neurological condition where the accuracy and consistency of speech movements are affected without the presence of neuromuscular impairments. Many autistic students using alternative communication devices report their usefulness. They have difficulties moving messages from their brain to their mouth because their muscles don't move predictably to make speech sounds (Higashida, 2016; Lebenhagen, 2022; Sparrow, 2017). Childhood apraxia of speech is prevalent in approximately one-third of younger autistic children (Ming et al., 2007) and more so in minimally and non-speaking school-aged children (Chenausky et al., 2019; Tager-Flusberg & Kasari, 2013). Examining the shared neurology between autism and childhood apraxia speech is still in its infancy, but future developments will continue to assist educators, practitioners, and parents in tailoring interventions to the individual abilities of autistic children (Conti et al., 2020).

Since music also follows rhythmic gestalt patterns, **Music Mediated Instruction** is a practical, fun, and inclusive approach to improving speech production in autistic students with limited spoken language (Lim, 2009; MacDonald-Prégent et al., 2023). Interactive music instruction includes sequences of structured learning that encourage students to participate in joint attention, imitation, and rhythmic activities (Benarous et al., 2021). In addition to improving speech, music-mediated instruction enhances attention, memory, mood, and behaviour in autistic children (Shi et al., 2016). Therefore, collaborative programming between music teachers, speech-language therapists, occupational therapists, and physical therapists is beneficial for language and communication development in autistic students but can also be used as a fun and meaningful learning opportunity for all students.

Sensory processing, specifically the ability to process auditory and visual stimuli, has also been found to impact language development in autistic children (Åkerlund, 2021). Autistic students' ability to attend to verbal and non-verbal communication is influenced by either under- or over-responsiveness to auditory and visual stimuli (Mallory & Keehn, 2021). For instance, in classrooms with constant background noise, clutter, and artificial lighting, autistic students report feeling distracted, which affects their ability to concentrate and communicate (Abineau & Blicharska, (2022); Hummerstone & Parsons, 2021). Repeated incidences of distractibility and poor concentration reduce the quantity and quality of communicative interactions available to autistic students, leading to fewer opportunities for autistic students to develop and practice language and social-communication skills in their natural social environments.

Minimally speaking and non-speaking autistic students benefit from **Augmentative and Alternative Communication (AAC)**, which can be unaided (i.e., no equipment) or aided (i.e., with equipment). Augmentative refers to strategies to supplement students' existing communication abilities, and their combined purpose is to help promote clarity (i.e., gestures and verbal speech), whereas alternative refers to tools used in place of verbal communication, which may include letter boards, picture symbols, and text-to-speech software. Communication success is not only affected by sensory aspects of students' learning environments but also by the frequency and predictability of exposure to such sensory stimuli and, consequently, feelings of physical discomfort and anxiety (Hummerstone & Parsons, 2021; Lebenhagen, 2022; Roberts & Simpson, 2016). While autistic students appreciate having access to flexible communication supports and predictable learning environments, some approaches make students feel more disabled when used rigidly or in ways that accentuate their differences, which interestingly is a view supported by autistic adults (Howard et al., 2021). For example, in a busy classroom, a speaking student may prefer to use typed communication over verbal face-to-face communication because typing provides additional time to process information and formulate responses without the added pressure of processing auditory and visual stimuli (Benford & Standen, 2011; Howard et al., 2021; Lebenhagen, 2022; Sequenzia & Grace, 2015). For autistic students who experience social anxiety, opportunities to interact with peers online reduce stress and stigma often associated with communication errors or breakdowns and help autistic students feel like they are viewed as equals by their teachers and peers (Scott-Berrett et al., 2019).

Research on educational approaches and technologies to improve the communication skills and experiences of autistic students is mixed due to the heterogeneity of autistic students' skills, knowledge of professionals, and consistent use, emphasising the need to avoid one-size-fits-all methods (Klefbeck, 2023). Multi-modal approaches that combine low-tech (i.e., picture symbols) and high-tech (i.e., speech-generating) are most effective because they support students' communication in personalised ways as they flex with the learning tasks, social preferences, and classroom environments (Ganz, 2015).

While strengthening and supporting autistic students' development and use of language and communication skills in school is a main priority, successful communication relies on more than student factors; it should be viewed as a shared responsibility that also depends on the skills of the listener. If listeners prioritise spoken communication over non-spoken communication, they are implying the relative importance of the person and their message and, therefore, risk overlooking genuine and insightful communication from minimally and non-speaking autistic students (Barber, 2008; Keen, 2005). The framework used in this chapter is meant to highlight ways educators, practitioners, parents, and autistic students can co-develop a shared understanding of the communication skills and preferences of autistic students.

Section Highlights

- Up to one-third of autistic people are minimally or non-speaking and, therefore rely on Augmentative and Alternative Communication support.
- Autistic students' language and communication abilities should not be associated with intelligence nor preclude them from accessing inclusive education with same-aged peers.
- Successful communication relies on the attitudes and abilities of both the speaker and the listener.
- Music Mediated Instruction is a fun, practical, and inclusive evidenced-based intervention to support skill development in language and communication.

Vignette 1: Student Voice

Teacher

Alex follows the classroom routines and participates in most activities. She has made so much progress this year; however, writing times are still the most difficult for her. We complete writing activities at least once a day, and I have talked with the students about how writing is another great way to communicate our ideas. I have tried a few different approaches, but I am still unsure how to help her with her frustration. For example, I have scheduled writing activities at different parts of the day, we also have a jar of fun pens in the class that any student can use during this time. Alex enjoys choosing a pen that has four different colours to write with. I have also provided Alex with opportunities to work in different quiet spots in the class. For the students who require it, I try to make her writing tasks shorter, provide sentence starters and writing checklists. Today during a journal writing activity, I suggested Alex write about dinosaurs as this was something she said that she liked. I asked Alex to join me at my table so I could help her alongside a few other students. As soon as we sat down to write, I gave Alex her favourite pen and wrote a sentence starter, "I like dinosaurs because..." Alex picked up her page, tore it in half and began to scream. She then hid under a table at the back of the room. I asked her to come out from under the table to talk, and she ran right out of the classroom. Later when she was able to return to the class, I tried to talk to her about the strategies that we were using and to get some more of her feedback. Report cards are coming up, and I am just trying to make sure I have enough writing samples to accurately assess what she can do.

Student

I don't like writing. I have a hard time putting the words I want to say on the paper. I try to tell my teacher, but then I get really frustrated sometimes. Once I get to this point, it is hard to get calm. I know that if I move away and take some time alone, I can usually come back to my class or group. I know my teacher tries to help. I like to be given a choice like using voice text, drawing, working with a friend, or even making a fun presentation on the computer that lets me show what I know. These choices take the pressure off of writing—I like the fancy pen, but sometimes my hand just won't move the way I want it to and then I can't remember the words I wanted to write. I feel so much calmer and can share my ideas when I don't have to write. At the beginning of the year, my teacher asked us all what our favourite things to learn and write about were. Back then, I said Dinosaurs and Space, but not no more—she thinks these are still my favourites. If she asked me this question again, I would tell her that video games are my favourite. My friend Laura likes video games too. When we work together, we share our ideas, and then she writes down what I say. After, I help draw the pictures in comic style.

Research Connections

In the classroom, many representations of student voice exist beyond speaking voice. Student voice includes spoken and unspoken messages and can be "listened to" through sound and action as they shift towards or away from people, spaces, and activities. For instance, Alex shares her preferences for communicating her ideas through augmentative voice-to-text software and drawing and resists or moves away from activities requiring written forms of expression. Recognising student voice outside spoken words challenges ableist norms on legitimate representations of student voice and conveys to students that alternative and augmentative forms of communication are equally valued as speaking. By encouraging students to use alternative and augmentative peaking and non-speaking methods, teachers and practitioners put into practice the principles of **Universal Design for Learning** (UDL) that have real-world benefits —including encouraging students to use multiple means of engagement, representation, expression, and action. To accommodate motor, sensory, and social factors, teachers and practitioners must seek ways to adapt their assessment methods and procedures so that autistic students more confidently and reliably can demonstrate their knowledge. In a practical sense, this may mean providing students with additional time to process information and including students' preferences on which school spaces enable them to listen, concentrate, process, and respond to information.

Combining UDL principles with evidence-based practices to support communication strengthens inclusionary practices and reduces ableist expectations that autistic students must conform to traditional methods and measures of communication competence. The psycho-social benefits of combining these approaches include fostering skill development and identity, agency, independence, confidence, and peer connections (Cooper, 2023; Rosa & Mountain, 2013). Autistic students who feel they have a voice and choice in their learning are more motivated to attend school and show increased engagement and achievement (Lebenhagen, 2022; Saggers et al., 2011; Saggers, 2015). Incorporating pedagogical practices encouraging speaking and non-speaking participation not only benefits autistic students but also benefits teachers as they deepen their understanding of student interests and abilities and become more confident in implementing support (Saggers, 2015; Woodfield & Ashby, 2016). For younger students, activities that encourage student voice outside of verbal language include I like/don't like activities like sorting photos and objects, and for older students, closed-ended questionnaires requiring yes/no responses and photo-journalism activities where students take photos of preferred and non-preferred school spaces, people, and activities (Rauvali & Riga, 2021). The learning and psycho-social benefits of including student voice and choice are not specific to autistic students; hence, the application of the following framework is helpful for a wide range of students and can be used as a class-wide or independent activity to promote individual understanding and classroom cultures of understanding and respect staff and students.

Section Highlights

- Legitimate forms of student communication include speaking and non-speaking forms, including words, gestures, interests, and actions.
- Combining Universal Design for Learning principles with evidence-based practices to support speaking and non-speaking communication encourages student voice and choice in learning.

Responsive Framework

💬 **Communication Preferences**	
Student Name: Alex **Grade:** Five	**Team Members:** Alex, Teacher
Identifies/Assessed as: ☑ Speaking ☐ Minimally-Speaking ☐ Non-Speaking	
Initial Date: February	**Review Dates:** March, April, May, and June

Preferred Methods	Preferred Space
☐ Gestures	☑ In-Person
☐ Body Language	☐ Online/Virtual
☐ Objects	☑ During School
☐ Emailing	☐ After School
☐ Texting	☑ Classroom
☑ Drawing/Art	☐ Hallway
☐ Voice Messages	☐ Library
☑ Text-to-Speech	☐ Hallway
☑ Speaking	☐ Office
☐ Online Chat	☐ Other:
☐ Assistive Device:	
Preferred People	**Preferred Time**
☑ Peers: Laura	☐ Daily Check-Ins
☑ Adults: Teacher	☐ Weekly Check-Ins
	☑ Monthly Check-Ins
	The teacher and Sarah will meet after school at 3:45 pm in the classroom on the 1st of each month.

Additional Information:
In place of writing, Alex will express her thoughts, ideas, and knowledge using text-to-speech on her laptop or drawing her responses. Each month we will meet to review the different methods Sarah has chosen to make sure they are working for her and to allow the teacher to provide feedback in relation to learning goals. During these meetings, Alex can share any updates on her passions and interests and any new peers she may want to work with.

Learning and Inclusionary Benefits

The learning and inclusionary benefits of using the Student Communication framework are:

- Alex and her teacher work together to co-develop a shared understanding of Alex's communication preferences.
- Alex has predictable opportunities to share her learning interests with her teacher and provide feedback on which communication methods and learning accommodations are the most effective for her as she progresses throughout the school year.
- Alex and the teacher develop an increased awareness of factors affecting Alex's communication success (methods, people, space, and time); therefore,

they are better positioned to identify strengths, future goals, and responsive support.

- When Alex has voice and choice (autonomy) in which communication methods (i.e., speech-to-text and drawing) best support her learner strengths, she will be better able to demonstrate her knowledge accurately and consistently, resulting in more accurate assessments of her knowledge and abilities.

Vignette 2: Disclosure

Therapist

My client Henry is a 14-year-old transgender male in grade 8. Henry is an excellent artist and has won awards for his artwork at school, he also enjoys playing online games with his peers and taking his dog for a walk. Henry came to family therapy with his mother and engages in the process when asked to do so. Upon initial observation, I notice that Henry is uncomfortable looking me in the eye when I am speaking with him and gains confidence in expressing himself when his mother is not present during the session. The presenting concerns that Henry and his mother brought up in our initial session consisted of issues within family dynamics, friendship and peer pressure concerns, parental separation concerns, and Henry's medical history and diagnoses. Henry has been through a lot in his 14 years and often weeps when he speaks about problems in our therapy sessions. Henry's mother is quick to place blame on Henry for the problems that are present in his life, and Henry often responds with emotional outbursts or shutting down. As part of my conceptualisation and intervention planning with this family, I focus on the interpersonal patterns between Henry and his mother in our work together. In our third session together, Henry gains enough courage to speak up and ask for time to meet with me alone. Reluctantly, Henry's mother agrees and leaves the room. During this time Henry discloses to me that he believes he might be autistic and explains that he is identifying with a lot he is learning about autism and being autistic online. Upon further exploration, I learn that Henry feels he does not understand social cues from his peers, which causes frustration and friendship issues. He explains that this often leads him to getting into situations he shouldn't be in because he feels he doesn't understand that people are trying to take advantage of him. Henry also explains that the noise in his classroom causes him physical pain, and he is only able to focus on what his teacher is talking about if he can move or work on his art during class. Henry's main reason for bringing this up with me is because he would like to have support in bringing up his wondering to his mother. I agree to support Henry with this, and we invite his mother back into the room. Henry's mother is quick to dismiss Henry's wondering about his identity and Henry becomes very emotional over the matter. I spend the rest of the session attempting to validate Henry and normalise neurodiversity with his mother.

Student

I agreed to come to family therapy with my mother because I thought she might give me a chance to talk and hear me out. During the first three sessions my mother spent most of her time blaming me for all the problems in my life. I don't have great friendships with kids in my school, but I find friendships hard to understand, and a lot of the kids I go to school with don't have the same interests as me. I really like spending time with my best friend Claire because we work on our art projects together. My mother tells my therapist that I should be making more friends and Claire is a bad influence on me. The one thing I like about this new therapist is she asks for my perspective on things, and when I do get upset, she just gives me space to collect my thoughts. One time she even asked my mom to wait until I was finished talking when my mom interrupted me (no one has ever stood up to my mom before). I have spent a lot of time on social media following people who I game with online, and a lot of them talk about being autistic. What they say really makes sense, and I think I might also be autistic. I really want my therapist to understand my experience and my feelings, but I can't tell her with my mom in the room. I know my mom won't like what I have to say and will probably get angry with me for bringing it up. I feel like such a burden to my mom with all my medical issues and my change in gender identity. In one session with our therapist, I got angry and asked if I could talk to our therapist alone. Surprisingly, my therapist agreed that this would be a good idea, and my mom left the room. When I told my therapist my idea about being autistic, she made me feel safe and told me she would help me tell my mom. Even though my mom acted as I expected she would, I felt so relieved to tell someone and feel understood. My therapist even told me she was proud of me for how brave I was to bring this up.

Research Connections

Research suggests that up to two-thirds of autistic students believe an autism diagnosis negatively affects their school experiences (Bottema-Beutel et al., 2020). This helps to explain why many autistic students struggle with disclosing their autism diagnosis, which tends to depend on personal preferences and sensitivities around social understanding and acceptance (Frost et al., 2019). Adding to the dilemma is that autistic students and their parents are uncertain if sharing an autism diagnosis with school team members will boost access to additional support or restrict educational opportunities (Aubineau & Blicharska, 2020). Others diagnosed as autistic may not identify as such and prefer to distance themselves from the label and the autism community, while others with reduced access to community health resources providing diagnostic assessments may not be formally diagnosed but identify as autistic.

Regardless of diagnosis or identification, both scenarios influence the formation of students' identities and views on acceptance, belonging, and inclusion (Woodfield & Ashby, 2016). Identity formation predominately develops during adolescence and is impacted by school life, peer connections, and a deep desire to fit in (Poon et al., 2014). Especially during adolescence and young adulthood, autistic individuals may attempt to mask or camouflage some of their autistic traits to conceal parts of themselves that they believe are unusual or result in negative feedback from others (Hull et al., 2021). Mental health support from trained psychologists helps autistic children and youth explore mindsets and social experiences where they internalise expectations to be less of themselves, which over the long term assists in reducing adverse mental health outcomes, including anxiety, depression, and thoughts of self-harm (Cassidy et al., 2018; Lai et al., 2017; Raymaker et al., 2020). Strategies autistic people use to conceal aspects of their autism differ according to gender, developmental stages, and situations (Hull et al., 2017). However, common signs of masking include mirroring facial expressions and body language, rehearsing scripts, rejecting supports, and difficulty refraining from autistic stims during unfamiliar social activities (Cook et al., 2021; Bargiela et al., 2016; Mesa & Hamilton, 2022). Some research suggests that female students mask more frequently than males (Wood-Downie et al., 2021) to appear more socially competent and to avoid ostracisation and bullying (Tierney et al., 2016). However, over time, autistic students report that the cognitive demands associated with masking are extremely fatiguing and that it eventually becomes too difficult and stressful to maintain an idealised version of themselves (Tierney et al., 2016).

Further complicating the problem of masking is unlike individuals with more visible disabilities, autistic students experience multiple instances across the lifespan where they weigh the advantages and disadvantages of disclosing their autism. For instance, when they change grades or schools, join extra-curricular activities or start a new job. Recognising the countless social pressures autistic students face to hide or turn off parts of their autism is imperative as stakeholders seek to understand factors impacting autistic students' behaviour and psychological states of well-being as well as for those responsible for ensuring schools are welcoming and safe spaces for autistic students to be their authentic selves. Research shows there are more positive life outcomes for autistic people the earlier they learn about their autism (Oredipe et al., 2022) and can develop support systems and strategies that promote self-acceptance and acceptance by others.

Section Highlights

- Disclosing an autism diagnosis is difficult for many parents and students because of fears of stigmatisation and reduced access to educational opportunities.
- In an attempt to avoid ostracisation and to feel accepted by others, many autistic students mask their autism, which over the long term leads to adverse mental health outcomes.

Responsive Framework

💬 Communication Preferences	
Student Name: Henry **Grade:** Eight	**Team Members:** Henry, Mom and Therapist
Identifies/Assessed as: ☑ Speaking ☐ Minimally-Speaking ☐ Non-Speaking	
Initial Date: April 17	**Review Dates:** Weekly
Preferred Methods	**Preferred Space**
☐ Gestures ☐ Body Language ☐ Objects ☐ Emailing ☐ Texting ☑ Drawing/Art ☐ Voice Messages ☐ Text-to-Speech ☑ Speaking ☑ Online Chat ☐ Assistive Device:	☑ In-Person ☑ Online/Virtual ☐ During School ☑ After School ☐ Classroom ☐ Hallway ☐ Library ☐ Hallway ☐ Office ☐ Other: Therapist's office
Preferred People	**Preferred Time**
☑ Peers: Claire ☑ Adults: Mom and therapist	☐ Daily Check-Ins ☑ Weekly Check-Ins Thursday's at 4:00 pm ☐ Monthly Check-Ins

Additional Information:
Henry, mom, and their therapist will continue to explore an autism diagnosis and the advantages and disadvantages of disclosure in the school setting. Together we will explore ways Henry can expand their social circle with people who have similar interests and preferences for connecting socially.

Learning and Inclusionary Benefits

The learning and inclusionary benefits of using the Student Communication framework are:

- A safe and predictable time and space (i.e., therapist's office on Thursdays at 4:00 p.m.) is available for Henry to discuss sensitive topics related to identity, disclosure, and friendships.
- Based on a shared understanding of Henry's social-communication preferences and desire for connection, a clearly defined social goal (i.e., to make new friends) is established that respects Henry's communication preferences (i.e., online) and interests (i.e., art).
- Descriptions of various communication methods, people, space, and time are made visible to Henry, which may prompt future discussion on ways to expand their communication toolkit and confidence in a variety of learning and social settings.

Vignette 3: Augmentative and Alternative Communication (AAC)

Parent

Our journey to support Marc's communication at home and school has been long and honestly, frustrating. But we know that Marc has struggled much more than we have. We started with picture symbols when he was little, and that was helpful for a while, especially when we used them to support routines like getting ready for bed. But after a few years we knew he needed something more than picture symbols, in a way limited his communication because they didn't always represent what he wanted to say, which was frustrating for him and us because then we ended up guessing, which seemed to escalate things even more. And to be honest, I think they are impractical in some ways, like in some situations, and he never liked to use them outside of home. At the beginning of grade 6, we had a new speech and occupational therapist team who introduced us to the idea of teaching Marc to type. At first, we tried an iPad, thinking that it was something he could carry with him, but he did better on an adapted keyboard with fewer and larger buttons, which now he uses a regular laptop. Sometimes, when I think back, I feel quite guilty that we didn't try typing sooner, I don't think we even realised how articulate Marc could be and how much of his environment (and our discussions on what we thought would work best for him) he was taking in and remembering. We have absolutely entered a whole new world, and in some ways we are still getting to know Marc because we now have access to his own ideas and interests and he can explain why and when he prefers some things and not others. The school is amazed at some of Marc's responses to group discussions, and it works well that we get the questions beforehand to help Marc prepare his response at home. It really is exciting to see the progress and Marc's confidence improve, and we are so happy that the school is so supportive. They have welcomed the support of our home therapists to show staff how to support Marc using his laptop and brainstorm ways to use typing at school to participate in discussions and assignments. For the most part, he still needs someone to sit beside him to help with attention and to break down parts of questions into smaller bits. Right now, we are working on developing a template so that Marc can type his responses and messages into defined areas on a document, which will help prevent frustration with formatting and the curser jumping around if he accidentally hits the wrong key, which has been a bit of an issue causing frustration for Marc.

Child

I don't know what I would do without my laptop. Finally, I am able to share with others what's in my mind. I felt depressed sometimes, not having a reliable way to talk to others and feeling understood 99% of the time. You end up just sitting there listening to people try to solve you like you are some great mystery. What's worse is that they think because I can't speak or when I stim and rock and hum, that I can't hear them talk, or I am not learning, or that I don't have thoughts and feelings. It's such a relief knowing that my teachers and Mr. B, the ed assistant, know how smart I am—well at least they are beginning to! It makes it so much easier to get out of bed and go to school. I know I am not easy, and I still need help getting my fingers to comply with my brain. Soon I hope to type more by myself and then join some online groups with other people like me. It's nice being with people who just get your struggles.

Research Connections

Very little research has been conducted on autistic students' use of augmentative and assistive communication technologies in inclusive classrooms because most research prioritises the views of students who speak to communicate (Fayette & Bond, 2017; Woodfield & Ashby, 2016). Combining this limitation with the scarcity of research on evidence-based communication tools to support autistic students in inclusive school settings has resulted in additional challenges for autistic students, teachers, and practitioners.

Potentially due to the limited, unreliable, or impractical use of technology-related tools, non-speaking students experience more exclusion from academically challenging lessons and age-appropriate social activities than students who speak to communicate (Courchesne et al., 2015; Kliewer & Biklen, 2006). However, teachers who receive adequate training and support are more likely to incorporate assistive technologies into their lessons and assessment practices, and report more confidence in their ability to modify learning objectives to accommodate students using speech-generating devices (Alsolami, 2022; Fernández-Batanero, 2022; Woodfield & Ashby, 2016). Issues related to communication technologies and school inclusion for minimally and non-speaking autistic students increase throughout the grades, where training for an array of staff and providing consistent support for students is challenging to coordinate and maintain (Light & McNaughton, 2012; Woodfield & Ashby, 2016). Even when a student's primary mode of communication is verbal speech, the opportunity to use non-speaking methods in times of fatigue or anxiousness is often overlooked because of educational biases, perceptions of convenience, and even interpreting student behaviour as avoidant or controlling (Donaldson et al., 2023).

Providing autistic students access to multimodal communication in various learning contexts reduces participation barriers and one-sided expectations that students conform to dominant speaking modes of communication (Ellsworth, 1997). Even more ideal is when autistic students have the option to self-select communication methods that are responsive to their regulation needs, the learning activity, and social context, which also means they are encouraged to exercise autonomy in decision-making and develop confidence in their ability to come up with responsive solutions to personal difficulties and changing circumstances (Woodfield & Ashby, 2016). Letter boards, word boards, picture symbols, texting, email, text-to-speech software, and online chats are readily available in most schools, with the benefit of being cost-effective and socially unobtrusive.

Providing students with various communication tools not only acknowledges the heterogeneity of autistic abilities and preferences, but also acts as an enabler in developing healthy relationships between autistic students and their teachers (Roberts & Simpson, 2016). The downstream effect of successful communication and connection with teachers is that when autistic students feel understood, they are more motivated to engage in learning and social activities (Goodall, 2018; Hummerstone & Parsons, 2021; Saggers, 2015).

Feeling connected to education assistants is also important as they frequently are the primary support people who assist autistic students with the logistic and functional aspects of augmentative and alternative technologies, including programming, maintenance, and availability across learning environments. The unique role of communication partners, including teachers and education assistants, is that, based on their connection with students, they are in an advantageous position to continually draw on a continuum of strategies that simultaneously provide support while encouraging student independence, which, over time, ensures that autistic students are ideally positioned to self-represent their voice and choice in a variety of contexts.

Section Highlights

- More research is needed to better understand the effectiveness and practical use of Augmentative and Alternative Communication tools in inclusive K–12 classrooms.
- When autistic students have voice and choice in their communication methods, they generally prefer access to various non-stigmatising tools that flex to the learning task and their social environment.

Responsive Framework

Communication Preferences	
Student Name: Marc **Grade:** Six	**Team Members:** Marc, teacher, parents, SLT
Identifies/Assessed as: ☐ Speaking ☐ Minimally-Speaking ☑ Non-Speaking	
Initial Date: November 1	**Review Dates:** Monthly

Preferred Methods	Preferred Space
☐ Gestures	☑ In-Person
☐ Body Language	☑ Online/Virtual
☐ Objects	☑ During School
☑ Emailing	☑ After School
☐ Texting	☐ Classroom
☐ Drawing/Art	☐ Hallway
☐ Voice Messages	☐ Library
☑ Text-to-Speech	☐ Hallway
☐ Speaking	☐ Office
☑ Online Chat	☐ Other:
☑ Assistive Device: Personal Laptop	
Preferred People	**Preferred Time**
☐ Peers:	☑ Daily Check-Ins
☑ Adults: Mom, teacher, Mr. B and SLT	☐ Weekly Check-Ins Day & Time:
	☐ Monthly Check-Ins

Additional Information:
Mr. B will check-in with Marc each day to determine what subject areas Marc will use his laptop (text-to-speech) to share his answers in class and will let the teachers know ahead of time if Marc is going to share his responses with the whole class or email them to the teacher. The school team will receive monthly updates from home and the SLT to ensure consistent practices and support are being offered to Marc as he continues to become a more independent typer. Mr. B is going to work with Marc in creating an after-school club where students meet online.

Learning and Inclusionary Benefihts

The anticipated learning and inclusionary benefits of using the Student Communication are:

- The school team collaborates with the home team to learn more about how assisted and augmentative communication (i.e., laptop and text-to-speech software) can support Marc's communication independence and participation in learning.
- Consistent expectations and support implementation are determined alongside Marc's perspective and priorities.
- Marc's self-esteem and confidence as a learner improved.
- The perspective of the school community, including staff and peers, shifts to view Marc as "smart" and capable.

- Opportunities to provide Marc with social activities (i.e., online after-school club) are re-examined using a strength-based lens that seeks to remove participation barriers that uphold meaningful participation relies on verbal communication.

SECTION TWO

Inclusionary Framework to Support Communication and Voice

💬 Communication Preferences	
Student Name: **Grade:**	**Team Members:**
Identifies/Assessed as: ☐ Speaking ☐ Minimally-Speaking ☐ Non-Speaking	
Initial Date:	**Review Dates:**
Preferred Methods	**Preferred Space**
☐ Gestures ☐ Body Language ☐ Objects ☐ Emailing ☐ Texting ☐ Drawing/Art ☐ Voice Messages ☐ Text-to-Speech ☐ Speaking ☐ Online Chat ☐ Assistive Device:	☐ In-Person ☐ Online/Virtual ☐ During School ☐ After School ☐ Classroom ☐ Hallway ☐ Library ☐ Hallway ☐ Office ☐ Other:
Preferred People	**Preferred Time**
☐ Peers ☐ Adults	☐ Daily Check-Ins ☐ Weekly Check-Ins ☐ Monthly Check-Ins
Additional Information:	

Reflective Questions for Teachers, Practitioners, and Parents

1. What opportunities do you provide to autistic students that encourage communication outside spoken words?
2. What strategies do you use during class discussions to prevent classmates from speaking "over" autistic students?
3. When an autistic student shows interest in responding to a question or sharing information but is unsuccessful, what is your responsive strategy?
4. How do you provide positive and constructive feedback to students who are non-speaking?
5. To help autistic students prepare to share their knowledge in class, do you provide learning material or discussion questions in advance?
6. How are autistic students involved in decision-making about communication goals and supports?
7. In what ways are the voices of speaking, minimally-speaking, and non-speaking students included in school-wide activities and initiatives?

Additional Readings and Resources

1. Heyworth, M. (2021). *Just right for you: A story about autism*. Reframing Autism Ltd.
2. Sparrow, M. *Unstrange mind: Autistic author, artist, advocate, and speaker*. https://unstrangemind.com
3. Crane, L., Lui, L. M., Davies, J., & Pellicano, E. (2021). Autistic parents' views and experiences of talking about autism with their autistic children. *Autism*. https://doi.org/10.1177/1362361320981317

Chapter Summary

Providing multiple opportunities to include autistic students' speaking and non-speaking voices in matters that affect them is an important considerations stakeholders must take to promote equity, inclusion, and accessibility in education. The benefit of including the unique views, interests, and priorities of autistic students is that it signals to students that they are recognised and valued as their authentic selves and that they do not have to conceal parts of their identity to belong or be granted equal and fair access to high-quality learning. Additionally, by regularly including student perspectives, stakeholders are better positioned to collect real-time information and assessment data that is contextually relevant and personally meaningful to autistic students. Evidence-based interventions to support autistic students' communication, learning, and well-being include Augmentative and Alternative Communication methods and Music-Mediated Instruction.

Notes & Reflections

References

Åkerlund, S., Håkansson, A., & Claesdotter-Knutsson, E. (2021). An auditory processing advantage enables communication in less complex social settings: Signs of an extreme female brain in children and adolescents being assessed for autism spectrum disorders. *Frontiers in Psychology, 13.* https://doi.org/10.3389/fpsyg.2022.1068001

Alsolami, A. S. (2022). Teachers of special education and assistive technology: Teachers' perceptions of knowledge, competencies and professional development. *SAGE Open, 12*(1). https://doi.org/10.1177/21582440221079900

American Psychiatric Association. (2013). *Diagnostic and statistical manual of mental disorders: DSM-5.* American Psychiatric Publishing.

Aubineau, M., & Blicharska, T. (2020). High-functioning autistic students speak about their experience of inclusion in mainstream secondary schools. *School Mental Health, 12*(3). https://doi.org/10.1007/s12310-020-09364-z

Bal, V. H., Fok, M., Lord, C., Smith, I. M., Mirenda, P., Szatmari, P., Vaillancourt, T.,... & Zaidman-Zait, A. (2020). Predictors of longer-term development of expressive language in two independent longitudinal cohorts of language-delayed preschoolers with autism spectrum disorder. *Journal of Child Psychology and Psychiatry, 61*(7), 826–835. https://doi.org/10.1111/jcpp.13117

Barber, M. (2008). Using intensive interaction to add to the palette of interactive possibilities in teacher–pupil communication. *European Journal of Special Needs Education, 23*(4), 393–402. https://doi.org/10.1080/08856250802387380

Bargiela, S., Steward, R., & Mandy, W. (2016). The experiences of late-diagnosed women with autism spectrum conditions: An investigation of the female autism phenotype. *Journal of Autism and Developmental Disorders, 46*(10), 3281–3294. doi: 10.1007/s10803-016-2872-8.

Benarous, X., Vonthron, F., & Cohen, D. (2021). Music therapy for children with autistic spectrum disorder and/or other neurodevelopmental disorders: A systematic review. *Frontiers in Psychiatry, 12,* 643234. https://doi.org/10.3389/fpsyt.2021.643234

Benford, P., & Standen, P. J. (2011). The use of email-facilitated interviewing with higher functioning autistic people participating in a grounded theory study. *International Journal of Social Research Methodology, 14,* 353–368. Doi: 10.1080/13645579.2010.534654.

Bottema-Beutel, K., Cuda, J., Kim, S. Y., Crowley, S., & Scanlon, D. (2020). High school experiences and support recommendations of autistic youth. *Journal of Autism and Developmental Disorders, 50*(9), 3397–3412. https://doi.org/10.1007/s10803-019-04261-0

Cassidy, S., Bradley, L., Shaw, R., & Baron-Cohen, S. (2018). Risk markers for suicidality in autistic adults. *Molecular Autism.* https://doi.org/10.1186/s13229-018-0226-4

Chenausky, K., Brignell, A., Morgan, A., & Tager-Flusberg, H. (2019). Motor speech impairment predicts expressive language in minimally verbal, but not low verbal, individuals with autism spectrum disorder. *Autism & Developmental Language Impairments.* https://doi.org/10.1177/2396941519856333

Cook, J., Hull, L., Crane, L., & Mandy, W. (2021). Camouflaging in autism: A systematic review. *Clinical Psychology Review, 89,* 102080. https://doi.org/10.1016/j.cpr.2021.102080

Cooper, K., Russell, A. J., Lei, J., & Smith, L. G. (2023). The impact of a positive autism identity and autistic community solidarity on social anxiety and mental health in autistic young people. *Autism: The International Journal of Research and Practice, 27*(3), 848–857. https://doi.org/10.1177/13623613221118351

Courchesne, V., Meilleur, A. A., Poulin-Lord, M. P., Dawson, M., & Soulières, I. (2015). Autistic children at risk of being underestimated: School-based pilot study of a strength-informed assessment. *Molecular Autism, 6,* 12. https://doi.org/10.1186/s13 229-015-0006-3

Donaldson, A. L., Corbin, E., Zisk, A. H., & Eddy, B. (2023). Promotion of communication access, choice, and agency for autistic students. *Language, Speech, and Hearing Services in Schools, 54*(1), 140–155. https://doi.org/10.1044/2022_LSHSS-22-00031

Ellsworth, E. (1997). *Teaching positions: Difference, pedagogy, and the power of address.* Teachers College Press, NY.

Faerman, A., Sakallah, A., Skiba, S., Kansara, S., Kopald, B. E., Lewine, J. D., & Demopoulos, C. (2023). Language abilities are associated with both verbal and nonverbal intelligence in children on the autism spectrum. *Developmental Neuropsychology, 48*(5), 248–257. https://doi.org/10.1080/87565641.2023.2225663

Fayette, R., & Bond, C. (2017). A systematic literature review of qualitative research methods for eliciting the views of young people with ASD about their educational experiences. *European Journal of Special Needs Education, 33*. https://doi.org/17. 10.1080/ 08856257.2017.1314111

Fernández-Batanero, J. M., Montenegro-Rueda, M., Fernández-Cerero, J., & Inmaculada, G. M. (2022). Assistive technology for the inclusion of students with disabilities: a systematic review. *Educational Technology Research & Development, 70,* 1911–1930. https://doi. org/10.1007/s11423-022-10127-7

Ganz, J. B. (2015). AAC interventions for individuals with autism spectrum disorders: State of the science and future research directions. *Augmentative and Alternative Communication, 31*(3), 203–214. https://doi.org/10.3109/07434618.2015.1047532

Goodall, C. (2018). 'I felt closed in and like I couldn't breathe': A qualitative study exploring the mainstream educational experiences of autistic young people. *Autism & Developmental Language Impairments, 3.* https://doi.org/10.1177/2396941518804407

Howard, P. L., & Sedgewick, F. (2021). 'Anything but the phone!': Communication mode preferences in the autism community. *Autism.* https://doi.org/10.1177/1362361321 1014995

Hull, L., Levy, L., Lai, M. C., Petrides, K. V., Baron-Cohen, S., Allison, C.... & Mandy, W. (2021). Is social camouflaging associated with anxiety and depression in autistic adults?. *Molecular Autism, 12*(1), 13. https://doi.org/10.1186/s13229-021-00421-1

Hummerstone, H., & Parsons, S. (2021). What makes a good teacher? Comparing the perspectives of students on the autism spectrum and staff. *European Journal of Special Needs Education, 36*(4). https://doi.org/10.1080/08856257.2020.1783800

Keen, D., Sigafoos, J., & Woodyatt, G. (2005). Teacher responses to the communicative attempts of children with autism. *Journal of Developmental and Physical Disabilities, 17*(1), 19–33. https://doi.org/10.1007/s10882-005- 2198-5

Klefbeck, K. (2023). Educational approaches to improve communication skills of learners with autism spectrum disorder and comorbid intellectual disability: An integrative systematic review. *Scandinavian Journal of Educational Research, 67*(1), 51–68. https://doi. org/10.1080/00313831.2021.1983862

Kliewer, C., Biklen, D., & Kasa-Hendrickson, C. (2006). Who may be literate? Disability and resistance to the cultural denial of competence. *American Educational Research Journal, 43*(2), 163–192. https://doi.org/10.3102/00028312043002163

Lai, C., Lombardo, M. V., Chakrabarti, B., Ruigrok, A. N., Bullmore, E. T., Suckling, J., Auyeung, B., Happé, F., Szatmari, P...., & Baron-Cohen, S. (2018). Neural self-representation in autistic women and association with 'compensatory camouflaging.' *Autism.* https://doi.org/10.1177/1362361318807159

Lebenhagen, C. (2022). Autistic students' views on meaningful inclusion: A Canadian perspective. *Journal of Education.* https://doi.org/10.1177_00220574221101378

Light, J., & McNaughton, D. (2012). The changing face of augmentative and alternative communication: Past, present, and future challenges. *Augmentative and Alternative Communication, 28*(4), 197–204. https://doi.org/10.3109/07434618.2012.737024

Lim, H. A. (2009). Use of music to improve speech production in children with autism spectrum disorders: Theoretical orientation, *Music Therapy Perspectives, 27*(20), 103–114. https://doi.org/10.1093/mtp/27.2.103

Lindsay, S., Proulx, M., Thomson, N., & Scott, H. (2013). Educators' challenges of including children with autism spectrum disorder in mainstream classrooms. *International Journal of Disability Development and Education, 60,* 347–362. https://doi.org/10.1080/1034912X.2013.846470

MacDonald-Prégent, A., Saiyed, F., Hyde, K., Sharda, M., & Nadig, A. (2023). Response to music-mediated intervention in autistic children with limited spoken language ability. *Journal of Autism and Developmental Disorders.* https://doi.org/10.1007/s10803-022-05872-w

Mallory, C., & Keehn, B. (2021). Implications of sensory processing and attentional differences associated with autism in academic settings: an integrative review. *Frontiers in Psychiatry, 12.* https://doi.org/10.3389/fpsyt.2021.695825

Mesa, S., & Hamilton, L. (2021). "We are different, that's a fact, but they treat us like we're different-er": Understandings of autism and adolescent identity development. *Advances in Autism.* https://doi.org/10.1108/AIA-12-2020-0071

Mitchell, D., & Sutherland, D. (2020). *What really works in special and inclusive education: Using evidence-based teaching strategies (3rd ed.).* Routledge.

Nicolaidis, C. (2020). 'Having all of your internal resources exhausted beyond measure and being left with no clean-up crew': Defining autistic burnout. *Autism in Adulthood, 2*(2), 1–12. https://doi.org/10.1089/aut. 2019.0079

Oredipe, T., Kofner, B., Riccio, A., Cage, E., Vincent, J., Kapp, S. K.... & Gillespie-Lynch, K. (2022). Does learning you are autistic at a younger age lead to better adult outcomes? A participatory exploration of the perspectives of autistic university students. *Autism.* https://doi.org/10.1177/13623613221086700

Paltra, K. P., & De Jesus, O. (2023). Echolalia. *National Library of Medicine.* https://www.ncbi.nlm.nih.gov/books/NBK565908/

Poon, K. K., Soon, S., Wong, M. E., Kaur, S., Khaw, J., Ng, Z., & Tan, C. S. (2014). What is school like? Perspectives of Singaporean youth with high-functioning autism spectrum disorders. *International Journal of Inclusive Education.* https://doi.org/10.1080/13603116.2012.693401

Prizant, B. M. (1983). Language acquisition and communicative behavior in autism: toward an understanding of the "whole" of it. *The Journal of Speech and Hearing Disorders, 48*(3), 296–307. https://doi.org/10.1044/jshd.4803.296

Prizant, B. M. (1996). Brief report: Communication, language, social, and emotional development. *Journal of Autism and Developmental Disorders, 26*(2), 173–178. https://doi.org/10.1007/BF02172007

Raymaker, D. M., Teo, A. R., Steckler, N. A., Lentz, B., Scharer, M., Delos Santos, A.... & Nicolaidis, C. (2020). "Having all of your internal resources exhausted beyond measure and being left with no clean-up crew": Defining autistic burnout. *Autism in Adulthood: Challenges and Management, 2*(2), 132–143. https://doi.org/10.1089/aut.2019.0079

Roberts, J., & Simpson, K. (2016). A review of research into stakeholder perspectives on inclusion of students with autism in mainstream schools. *International Journal of Inclusive Education, 20*(10), 1084–1096. https://doi.org/10.1080/13603116.2016.1145267

Rosa, M., & Mountain, I. (2013). Psychoanalytic listening to socially excluded young people. *Psychoanalysis, Culture & Society, 18*, 1–16. https://doi.org/10.1057/pcs.2012.2

Rouvali, A., & Riga, V. (2021) Listening to the voice of a pupil with autism spectrum condition in the educational design of a mainstream early years setting. *Education, 3–13, (49)*4, 464–480. https://doi.org/10.1080/03004279.2020.1734042

Saggers, B. (2015). Student perceptions: Improving the educational experiences of high school students on the autism spectrum. *Improving Schools*. https://doi.org/10.1177/1365480214566213

Saggers, B., Hwang, Y. S., & Mercer, K. L. (2011). Your voice counts: Listening to the voice of high school students with autism spectrum disorder. *Australasian Journal of Special Education, 35*(2), 173–190. https://doi.org/10.1375/ajse.35.2.173

Schuler, A. L. (1979). Echolalia: Issues and clinical applications. *Journal of Speech and Hearing Disorders, 44*(4), 411–34.

Scott-Barrett, J., Cebula, K., & Florian, L. (2018). Listening to young people with autism: Learning from researcher experiences. *International Journal of Research & Method in Education, 42*, 1–22. https://doi.org/10.1080/1743727X.2018.1462791

Sequenzia, A., & Grace, E. (2015). *Typed words, loud voices*. Autonomous Press.

Shi, Z., Lin, G., & Xie, Q. (2016). Effects of music therapy on mood, language, behavior, and social skills in children with autism: A meta-analysis. *Chinese Nursing Research, 3*(3), 137–141. https://doi.org/10.1016/j.cnre.2016.06.018

Tierney, S., Burns, J., & Kilbey, E. (2016). Looking behind the mask: Social coping strategies of girls on the autistic spectrum. *Research in Autism Spectrum Disorders, 23*, 73–83. https://doi/10.1016/j.rasd.2015.11.013

van Santen, J. P., Sproat, R. W., & Hill, A. P. (2013). Quantifying repetitive speech in autism spectrum disorders and language impairment. *Autism Research: Official Journal of the International Society for Autism Research, 6*(5), 372–383. https://doi.org/10.1002/aur.1301

Wood-Downie, H., Wong, B., Kovshoff, H., Mandy, W., Hull, L., & Hadwin, J. A. (2021). Sex/gender differences in camouflaging in children and adolescents with autism. *Journal of Autism and Developmental Disorders, 51*(4), 1353–1364. https://doi.org/10.1007/s10803-020-04615-z

Woodfield, C., & Ashby, C. (2016). 'The right path of equality': Supporting high school students with autism who type to communicate. *International Journal of Inclusive Education, 20*(4), 435–454. https://doi.org/10.1080/13603116.2015.1088581

Chapter 5

Connection

DOI: 10.4324/9781032687926-5

SECTION ONE

The 5Cs of Inclusion | *Connection*

Review of the Research	• Autistic students feel more connected with teachers who are fun, fair, patient, and understanding. • Autistic students who feel disconnected report being more stressed, anxious, and socially and academically withdrawn. • Autistic students feel more connected with peers who are accepting of their differences and recognise their strengths. • Positive connections with peers and teachers are a protective measure against bullying.

Like most students, autistic students desire and value quality connections with their teachers and peers (Creswell et al., 2019; Locke et al., 2017), which are known to improve student school engagement and graduation rates and are a protective measure against school absenteeism and bullying (Breault, 2013; Caplan et al., 2016; Howell et al., 2022). However, autistic students have fewer quality friendships than their neurotypical peers due to communication barriers and misinterpreting autistic mannerisms (Horgan et al., 2022; Sasson et al., 2017; Taheri et al., 2016). Autistic students report the simplest of actions made by teachers have the most meaningful impact, including teachers greeting them in the hallway, sharing jokes, and telling stories about personal interests (Bolourian et al., 2022; Lebenhagen, 2022; Saggers, 2015; Van der Steen et al., 2019).

Researchers Esqueda Villegas et al. (2022) reviewed factors enabling or preventing positive interactions between teachers and autistic students in secondary settings and found that teachers perceived a) training and knowledge, b) getting to know the student's strengths and interests, c) assistance from other professionals and parents, d) teacher practice, and e) teacher emotions as factors impacting the development of relationships with autistic students. Autistic students viewed a) school environments (i.e., calm and smaller class sizes), b) material and social support (i.e., technology and one-to-one learning assistance), c) didactic strategies (i.e., workload and group work), and d) student characteristics (i.e., communication skills and emotional regulation) as main factors impacting their relationship with teachers (Esqueda Villegas et al., 2022). While commonalities exist between teachers' and autistic students' views on factors enabling positive relationships, autistic students describe the preferred actions of teachers based on personal attributes, for example, "fun," "patient," "kind," "friendly," and "passionate" about teaching (Lebenhagen, 2022). In contrast, teachers tend to identify broad-based systemic factors preventing the development of relationships with autistic students, including inadequate training (Simó-Pinatella et al., 2021; Young et al., 2017), teaching demands and time constraints (Carrington et al., 2016; Stephenson et al., 2020), and limited access to resources (Han & Cumming, 2022). Autistic students' descriptions of preferred inclusive actions made by peers are similar to ones identified for teachers and include friendly, understanding, and considerate (Deckers et al., 2014; Howard et al., 2006; Lebenhagen, 2022; Locke et al., 2017; Vine Foggo & Webster, 2016).

Attending to the everyday actions of teachers and peers that support autistic students' feelings of school connectedness is noteworthy not only because of the beneficial outcomes for autistic students but also because these actions do not require specialised training or additional time and resources. Universally applied actions such as these are examples of **naturalistic** approaches since, they occur in a student's natural learning environment and regularly within school routines (Ashbaugh & Koegel, 2021; Bateman et al., 2023). Developing social connections is based on being relatable, which is more likely to occur when autistic students are viewed as valuing and benefiting from everyday interactions such as greetings, talking about interests, and using humour. Connecting with autistic students at any age is critically important, but it requires more attention in high school, where the quality of student-teacher relationships is poorer due to increased class sizes and the increased number of teachers students interact with over a school year—all of whom have different perceptions of autism and effective approaches to support autistic students (Able et al., 2015). Additionally, as students mature, the complexity of social rules and dynamics increases, making it more challenging for autistic people to develop and maintain friendships with peers (Creswell et al., 2019). Often referred to as social breakdowns, many autistic students have trouble interpreting implicitly governed social rules (Berenguer et al., 2017), which can be further inhibited by sensory processing, regulation, and communication skills. The inability or difficulty of understanding the implicit beliefs of others has been termed as a lack of theory of mind (Baron-Cohen et al., 1985). However, many autistic people challenge neurotypical interpretations of social-communication breakdowns, proposing that the issue is not one-sided but, more accurately, the result of mutual misunderstandings, identified as the double empathy problem by autistic scholar Damian Milton (2012).

Re-evaluating traditional views on typical social interactions and whose responsibility it is to adapt to neurotypically normed social expectations suggests that more balanced perspectives and approaches are needed, which may result in more autistic students feeling motivated and confident to engage in social interactions with their teachers and peers. To draw attention to and encourage shared responsibility for the social acceptance and inclusion of all students, stakeholders might consider ways to consult with autistic students to co-identify inaccurate stereotypes, preventing the development of positive relationships and, by doing so, more easily identify systemic barriers that perpetuate harmful and inaccurate stereotypes; including that autistic students do not desire or benefit from ordinary social connections with teachers and peers. The framework titled *Connection* is used throughout this chapter to highlight ways stakeholders can proactively work together to connect meaningfully.

Section Highlights

- Autistic students desire simple but meaningful connections with teachers and peers who are fun, patient, understanding, and compassionate.
- Autistic students appreciate when teachers and peers connect with them naturally, including being greeted in the hallway, telling jokes, and sharing stories about shared interests.
- School connectedness improves school attendance and graduation rates for autistic students and reduces incidences of bullying.

Vignette 1: Connecting with Teachers and Peers as a Non-Speaker

Speech-Language Therapist

Jack is new to the class. His neurodivergent classmates tell me that he can't speak sometimes. They adopt a caregiver role with him, and they often speak for him. Jack takes longer to process language, and he is easily overwhelmed. He will stand and stare until someone directs him; a year of behavioural training methods has further eroded his spontaneity. He echoes the words of his peers and adults, but he can't initiate words independently yet.

At home, we look at communication options, and Jack is captivated by a robust AAC app. He uses his monotropic and gestalt capacities to teach himself about the words and pre-programmed phrases in the app over the next few months. He can quickly find phrases that he wants to say to take turns in a conversation with me. He responds to interaction quickly and confidently using the AAC. His hyperlexia and the predictive text are a fruitful combination; soon, he is typing.

Jack is pleased that he can bring his AAC to school. The teacher and I explain to the students about different ways that people communicate. With Jack, we explain the rules around his ownership of the iPad and remind them to seek consent from Jack if they want to use his iPad. The children accept this boundary. The teacher communicates with the students, at moments during the day, using the AAC app on her iPad and she makes it available for the children to explore, when she remembers.

Jack is proud to have his AAC in the class and he is encouraged by his peers' interest and their acceptance of it. At playtime, the teacher's AAC is made available for Jack's peers, I join Jack and his peers, and we play games together. Conversations are a mix of mouth words and typed words. The students enjoy having random AAC conversations with Jack. They laugh heartily as they take turns in the "silly" conversations which flows back and forth. Jack is beginning to find a way to participate equitably with his peers; communicating using the AAC app is a new experience for everyone, they are all novices. I see Jack beginning to make connections and enjoy mutuality in communication.

Student

When I started, there were so many new people and new rules. I could hear people talking to me, but I couldn't understand what they said. Ruby reminds me of the rules. When I got stuck, she would tell me again. I don't always get the words to come out right and sometimes I repeat. Like I kept repeating what other people said. I don't like this. I want to say my own words out of my own mouth. I liked pressing the buttons and hearing the phrases. It felt good when my teacher spoke about my device to the kids. When Bea came to see me in class, she talked with me using my device. It took a long time before someone else would talk to me using my device. I like to talk about everybody's birthday. When Bea comes, we say silly things a lot of the time with some kids. This was so funny. I didn't make friends in my last school.

Research Connections

With ongoing support from speech-language therapists, students with complex communication needs are considered easier to support in mainstream school settings (Light & McNaughton, 2012). Speech therapists, teachers, and teaching assistants work together to identify ways autistic students can develop their language and communication skills to interact meaningfully with peers and participate in learning. Jack first learned to use his alternative communication device at home through direct instruction from his speech therapist. **Direct instruction** is a teaching approach comprised of careful sequencing of small prerequisite skills until student mastery before introducing more advanced learning objectives (Mason & Otero, 2021). Over time, as Jack's proficiency and confidence increase, the speech therapist supports Jack in generalising the use of his device from the home setting to the classroom setting and **models** to his teachers and peers the different ways they, too, can use assistive technology to interact with Jack during structured and unstructured activities. Using a **Universal Design for Learning** approach, Jack's teacher integrates a text-to-speech app on her iPad during whole-class instruction, which provides an equal opportunity for Jack to participate in non-stigmatising ways because peers are also encouraged to use the iPad to interact with Jack in fun self-directed ways.

Peer-based instruction is a strength-based approach that promotes understanding and acceptance of differences between students and encourages students to view each other as equals (Vidal & DeThorne, 2021). Proactively teaching Jack's peers about his communication abilities and assistive device creates a classroom culture of respect and understanding and signals to Jack that he is accepted and capable. Additionally, because of the supported generalisation of Jack's skills to the classroom, along with the teacher's enthusiasm to incorporate technology-assisted pedagogies, peer curiosity, excitement, and supports are activated. Jack's parents, speech-language therapist, and teacher worked collaboratively to support Jack's communication needs and abilities in the context of his learning and social environment, resulting in an approach that demonstrates effectiveness and fosters a culture of inclusion.

Section Highlights

- Speech-language therapists are instrumental in providing direct instruction to students on using augmentative and alternative communication devices to support learning and socialisation.
- Teachers can reduce the stigma associated with using communication technologies by applying technology-aided pedagogies and principles of Universal Design for Learning.
- Peer-mediated instruction is a natural, strengths-based approach that encourages bi-directional skill development between students with different abilities and helps develop a shared understanding and respect for differences.

Responsive Framework

Connection	
Student Name: Jack **Grade:** Three	**Primary Teacher Connection:** Jack, Teacher, Ms. Bea (SLT) **Secondary Connection:** Education Assistant
Identifies/Assessed as: ☐ Speaking ☐ Minimally-Speaking ☑ Non-Speaking	
Initial Date: October	**Review Dates:** December, February, April, May, June

Teacher	Peers
☑ Key staff take the time to get to know the student ☑ Student is greeted by multiple staff ☑ Student has regular opportunities to talk about their interests and share stories ☐ The school community celebrates student's skills and passions ☑ Student's interests and passions are: Learning about classmates' birthdays, typing on his iPad ☐ School activities that are fun for the student: ☑ Things/activities/people that bring joy/make the student laugh: Spending time using the iPad to communicate with him, being silly, telling jokes	☑ Peers have a basic understanding of neurodiversity and neurodiversity-affirming attitudes and actions ☐ Student has a peer mentor ☐ Student has an opportunity to provide leadership/mentorship to others ☐ Student is included in extra-curricular clubs and activities ☑ Student has the opportunity to participate in activities alongside peers that do not require speaking communication for participation ☑ Student has a choice to participate in social skill development activities alongside neurotypical peers ☐ Other:

Additional Information:
Teacher and the education assistant will work together to learn more about Jack's interests from Jack's perspective and will explore with Jack ways to showcase his interests and skills during a school celebration with a peer mentor.

Learning and Inclusionary Benefits

The anticipated learning and inclusionary benefits of using the Connection framework are:

- Team members collaboratively identify inclusionary actions currently in place and identify future priorities to ensure Jack continues to be meaningfully included in learning and social activities.
- Jack's development of social-communication skills and experiences are supported through direct instruction and teacher and peer modeling, emphasising a shared responsibility to support Jack's inclusion.
- Predictable times are set for team members to co-evaluate Jack's skills and progress in the context of his learning and social environment.

- Identifying future goals is based on contextually relevant data from multiple perspectives, thus helping to ensure consistency in the implementation of evidence-based practices.

Vignette 2: Peer Connections and the Stigma of Support

Teacher

I don't know what to do anymore. The strategies I create for Ben seem to work for a week or two, and then he doesn't want to use them. The speech-language therapist and I met last week and came up with a great plan to help Ben remember his morning and afternoon schedule, which we thought would help make his day predictable. We found some extra time and created a visual schedule using brightly coloured PECS [Picture Exchange Communication System] and laminated it so that it would last for a long time. Ben loves science class so we thought this would be a good time to introduce the schedule, which seemed helpful when Ben was working at his desk. But today in science class, there was a group work activity where students found a space in the class-room to discuss their ideas for a presentation they would do on cell biology. After about 10 minutes, Ben became visibly upset and crumpled his paper on his presentation ideas. As I approached him, he ran out of the room. Another teacher heard Ben crying in the bathroom and when asked, "What's the problem?" Ben yelled, "Everyone hates me!" After 20 minutes, Ben reluctantly returned to the classroom but insisted on sitting by himself at the back until lunch break. Since the beginning of the year, I have followed recommendations from the speech therapist, occupational therapist, and autism consultant—we even have a behaviour support plan in place. I feel like I consistently use sensory breaks and visuals to support Ben. Maybe I need to find time to teach him social skills so he can learn to interact more successfully with his peers.

Student

I like to research and talk about plant classification systems. Science class is my favourite subject and I am really good at it, it's my highest grade. I like my friends, but I dread working in groups. I hate the chaos when everyone moves around looking for a space to sit or when people move desks around—that sound...argh! I never know where I should sit. The other thing that I hate about group work is all the random talking and having to face each other and all the other stuff. It makes it really hard to concentrate on what people are talking about when the whole class is talking at once and we are so close together. When it's hard to hear, and people are laughing and talking over each other, I start to feel anxious because of the noise, but also because

I never know when someone is going to ask me a question. It's a lot. When I can't think of an answer quickly enough, while everyone is looking at me, then by brain starts thinking about the plant classification system. I know it doesn't always fit or what I want to say, but those are the words that come out. It's embarrassing. So is the big bright schedule. Nobody else uses one in my group, why do I have to? It reminds me of being in grade 2 again. I wish my teacher would just write down what I am supposed to do and I would keep it at my desk and check it off as I go. Sometimes my body just explodes from it all, and I need to get out of the class and away from everyone looking at me. I just need some space and quiet to calm my brain and body. It's frustrating that my teacher wants to talk about it in front of everyone.

Research Connections

Autistic students have fewer friends and receive less support from neurotypical peers, causing them to feel more alone and likely to view themselves negatively (Crompton et al., 2023; Symes & Humphrey, 2011; Williams et al., 2019). The benefits of friendships cannot be understated, as one to two close friendships lead to improved psychological and well-being benefits for autistic students, including feeling recognised, included, valued, and confident and fewer feelings of loneliness and depression (Aubineau & Blicharska, 2020; Choi et al., 2020; Goodall, 2018). Common approaches to support autistic students in making friends include social skills interventions focusing on breaking down social expectations and providing examples of expected and unexpected social behaviours. However, traditional social skills programs have been criticised by the autistic community for perpetuating ableist norms on the "right way" to think and behave (Bottema-Beutel et al., 2018; Lorenc et al., 2018; O'Donoghue et al., 2020; Wilkenfeld & Mcarthy, 2020). Repeated exposure to social skills interventions that have a restricted view of socially appropriate behaviours may inadvertently teach autistic students to suppress or mask their authentic selves to be viewed as more neurotypical, which over time may lead to feelings of anxiety, depression, and even thoughts of self-harm (Belcher, 2022; Cage et al., 2018; Hebron & Humphrey, 2014).

Social narratives are instructional tools that provide concise and straightforward statements related to a social situation and are intended to teach autistic students social skills and help them interpret different situations (Gray & Garand, 1993). Over the last 25 years, the original social story concept has grown to include social scripts (Loveland & Tunali, 1991), social autopsies (Bieber, 1994), cartooning (Coogle et al., 2017), comic strips (Gray, 1994), and power cards (Campbell & Tincani, 2011); however, current research on the usefulness of social narratives on promoting positive and generalisable skill development is weak (Camilleri et al., 2021; Leaf et al., 2020). Researchers have attributed environmental factors, including educational context, staff knowledge and training, inconsistent use and insufficient comprehension checks, and student factors such as age, gender, reading ability, verbal comprehension, and intellectual ability, as affecting the efficacy of social narratives (Camilleri et al., 2021). Furthermore, limited research on the usefulness of social narratives from the perspective of autistic students is available.

Peer-based support is another **naturalistic** teaching approach, where both the mentor and mentee develop social, emotional, and academic skills through shared understanding and mutual respect (Chang & Locke et al., 2016; Hillier et al., 2019; Houlston et al., 2009). Peer-based interventions are beneficial because they strengthen school cultures based on mutual understanding, respect, and valuing of differences (Kasari et al., 2012; Crompton et al., 2023). Furthermore, peer-based support helps students develop pro-social behaviours because strategy use occurs in the context of students' natural environments (Chan et al., 2009). **Peer-support** groups are another effective approach for social skill development as they include students with diverse backgrounds and encourage students to interact based on shared interests (Aubineau & Blicharska, 2020; Botha et al., 2020; Crompton et al., 2023). Providing autistic students with opportunities to connect with like-minded peers, including other autistic students, has short- and long-term benefits, including school connectedness and improved life outcomes (Botha et al., 2020; Crane et al., 2021; Hebron, 2018; Shochet et al., 2022). Autistic adults who reflect on their school experiences share that they would have appreciated spending time with autistic peers to help minimise feelings of isolation, to be able to talk about issues related to their diagnosis, and to feel a sense of autistic pride (Crompton et al., 2023).

Video modeling is a **technology-aided** tool used to promote social skill development through observational learning, where autistic people can learn to interpret the facial expressions and emotions of others in the context of specific situations (Wong et al., 2015). Under the supervision of adults, autistic students may record role-playing scenarios to practice interpreting social cues, perspective-taking and problem-solving. Other video-based activities autistic students report as helpful for learning to interpret emotions is watching television programs or videos with real-life or animated characters such as those found in soap operas, anime, and cartoons (Cook, & Smagorinsky, 2016; Cross et al., 2022; Gould & Ashton-Smith, 2011). Minecraft is another popular technology-aided instruction tool that has been found to improve social skills in autistic people, including reciprocity, problem-solving, and collaboration, because it reduces stress and anxiety associated with traditional face-to-face social interactions (Dorn & Truong, 2021; Dundon, 2019).

Section Highlights

- Although autistic students desire friendships, they have fewer quality friendships and receive less social support than their peers.

- Social narratives and peer-based supports are naturalistic approaches schools can use to support skill development in real-world contexts and promote a shared understanding and responsibility for including autistic students.

Responsive Framework

Connection	
Student Name: Ben **Grade:** Six	**Primary Teacher Connection:** Homeroom Teacher **Secondary Connection:** Science Teacher
Identifies/Assessed as: ☑ Speaking ☐ Minimally-Speaking ☐ Non-Speaking	
Initial Date: October 15	**Review Dates:** Monthly
Teacher	**Peers**
☑ Key staff take the time to get to know the student ☑ Student is greeted by multiple staff ☑ Student has regular opportunities to talk about their interests and share stories ☐ The school community celebrates student's skills and passions ☑ Student's interests and passions are: Science class and plant classification systems ☑ School activities that are fun for the student: Helping to set up and attend school science fairs. ☑ Things/activities/people that bring joy/make the student laugh: Creating individual presentations on PowerPoint, telling jokes, watching	☑ Peers have a basic understanding of neurodiversity and neurodiversity-affirming attitudes and actions ☐ Student has a peer mentor ☐ Student has an opportunity to provide leadership/mentorship to others ☑ Student is included in extra-curricular clubs and activities ☐ Student has the opportunity to participate in activities alongside peers that do not require speaking communication for participation ☐ Student has a choice to participate in social skill development activities alongside neurotypical peers ☐ Other: _____ _____

> **Additional Information:**
> Teacher and Ben will select which science presentations he will complete independently and will look at opportunities where he can teach others and share his knowledge on plant classification systems. Class-wide agendas will be provided to guide group work activities, with clearly stated roles of speakers, time-keepers, note-takers, and listeners.

Learning and Inclusionary Benefits

The anticipated learning and inclusionary benefits of using the Connection framework are:

- It provides Ben and his teacher predictable opportunities to proactively identify preferred interests and learning activities and, thus, select effective and non-stigmatising supports for Ben.
- Ben has voice and choice (autonomy) in which science presentations he will complete individually or in a small group setting.
- The teacher uses Ben's feedback to develop a universal approach to provide the entire class with agendas and clear descriptions of group roles and responsibilities.
- Incorporating Ben's views on the situation deepens his teacher's awareness of factors affecting Ben's regulation and how his behaviour represents his desire for structure, predictability, and social belonging, thus prevents unnecessary social skills or behavioural-based interventions.

Vignette 3: Bullying Prevention

Parent

Elise seemed to have more friends in elementary school than she does now in middle school. We noticed a big shift when she started her new school, but it was hard to tell if her moodiness was because of the transition to a new school or from changes that come with adolescence. Once Elise stopped eating her lunches and started making excuses not to go to school. I asked Elise more questions about what she was doing during her free time during the school day, like before school and during lunch break. I don't think I have the whole story, but I learned that Elise doesn't have many friends, if any, at her new school and is by herself a lot during lunchtime—which is really difficult to hear as parents. She avoids going into the cafeteria because of the noise and how busy it gets. The sound of other people eating also bothers her, which means that she either doesn't eat her lunch or only eats with what she can hold in her hands as she walks around outside. After meeting with her homeroom teacher to talk about my concerns, I learned about a couple of incidents where Elise was called names by another student, like "weirdo" and "goth girl." I think the other part of the story is that this name-calling also happens online, although Elise shuts down if I ask too many questions because she doesn't want the other kids to get in trouble. We haven't come up with a clear plan. Still, the school has been good at listening to our concerns and seems to want to take the time to get to know Elise better to find out her interests so that they can connect her with someone in their school mentorship program and find a space and a few other students she can eat with at lunch.

Child

My new school is okay. I had more friends at my last school because everyone knew each other since kindergarten. It seems like everyone has known each other for a long time at this school, too, which means they aren't really looking for someone else to hang out with. I would consider myself pretty quiet. I do have a few friends online, it's an anime group. My favourite character is Renge Miyauchi, I like her purple hair and she is really outgoing, which is different from me. Some of us think that she is autistic too. A few kids at school have called me names for liking anime, it doesn't bother me too much, I just learn to ignore it. I am not sure if I will make any good friends at this school, but I am open to doing that mentorship club just to see. I know that my mom is trying to help, but telling on those kids won't do me any good and it definitely won't put me in the good books of people at school.

Research Connections

Autistic students experience more peer rejection and bullying than other students with disabilities (Fink et al., 2015; Humphrey & Symes, 2010; Schroeder et al., 2014; Zeedyk et al., 2014); however, social difficulties leading to bullying behaviours also occur between autistic students (Crompton et al., 2023). The reported prevalence of in-school bullying varies, with autistic students and teachers reporting up to 65% and parents reporting between 60–78% (Chen & Schwartz, 2012; Hebron & Humphrey, 2014; Lebenhagen, 2022). The emotional effects of bullying include low self-esteem, social withdrawal, increased maladaptive behaviour, such as anger and sadness, higher absenteeism, decreased academic engagement, and generally poorer mental health states (Chen & Schwartz, 2012; Fink et al., 2015; Zeedyk et al., 2014). Potential risk factors for bullying include social-communication and emotional regulation difficulties that lead to breaking social rules (Schroeder et al., 2014; Tierney et al., 2016).

Positive peer relationships are a known protective factor against bullying (Symes & Humphrey, 2011), as are strong relationships between teachers and autistic students (Saggers, 2015). Researchers have investigated associations between autism characteristics and experiences of bullying and found that autistic students with a co-occurring diagnosis of depression experience more incidents of cyberbullying, and autistic students with co-occurring diagnosis of anxiety disorders experience more incidents of face-to-face bullying (Ashburner et al., 2019). Strategies autistic students report useful in their attempts to avoid uncomfortable and harmful interactions with peers include seeking out friendships with female peers as they tend to be more nurturing, reporting incidences of bullying to trusted teachers, and seeking support from parents to schedule activities with preferred peers outside of school (Fisher et al., 2015; Howard et al., 2006; Tierney et al., 2016). Efforts to address higher rates of bullying amongst autistic students should not become the primary responsibility of autistic students or negatively affect their involvement in preferred subjects and activities (i.e., missing art class to attend targeted social skills training). Instead, social understanding and skill development should be based on shared responsibility and co-production of universal preventative strategies (Bottema-Beutel et al., 2018; Jones, 2022). For example, **peer-mediated interventions** such as Circle of Friends have positively impacted inclusive attitudes and led to greater peer acceptance between neurotypical and autistic students in school and the community (Schlieder et al., 2014).

The benefit of using school-wide universal approaches to reduce incidences of bullying is it prevents singling out victims (Hebron et al., 2015), promotes a deeper understanding and acceptance of diversity, and encourages innovative solutions relevant to people and priorities of the school community. Research on school-wide anti-bullying initiatives, such as the KiVa program used in the Netherlands, has found that after two years of use, students' self-reported victimisation and bullying significantly declined compared to schools that did not use the program, where the potential for being bullied were 1.29–1.63 greater, and the likelihood of being a bully were 1.19–1.66 greater in schools that did not use the KiVa anti-bullying program (Huitsing et al., 2020).

Section Highlights

- Autistic students experience more instances of bullying than their neurotypical peers and other students with disabilities.
- In-school and cyberbullying is a major parental concern.
- Successful bullying prevention includes school-wide approaches, peer-mediated interventions, and family support.

Responsive Framework

⚛ **Connection**	
Student Name: Elise **Grade:** Eight	**Primary Teacher Connection:** Homeroom Teacher **Secondary Connection:** Teacher leading school mentorship program
Identifies/Assessed as: ☑ Speaking ☐ Minimally-Speaking ☐ Non-Speaking	
Initial Date: October 1	**Review Dates:** Monthly
Teacher	**Peers**
☑ Key staff take the time to get to know the student ☑ Student is greeted by multiple staff ☑ Student has regular opportunities to talk about their interests and share stories ☐ The school community celebrates student's skills and passions ☐ Student's interests and passions are: ☐ School activities that are fun for the student: ☐ Things/activities/people that bring joy/make the student laugh:	☐ Peers have a basic understanding of neurodiversity and neurodiversity-affirming attitudes and actions ☑ Student has a peer mentor ☐ Student has an opportunity to provide leadership/mentorship to others ☐ Student is included in extra-curricular clubs and activities ☐ Student has the opportunity to participate in activities alongside peers that do not require speaking communication for participation ☐ Student has a choice to participate in social skill development activities alongside neurotypical peers ☑ Other: Elise will be provided a separate space to eat lunch alongside a few other peers.

Additional Information:

To support Elise's transition to the school, her homeroom teacher and mentor teacher will make sure to greet Elise in the hallways and will take the time to get to know Elise's interests. Elise will try the peer mentor program for two weeks, and we will meet again with Mom for everyone to provide their feedback. The mentor teacher will speak with the school admin about a school-wide approach to teach all students more about diversity, acceptance, and belonging.

Learning and Inclusionary Benefits

The anticipated learning and inclusionary benefits of using the Connection framework are:

- Accommodations are provided to support Elise's sensory preferences at lunchtime alongside peers who also benefit from having access to a separate space.
- Access to a separate space with peers with similar interests and preferences for unstructured school time provides a safe space for students and reduces social stigma based on the visibility of being socially isolated in larger school spaces like the cafeteria or outside on school grounds.
- Teachers use an intentional approach to connect with Elise through greetings and learning about her interests, a proactive strategy to build connection and a visible sign to peers that Elise is a valuable member of the school community.
- The peer mentorship program allows Elise to make positive peer connections, which are a protective measure against peer bullying.
- The framework identifies a gap in school-wide practice where more attention is needed on school-wide diversity and inclusion approaches to reduce bullying.

SECTION TWO

Inclusionary Framework to Support Student Connection

Connection	
Student Name: **Grade:**	**Primary Teacher Connection:** **Secondary Connection:**
Identifies/Assessed as: ☐ Speaking ☐ Minimally-Speaking ☐ Non-Speaking	
Initial Date:	**Review Dates:**
Teacher	**Peers**
☐ Key staff take the time to get to know the student ☐ Student is greeted by multiple staff ☐ Student has regular opportunities to talk about their interests and share stories ☐ The school community celebrates student's skills and passions ☐ Student's interests and passions are: ☐ School activities that are fun for the student: ☐ Things/activities/people that bring joy/make the student laugh:	☐ Peers have a basic understanding of neurodiversity and neurodiversity-affirming attitudes and actions ☐ Student has a peer mentor ☐ Student has an opportunity to provide leadership/mentorship to others ☐ Student is included in extra-curricular clubs and activities ☐ Student has the opportunity to participate in activities alongside peers that do not require speaking communication for participation ☐ Student has a choice to participate in social skill development activities alongside neurotypical peers ☐ Other:
Additional Information:	

Reflective Questions for Teachers, Practitioners, and Parents

1. In what ways (look, feel, sound) does school staff convey to autistic students that they are welcome and valued members of the school community?
2. What school-wide events and activities are neuro-affirming? Are neurodivergent students involved in the planning of neuro-affirming events and activities?
3. Do you provide opportunities for students to work together in groups using in-person and online formats? What supports are provided to enable flexible student participation?
4. What opportunities do autistic students have to showcase their interests and abilities in classroom and school-based leadership and mentorship roles?
5. What school-wide approaches are used to develop a shared understanding of diversity and to encourage collective responsibility for ensuring school connectedness is attained for all students?

Additional Readings and Resources

1. Reyes, P. (2016). *My voice is all mine.* https://autismacceptance.com/my-voice-is-all-mine/
2. Leedham, A. T., Thompson, A. R., & Freeth, M. (2020). A thematic synthesis of siblings' lived experiences of autism: Distress, responsibilities, compassion and connection. *Research in Developmental Disabilities, 97*, 103547. https://doi.org/10.1016/j.ridd.2019.103547
3. Crompton, C. J., DeBrabander, K., Heasman, B., Milton, D., & Sasson, N. J. (2021). Double empathy: Why autistic people are often misunderstood. *Neuroscience, 9*(554875), 4–11. https://doi.org/10.3389/frym.2021.554875

Chapter Summary

A main factor affecting school inclusion for autistic students is feeling connected to teachers and peers. Autistic students want to be considered equal and valuable members of their school community and appreciate the simple actions taken by teachers and peers that show them they are. Everyday actions like being greeted in the hallway, having special interests and abilities celebrated, and being offered leadership opportunities, autistic students receive messages from the school community that they make a valuable contribution to the school community. There are several learning and

psychological benefits for autistic students who are socially connected with teachers and peers, including a more positive sense of
self, increased engagement in learning, lower absenteeism, and fewer
experiences of bullying. Evidence-based practices to promote positive social connections between autistic students and members of
their school community include naturalistic, direct, and peer-based
instruction, social narratives, social skills training, video modeling,
and technology-aided instruction.

Notes & Reflections

References

Able, H., Sreckovic, M., Schultz, T., Garwood, J., & Sherman, J. (2015). Views from the trenches: Teacher and student supports needed for full inclusion of students with ASD. *Teacher Education and Special Education, 38*(1), 44–57. https:// doi. org/ 10. 1177/08884 06414 558096

Ashbaugh, K., & Koegel, R. L. (2021). Naturalistic interventions. In F. R. Volkmar (Eds.), *Encyclopedia of autism spectrum disorders.* Cham; Springer. https://doi.org/10.1007/978-3-319-91280-6_124

Ashburner, J., Saggers, B., Campbell, M. A., Dillon-Wallace, J. A., Hwang, S., Carrington, S., & Bobir, N. (2019). How are students on the autism spectrum affected by bullying? Perspectives of students and parents. *Journal of Research in Special Educational Needs, 19*(1), 27–44. https://doi.org/10.1111/1471-3802.12421

Aubineau, M., & Blicharska, T. (2020). High-functioning autistic students speak about their experience of inclusion in mainstream secondary schools. *School Mental Health, 12.* 10.1007/s12310-020-09364-z.

Baron-Cohen, S., Leslie, A. M., & Frith, U. (1985). Does the autistic child have a "theory of mind"? *Cognition, 21*(1), 37–46. https://doi.org/10.1016/0010-0277(85)90022-8

Bateman, K., Wilson, S. E., Matthews, K., Gauvreau, A., Gucwa, M., Therrien, W. J., Nevill, R., et al. (2023). Keeping teachers engaged during non-instructional times: An analysis of the effects of a naturalistic intervention. *Education Sciences, 13*(6), 534. http://dx.doi.org/10.3390/educsci13060534

Belcher, H. (2022. On being autistic and in mental health crisis care. *Autism in Adulthood,* 179 –182. http://doi.org/10.1089/aut.2022.0044

Berenguer, C., Miranda, A., Colomer, C., Baixauli, I., & Roselló, B. (2018). Contribution of theory of mind, executive functioning, and pragmatics to socialization behaviors of children with high-functioning autism. *Journal of Autism and Developmental Disorders, 48*(2), 430–441. https://doi.org/10.1007/s10803-017-3349-0

Bieber, J. (1994). *Learning disabilities and social skills with Richard LaVoie: Last one picked... First one picked on.* Washington, DC: Public Broadcasting Service.

Bolourian, Y., Losh, A., Hamsho, N., Eisenhower, A., & Blacher, J. (2022). General education teachers' perceptions of autism, inclusive practices, and relationship building strategies. *Journal of Autism and Developmental Disorders, 52*(9), 3977–3990. https://doi.org/10.1007/s10803-021-05266-4

Botha, M., Dibb, B., & Frost, D. M. (2020). 'Autism is me': An investigation of how autistic individuals make sense of autism and stigma. *Disability & Society,* 1–27. https://doi.org/10.1080/09687599.2020.1822782

Bottema-Beutel, K., Park, H., & Kim, S. Y. (2018). Commentary on social skills training curricula for individuals with ASD: Social interaction, authenticity, and stigma. *Journal of Autism and Developmental Disorders, 48*(3), 953–964. https://doi.org/10.1007/s10 803-017-3400-1

Breault, R. (2013). "She was great, but...": Examining preservice recollections of favorite and most effective teachers. *Professional Educator, 37*(1). https://files.eric.ed.gov/fulltext/EJ1019125.Pdf

Cage, E., Di Monaco, J., & Newell, V. (2018). Experiences of autism acceptance and mental health in autistic adults. *Journal of Autism and Developmental Disorders, 48*(2), 473–484. https://doi.org/10.1007/s10803-017-3342-7

Camilleri, L. J., Maras, K., & Brosnan, M. (2022). Autism Spectrum Disorder and social story research: A scoping study of published, peer-reviewed literature reviews. *Review Journal of Autism and Developmental Disorders, 9*, 21–38. https://doi.org/10.1007/s40 489-020-00235-6

Caplan, B., Feldman, M., Eisenhower, A., & Blacher, J. (2016). Student–teacher relationships for young children with autism spectrum disorder: Risk and protective factors. *Journal of Autism and Developmental Disorders, 46*(12). https://doi.org/10.1007/s10 803-016-2915-1

Carrington, S., Berthelsen, D., Nickerson, J., Nicholson, J. M., Walker, S., & Meldrum, K. (2016). Teachers' experiences of inclusion of children with developmental disabilities across the early years of school. *Journal of Psychologists and Counsellors in Schools, 26*(2), 139–154. https://doi.org/10.1017/jgc. 2016.19

Chan, J., Lang, R., Rispoli, M., O'Reilly, M., Sigafoos, J., & Cole, H. (2009). Use of peer-mediated interventions in the treatment of autism spectrum disorders: A systematic review. *Research in Autism Spectrum Disorders, 3*, 876–889. Https://doi.org/10.1016/ j.rasd.2009.04.003

Chang, C., & Locke, J. (2016). A systematic review of peer-mediated interventions for children with autism spectrum disorder. *Research in Autism Spectrum Disorders, 27*, 1. https://doi.org/10.1016/j.rasd.2016.03.010

Chen, P., & Schwartz, I. S. (2012) 'Bullying and victimisation experiences of students with autism spectrum disorders in elementary schools.' *Focus on Autism and Other Developmental Disabilities, 27*, 200–212. https://doi.org/10.1177/1088357612459556

Choi, K. W., Stein, M. B., Nishimi, K. M., Ge, T., Coleman, R. I., Chen, Y.... & Smoller, J. W. (2020). An exposure-wide and Mendelian randomization approach to identifying modifiable factors for the prevention of depression. *The American Journal of Psychiatry, 177*(10), 944. https://doi.org/10.1176/appi.ajp.2020.19111158

Coogle, C. G., Ahmed, S., Aljaffal, M. A., Alsheef, M. Y., & Hamdi, H. A. (2017). Social narrative strategies to support children with autism spectrum disorder. *Early Childhood Education Journal, 46*, 445–450. https://doi.org/10.1007/s10643-017-0873-7

Cook, L. S., & Smagorinsky, P. (2016). The collaborative online anime community as positive social updraft. In P. Smagorinsky (Ed.). *Creativity and community among autism-spectrum youth. Palgrave studies in play, performance, learning, and development*. Palgrave Macmillan, New York. https://doi.org/10.1057/978-1-137-54797-2_9

Crane, L., Hearst, C., Ashworth, M., Davies, J., & Hill, E. L. (2021). Supporting newly identified or diagnosed autistic adults: An initial evaluation of an autistic-led programme. *Journal of Autism and Developmental Disorders, 51*(3), 892–905. https://doi.org/10.1007/ s10803-020-04486-4

Cresswell, L., Hinch, R., & Cage, E. (2019). The experiences of peer relationships amongst autistic adolescents: A systematic review of the qualitative evidence. *Research in Autism Spectrum Disorders, 61*, 45–60. https://doi.org/10.1016/j.rasd.2019.01.003

Crompton, C. J., Hallett, S., Axbey, H., McAuliffe, C., & Cebula, K. (2023). 'Someone like-minded in a big place': Autistic young adults' attitudes towards autistic peer support in mainstream education. *Autism: The International Journal of Research and Practice, 27*(1), 76–91. https://doi.org/10.1177/13623613221081189

Cross, L., Piovesan, A., & Atherton, G. (2022). Autistic people outperform neurotypicals in a cartoon version of the Reading the Mind in the Eyes. *Autism Research: Official*

Journal of the International Society for Autism Research, 15(9), 1603–1608. https://doi.org/10.1002/aur.2782

Deckers, A., Roelofs, J., Muris, P., & Rinck, M. (2014). Desire for social interaction in children with autism spectrum disorders. *Research in Autism Spectrum Disorders, 8*(4). https://doi.org/10.1016/j.rasd.2013.12.019

Dorn, S., & Truong, L. (2021). Assessing effectiveness of Minecraft-based interventions to improve interpersonal skills of youth with autism spectrum disorder. Poster presented at the 19th Annual Psychology, Family, Community Research Conference. Online.

Dundon, R. (2019). *Teaching social skills to children with autism using Minecraft®: A step by step guide.* Jessica Kingsley Publishers.

Esqueda Villegas, F., van der Steen, S., & Minnaert, A. (2022). Interactions between teachers and students with autism spectrum disorder in mainstream secondary education: Fundamental, yet under-researched. *Review Journal of Autism and Developmental Disorders.* https://doi.org/10.1007/s40489-022-00346-2

Fink, E., Deighton, J., Humphrey, N., & Wolpert, M. (2015). Assessing the bullying and victimisation experiences of children with special educational needs in mainstream schools: Development and validation of the Bullying Behaviour and Experience Scale. *Research in Developmental Disabilities, 36C,* 611–619. https://doi.org/10.1016/j.ridd.2014.10.048

Fisher, M. H., & Taylor, J. L. (2015). Let's talk about it: Peer victimisation experiences as reported by adolescents with autism spectrum disorder. *Autism, 20*(4), 402–411. https://doi.org/10.1177/1362361315585948.

Goodall, C. (2018). 'I felt closed in and like I couldn't breathe': A qualitative study exploring the mainstream educational experiences of autistic young people. *Autism & Developmental Language Impairments.* https://doi.org/10.1177/2396941518804407

Gould, J., & Ashton-Smith, J. (2011). Missed diagnosis or misdiagnosis? Girls and women on the autism spectrum. *Good Autism Practice, 12*(1), 34–41.

Gray, C. (1994). *Comic strip conversations: Illustrated interactions that teach conversation skills to students with autism and related disorders.* Jenison: Jenison Public Schools.

Gray, C. A., & Garand, J. D. (1993). Social stories: Improving responses of students with autism with accurate social information. *Focus on Autism and Other Developmental Disabilities, 8*(1), 1–10

Han, C., & Cumming, T.M. (2022). Teachers' beliefs about the provision of education for students with autism spectrum disorder: A systematic review. *Review Journal of Autism and Developmental Disorders* https://doi.org/10.1007/s40489-022-00350-6

Hebron, J., & Humphrey, N. (2014) Exposure to bullying among students with autism spectrum conditions: A multi-informant analysis of risk and protective factors. *Autism, 18,* 618–30. https://doi.org/10.1177/1362361313495965

Hebron, J., Humphrey, N., & Oldfield, J. (2015). Vulnerability to bullying of children with autism spectrum conditions in mainstream education: A multi-informant qualitative exploration. *Journal of Research in Special Educational Needs, 15*(3), 185–193. https://doi.org/10.1111/1471-3802.12108

Hillier, A., Goldstein, J., Tornatore, L., Byrne, E., & Johnson, H. (2019). Outcomes of a peer mentoring program for university students with disabilities. *Mentoring & Tutoring: Partnership in Learning,* 27, 1–22. https://doi.org.10.1080/13611267.2019.1675850

Horgan, F., Kenny, N., & Flynn, P. (2022). A systematic review of the experiences of autistic young people enrolled in mainstream second-level (post-primary) schools. *Autism*, https://doi.org/10.1177/13623613221105089

Houlston, C., Smith, P., & Jessel, J. (2009). Investigating the extent and use of peer support initiatives in English schools. *Educational Psychology, 29,* 325–344. https://doi.org/10.1080/01443410902926751

Howard, B., Cohn, E., & Orsmond, G. I. (2006). Understanding and negotiating friendships: Perspectives from an adolescent with Asperger syndrome. *Autism. The International Journal of Research and Practice, 10*(6), 619–627. https://doi.org/10.1177/1362361306068508

Howell, M., Bradshaw, J., & Langdon, P. E. (2022). 'There isn't a checklist in the world that's got that on it': Special needs teachers' opinions on the assessment and teaching priorities of pupils on the autism spectrum. *Journal of Intellectual Disabilities, 26*(1), 211–226. https://doi.org/10.1177/1744629520972901

Huitsing, G. A., Lodder, G. M., Browne, W. J., Oldenburg, B., & Veenstra, R. (2020). A large-scale replication of the effectiveness of the KiVa antibullying program: A randomized controlled trial in the Netherlands. *Prevention Science, 21*(5), 627–638. https://doi.org/10.1007/s11121-020-01116-4

Humphrey, N., & Lewis, S. (2008). "Make me normal": The views and experiences of pupils on the autistic spectrum in mainstream secondary schools. *Autism, 12*(1), 23–46. https://doi.org/10.1177/1362361307085267

Humphrey, N., & Symes, W. (2010). Perceptions of social support and experience of bullying among pupils with autistic spectrum disorders in mainstream secondary schools. *European Journal of Special Needs Education, 25*(1), 77–91. https://doi.org/10.1080/08856250903450855

Jones, S. C. (2022). Measuring the wrong thing the right way? Time to rethink autism research tools. *Autism in Adulthood, 4*(2), 104–109. https://doi.org/10.1089/aut.2021.0050

Kasari, C., Rotheram-Fuller, E., Locke, J., & Gulsrud, A. (2012). Making the connection: Randomized controlled trial of social skills at school for children with autism spectrum disorders. *Journal of Child Psychology and Psychiatry, and Allied Disciplines, 53*(4), 431–439. https://doi.org/10.1111/j.1469-7610.2011.02493.x

Leaf, J. B., Ferguson, J. L., Cihon, J. H., Milne, C., Leaf, R., & McEachin, J. (2020). A critical review of social narratives. *Journal of Developmental and Physical Disabilities, 32,* 241–256. https://doi.org/10.1007/s10882-019-09692-2

Lebenhagen, C. (2022). Autistic students' views on meaningful inclusion: A Canadian perspective. *Journal of Education.* https://doi.org/10.1177_00220574221101378

Light, J., & McNaughton, D. (2012). The changing face of augmentative and alternative communication: Past, present, and future challenges. *Augmentative and Alternative Communication, 28*(4), 197–204. https://doi:10.3109/07434618.2012.737024

Locke, J., Williams, J., Shih, W., & Kasari, C. (2017). Characteristics of socially successful elementary school-aged children with autism. *Journal of Child Psychology and Psychiatry, and Allied Disciplines, 58*(1), 94–102. https://doi.org/10.1111/jcpp.12636

Lorenc, T., Rodgers, M., Marshall, D., Melton, H., Rees, R., Wright, K., & Sowden, A. (2018). Support for adults with autism spectrum disorder without intellectual impairment: Systematic review. *Autism: The International Journal of Research and Practice, 22*(6), 654–668. https://doi.org/10.1177/1362361317698939

Loveland, K. A., & Tunali, B. (1991). Social scripts for conversational interactions in autism and down syndrome. *Journal of Autism and Developmental Disorders, 21*(2), 177–186.

Mason, L., & Otero, M. (2021). Just how effective is direct instruction? *Perspectives on Behavior Science, 44*(2–3), 225–244. https://doi.org/10.1007/s40614-021-00295-x

Milton, D. E. (2012). On the ontological status of autism: the 'double empathy problem'. *Disability & Society, 27*(6), 883–887. https://doi.org/10.1080/09687599.2012.710008

O'Donoghue, M I., O'Dea, A., O'Leary, N., Kennedy, N., Forbes, J., & Murphy, C. (2021). Systematic review of peer-mediated intervention for children with autism who are minimally verbal. *Review Journal of Autism and Developmental Disorders. 8*, 1–16. https://doi.org//10.1007/s40489-020-00201-2

Saggers, B. (2015). Student perceptions: Improving the educational experiences of high school students on the autism spectrum. *Improving Schools.* https://doi.org/10.1177/1365480214566213

Sasson, N. J., Faso, D. J., Nugent, J., Lovell, S., Kennedy, D. P., & Grossman, R. B. (2017). Neurotypical peers are less willing to interact with those with Autism based on thin slice judgments. *Scientific Reports, 7.* https://doi.org/10.1038/srep40700

Schlieder, M., Maldonado, N., & Baltes, B. (2014). An investigation of "Circle of Friends" peer-mediated intervention for students with autism. *The Journal of Social Change, 6*(1), 27–40. https://doi.org/10.5590/JOSC.2014.06.1.0

Schroeder, J. H., Cappadocia, M. C., Bebko, J. M., Pepler, D. J., & Weiss, J. A. (2014). Shedding light on a pervasive problem: a review of research on bullying experiences among children with autism spectrum disorders. *Journal of Autism and developmental Disorders, 44*(7), 1520–1534. https://doi.org/10.1007/s10803-013-2011-8

Scott-Barrett, J., Cebula, K., & Florian, L. (2018). Listening to young people with autism: learning from researcher experiences. *International Journal of Research & Method in Education, 42*, 1–22. https://doi.org.10.1080/1743727X.2018.1462791

Shochet, I. M., Saggers, B. R., Carrington, S. B., Orr, J. A., Wurfl, A. M., Kelly, R. L., & Duncan, B. M. (2022). A school-based approach to building resilience and mental health among adolescents on the autism spectrum: A longitudinal mixed methods study. *School Mental Health: A Multidisciplinary Research and Practice Journal.* https://doi.org/10.1007/s12310-022-09501-w

Simó-Pinatella, D., Günther-Bel, C., & Mumbardó-Adam, C. (2021). Addressing challenging behaviours in children with autism: A qualitative analysis of teachers' experiences. *International Journal of Disability, Development and Education.* https://doi.org/10.1080/1034912X.2020.1870664

Stephenson, J., Browne, L., Carter, M., Clark, T., Costley, D., Martin, J., William, K.,... & Sweller, N. (2020). Facilitators and barriers to inclusion of students with ASD: Parent, teacher, and principal perspectives. *Australasian Journal of Special and Inclusive Education, 45*(1), 1–17. https://doi.org/10.1017/jsi. 2020.12

Symes, W., & Humphrey, N. (2011). The deployment, training and teacher relationships of teaching assistants supporting pupils with autistic spectrum disorders (ASD) in mainstream secondary schools. *British Journal of Special Education, 38*(2), 57–64. https://doi.org/10.1111/j.1467-8578.2011.00499.x

Taheri, A., Perry, A., & Minnes, P. (2016). Examining the social participation of children and adolescents with intellectual disabilities and autism spectrum disorder in relation to peers. *Journal of Intellectual Disability Research, 60*(5). https://doi.org/10.1111/jir.12289

Tierney, S., Burns, J., & Kilbey, E. (2016). Looking behind the mask: Social coping strategies of girls on the autistic spectrum. *Research in Autism Spectrum Disorders, 23,* 73–83. https://doi.org/10.1016/j.rasd.2015.11.013

Van der Steen, S., Steenbeek, H., Den Hartigh, R. J. R., & Van Geert, P. (2019). The link between microdevelopment and long-term learning trajectories in science learning. *Human Development, 63,* 4–32. https://doi.org/10.1159/000501431

Vidal, V., & DeThorne, L. (2021). Effectiveness of a supports-based approach to peer interactions of an autistic student in the classroom: A mixed-methods study. *Perspectives, 6*(2), 327–343. https://doi.org/10.1044/2021_PERSP-20-00223

Vine Foggo, R. S., & Webster, A. A. (2016). Understanding the social experiences of adolescent females on the autism spectrum. *Research in Autism Spectrum Disorders, 35,* 74–85. https://doi.org/10.1016/j.rasd.2016.11.006

Wilkenfeld, D. A., & McCarthy, A. M. (2020). Ethical concerns with applied behavior analysis for Autism Spectrum "Disorder". *Kennedy Institute of Ethics Journal, 30*(1), 31–69. https://doi.org/10.1353/ken.2020.0000

Williams, E. I., Gleeson, K., & Jones, B. E. (2019). How pupils on the autism spectrum make sense of themselves in the context of their experiences in a mainstream school setting: A qualitative meta synthesis. *Autism, 23*(1), 8–28. https://doi.org/10.1177/1362361317723836

Woodfield, C., & Ashby, C. (2016). 'The right path of equality': Supporting high school students with autism who type to communicate. *International Journal of Inclusive Education, 20*(4), 435–454. https://doi.org/10.1080/13603116.2015.1088581

Young, K., McNamara, P. M., & Coughlan, B. (2017). Authentic inclusion-utopian thinking? – Irish post-primary teachers' perspectives of inclusive education. *Teaching and Teacher Education,68,* 1–11. https://doi.org/10.1016/j.tate.2017.07.017

Zeedyk, S., Rodriguez, G., Tipton, L. A., Baker, B. L. & Blacher, J. (2014). Bullying of youth with autism spectrum disorder, intellectual disability, or typical development: victim and parent perspectives. *Research in Autism Spectrum Disorders, 8,* 1173–83. https://doi.org/10.1016/j.rasd.2014.06.001

Chapter 6

Classroom Environment

CHAPTER OVERVIEW

SECTION ONE

1. The 5Cs of Inclusion | Classroom Environment
2. Vignette 1: The Difficulties with Gym Class
3. Vignette 2: Inattention or Distraction?

SECTION TWO

4. Inclusionary Framework to Support Student Connection
5. Reflective Questions for Teachers, Parents, and Practitioners
6. Additional Readings and Resources
7. Chapter Summary

DOI: 10.4324/9781032687926-6

SECTION ONE

The 5Cs of Inclusion | *Classroom Environment*

Review of the Research	• Classroom environments affect autistic students' physical and psychological well-being and, thus their ability to successfully participate in school. • Sensory processing impacts autistic students' communication, attention, concentration, regulation, and achievement. • Autistic students like to have flexible choices in sensory supports and classroom accommodations.

A majority of autistic individuals (87–95%) report hyper and hypo sensitivities to sensory stimuli (Foley & Baz, 2021; Marco et al., 2011), which has been a diagnostic feature of autism since the 1940s, as described by Leo Kanner (1943) and Hans Asperger (1944). Hyper-sensitive means that a person is over-reactive or has a low threshold to a particular sensory stimulus, and hypo-sensitive means that a person is under-reactive or has a high threshold to a specific sensory stimulation, which includes auditory (hearing), visual (seeing), and tactile (feeling) stimuli (Marco et al., 2011). Autistic students who have difficulty regulating their response to environmental stimuli may compensate by seeking stimulation (i.e., swings) or avoiding stimulation (i.e., running from the sound of toilets flushing) (Roberts et al., 2007). Multisensory integration refers to the brain's ability to integrate various aspects of sensory stimuli into meaningful information and is considered essential for high-level cognitive functions (Stein & Stanford, 2008). However, the term multisensory is often misused when it implies that a person is being exposed to or uses two different sensory modalities (i.e., seeing and hearing), more accurately referred to as cross-modal stimuli (Stein & Stanford, 2008). Most autistic people experience difficulties with multisensory integration (Marco et al., 2011; Parmar et al., 2020), which has been found to impact the severity of autistic traits and the development of speech and social-communication skills (Cascio et al., 2016; Feldman et al., 2018; Gonçalves & Monterio, 2023; Marco et al., 2011; Turi et al., 2016). For instance, the integration of auditory stimuli (i.e., voice) and visual stimuli (i.e., facial expressions) is an integral aspect of speech development and one's ability to interpret the emotions of others (Stevenson et al., 2014). The observed behaviours of autistic students with sensory processing challenges may include covering their ears in a seemingly quiet classroom, refusing to wear socks and shoes, avoiding touch, and preferring to work with the lights turned off. In addition to hyper/hypo sensitivities, autistic students may have fixed sensory interests in objects or aspects of their environment, such as spinning toys and reflections (Simmons et al., 2009).

Sensory Integration therapies are developed by occupational therapists who provide carefully selected sensory stimuli during planned activities to ensure autistic students receive "just-right" sensory stimulation (Pfeiffer et al., 2013). The goal of sensory integration is to alter autistic children's responses to sensory stimulation by re-teaching the nervous system to interpret, organise, and integrate environmental stimuli so that they can more easily and successfully participate in learning, communication, socialisation, and aspects of daily living (Baranek, 2002). In research, discrepancies exist in findings on the positive effects of multisensory integration and autism severity, which have been attributed to differences in study design, age and development of participants, and the differences in stimuli used with participants (Beker et al., 2018; Chan et al., 2016; Stevenson et al., 2016). For example, some research finds inconsistencies and challenges with multisensory integration in autistic children may be due to delayed maturation, not impairment (Crosse et al., 2022; Becker et al., 2018). Other studies report that following carefully planned and individualised sensory integration therapies, autistic children generally display less stereotyped or self-stimulatory behaviours and are better able to process sensory stimuli, regulate their emotions, and employ fine motor skills (Pfeiffer et al., 2013). However, the generalisability of outcomes among autistic children is mixed, possibly due to the heterogeneity of autistic people and because little research has been conducted on the efficacy of sensory integration in school settings (Dynia et al., 2022). Several sensory-based interventions have little to no evidence of effectiveness and should not be used in school settings due to safety concerns (Dynia et al., 2022). These include joint compression, body brushing, and weighted vests (Moore et al., 2015; Reichow et al., 2010).

Sensory Phenotypes

To assist educators, practitioners, and parents in developing a more accurate understanding of autistic children's sensory preferences and aversions, sensory data was collected from 599 autistic children and adults between the ages of 1 and 21 years by researchers Scheerer et al. (2021), who identified five main sensory phenotypes: (1) sensory adaptive, (2) generalised sensory differences, (3) taste and smell sensitivity, (4) under-responsive and sensation seeking, and (5) movement difficulties. Interestingly, researchers also found that "age, adaptive behaviour, and traits associated with autism, attention-deficit and hyperactivity disorder, and obsessive and compulsive disorder were found to differ significantly across the five phenotypes" (Scheerer et al., 2021, p.1). Particularly relevant to discussions on behavioural-based interventions, researchers also state that behavioural challenges experienced by autistic children, youth, and young adults are strongly related to their sensory processing difficulties, suggesting that behavioural-based interventions that account for a student's unique sensory phenotype may be more effective in promoting skill development and generalised use (Scheerer et al.,

2021). To prevent misconceptions about the relationship between the severity of an autistic person's sensory symptoms and cognitive abilities, researchers find no predictive relationship exists between the two variables (Ben-Sasson et al., 2021; O'Donnell et al., 2012; Scheerer et al., 2021), and instead, sensory seeking and under-responsiveness is associated with academic underachievement (Ashburner et al., 2008). A synthesis of the five sensory phenotypes and descriptive characteristics of the associated learner profile is presented below in Table 1: Sensory Phenotypes and Learner Characteristics and is conceptually integrated within the responsive framework used throughout this chapter.

Section Highlights

- Most autistic students are hypo/hypersensitive to sensory stimuli and struggle with multisensory processing.
- Difficulties associated with multisensory integration affect autistic students' communication, socialisation, concentration, and states of psychological and physical states of well-being.
- Understanding autistic students' sensory phenotype is useful for informing which environmental accommodations will most respond to student needs.

Vignette 1: Gym Class

Teacher

My co-teacher and I have been working with Charlie and his physical education teacher throughout the school year to try and develop a plan to help Charlie feel less anxious about participating in gym class. Recently Charlie verbalised his thoughts on a few of the barriers that he thinks are preventing him from being in the gymnasium, let alone participating. Charlie shared that he does not like changing in the general changing room, and he really does not like to be touched by peers or be in a situation where he is at risk of being touched. Charlie also shared that the noise can be overwhelming, with all the yelling from the other kids, squeaking shoes, and bouncing balls. He also feels anxious when he is randomly asked to pick a partner. Charlie's anxiety around gym class has increased significantly, and his parents shared that the thought of it consumes him throughout the day and on weekends. We have tried several strategies, but none have been genuinely effective. For instance, we have arranged for Charlie to change in a smaller space to avoid changing in front of peers and to help alleviate his fear of being touched, Charlie wears his air pods during gym class to help drown out the noise. However, with these accommodations, Charlie thinks he "sticks out" from his peers, which in turn increases his anxiety. To help with his anxiousness and discomfort with being touched, the physical education teacher provides Charlie with an alternate activity to minimise his anticipation or risk of being touched by

Table 1 Sensory Phenotypes and Learner Characteristics

Sensory Phenotype	Description	Learner Characteristics
Sensory Adaptive (SA)	• Typical tactile, taste/ smell, movement, sensory seeking, and auditory/visual processing • Probable differences in low energy/weakness	• Highest adaptive functioning
Generalised Sensory Difference (GSD)	• Differences in tactile, taste/ smell, movement, sensory seeking, and auditory/visual processing	• Lowest adaptive functioning • Most restricted and repetitive behaviours, communication difficulties, hyperactive, inattentive, and compulsive behaviours • While most sensory processing difficulties, **not** most cognitively impaired
Taste and Smell Sensitivity (TSS)	• Typical movement and low energy/weakness • Differences in tactile, taste/ smell, movement, sensory seeking, and auditory/visual processing	• Higher repetitive behaviours and hyperactivity
Under-Responsive/ Sensory Seeking (URRS)	• Typical taste/smell, movement, low energy/ weakness • Differences in sensory seeking and auditory filtering • Probable differences in auditory/visual and tactile processing	• Lower adaptive functioning • May benefit from supports to promote physical accessibility and access to diverse sensory input activities and environments
Movement Difficulties and Low Energy/Weak (M/LEW)	• Differences in movement, under responsiveness, sensory seeking, auditory filtering, and low energy/ weakness • Probable differences in tactile, taste/smell, and visual and auditory processing	• Lower adaptive functioning • May benefit from supports to promote physical accessibility and access to diverse sensory input activities and environments

others. The teacher also now chooses a partner or group for Charlie so that Charlie feels less pressure to talk to multiple people in search of a partner. As a team, we decided to gradually increase Charlie's participation in gym by chunking time, starting with 5–10 minutes, and then gradually increasing with his input. The last thing that we have tried, which seems to have helped reduce Charlie's anxiety at home, is to send home weekly schedules, which allows Charlie to see what his class will be doing the following week in gym class, making it more predictable for him. However, I must say, even with all of these strategies and accommodations, we are still struggling to get Charlie actively involved in gym class.

Student

I am getting so frustrated and consumed by gym class and it is taking an emotional toll on my health not only at school, but at home too. I am constantly thinking about what we will be doing in gym class if I will feel comfortable participating. I finally opened up to my teachers, explaining the triggers that set me off. My teachers have tried to help me and have offered many solutions, but the anxiety and sensory overload I feel is still too much for me when I try to go to gym class. It's really tough because I love sports, but I cannot find ways that don't immediately increase my anxiety and sensory difficulties. One of the main things that increases my anxiety is when I have to pick a partner or a group— it's something that I have always had trouble with, but it seems worse now. Thankfully, my teachers now know this trigger and pick my partners and groups for me. Also, I wouldn't say I like the thought of being touched, so when we are doing activities that touch may be involved, it immediately increases my anxiety. The noise also makes me not able to think straight. I cannot stand the kids screaming, balls bouncing on the floor, or shoes squeaking across the gym. The noise usually becomes too much that I have to leave, which makes me feel guilty about missing class. My teacher has suggested wearing my earbuds in class to help with the noise, but then I feel like everyone is looking at me. I don't want to stand out to the rest of my class. I already feel like everyone is always watching me and will make fun of me if I make a mistake, like missing catching or hitting the ball in baseball. I want to participate and fit in, but I don't know how, so it's better to just not go to gym class.

Research Connections

A common yet frequently overlooked barrier to autistic students' participation in non-academic classes, such as physical education and music class, is the impact of unpredictable sensory stimuli, including lighting, bright colours and patterns, smells, sounds, motions, and people (Goodall, 2018; Lebenhagen, 2022; Parmar et al., 2020; Roberts & Webster, 2020; Zanuttini, 2023). Transitions involving themselves, peers, or staff within and in and out of classrooms and corridors mean autistic students are constantly exposed to ever-changing sensory stimuli. Throughout a school day, eventually leading to weeks and years of distressing experiences, it is easy to understand why school environments significantly affect autistic students' learning, communication, behaviour, and physical and psychological well-being. Furthermore, without input from autistic students, their actions easily become misinterpreted and viewed as task avoidance, attention-seeking, or manipulation. Charlie's fear of being touched, his dislike of screeching shoes and echoing balls, and the unpredictability of partner work affected his ability to transition to and participate in gym class. However, the distinction is noteworthy: a student's desire to participate versus a student's ability to participate without personalised support. If teachers, practitioners, and parents do not recognise the distinction between student interest and ability, the accumulation of misunderstandings may amount to high levels of anxiety and frustration, and eventually disengagement by autistic students, who become overwhelmed by the personal responsibility of overcoming barriers to participation despite their interest.

Difficulties associated with navigating the sensory aspects of school environments are at the core of many autistic students' negative emotional states, including irritability, fatigue, anxiousness, self-harm, and even physical pain, such as headaches (Neal & Frederickson, 2016; Parmer et al., 2020; Roberts & Simmons, 2015; Saggers et al., 2011; Skafle et al., 2020). Extreme and frequent exposure to uncomfortable and painful environmental stimuli can trigger fight, flight, and freeze responses, even "dysregulation-aggression" in autistic students (Foley & Baz, 2021). Uncustomary reactions from autistic students to commonplace school activities are difficult for neurotypical teachers and practitioners to comprehend, emphasising the importance of seeking the perspectives of autistic students to identify which aspects of the school environment are helpful or harmful to them. Additionally beneficial for staff and autistic students is connecting with and learning from other neurodivergent staff members who once faced similar challenges (StEvens, 2022) and can offer alternative perspectives and insights on solutions they found helpful.

To help reduce stress autistic students experience from overwhelming school environments, autistic students report wanting choice in seating, being able to transition between classes before or after large crowds, flexibility in participating in independent or small group work, and access to quiet and visually calm spaces where they do not have to earn or seek permission to access (Costley et al., 2021; Lebenhagen, 2022; Roberts & Simpson, 2016; Saggers, 2015; Scheerer et al., 2021). To strengthen the effectiveness of sensory supports, autistic students also want autonomy in decision-making, meaning they want a voice in what supports they will use at different times, in different activities and social contexts so that they can better support their fluctuating regulatory states and prevent embarrassment (Aubineau & Blicharska, 2020; Zanuttini, 2023). Research finds the provision of sensory supports and accommodations, whether they are individual (i.e., noise cancelling headphones) or universal (i.e., natural lighting), is one of the most

effective ways to reduce participation barriers for autistic students and, thus, max-
imises their potential to demonstrate their adaptive functioning, communication,
and social abilities (Nagib & Williams, 2017) more accurately and predictably.

Section Highlights

- School environments significantly affect autistic students' learning, communication, behaviour, and physical and psychological well-being in academic and
  non-academic activities.
- Frequent exposure to uncomfortable and painful environmental stimuli can
  trigger fight, flight, and freeze responses, even "dysregulation-aggression" in
  autistic students.
- Including autistic students' views in the selection and use of sensory supports
  and environmental accommodations ensures that they are both helpful and
  non-stigmatising.

Responsive Framework

Classroom Environment			
Student Name: Charlie **Grade:** Eleven	**Initial Date:** November **Review Dates:** January, March, May	**Team Members:** Charlie, Gym and classroom teachers, OT (need to contact)	
	Sensory Seeks	**Sensory Avoids**	**Accommodations**
Auditory		Loud spaces (gym), squeaking shoes and balls bouncing, screaming from kids	Earbuds and a schedule of gym activities so that Charlie can choose which sensory-friendly units he will participate in.
Visual			
Tactile		Being touched by peers	Separate change room, partner chosen prior to class or no partner option

Taste/Smell
Universal Supports

- ☐ Students have a choice of seating
- ☐ Learning tools, resources, supplies, and activities are minimal and well organised
- ☐ Desks/tables are organised with spaces for sitting, standing, and moving
- ☐ Classroom walls, shelves, and desks are free from clutter
- ☐ Walls are a neutral background, and displays use soft colours and low sheen
- ☐ Space is provided for visual information (i.e., daily schedule and announcements)
- ☐ Lighting is natural and diffused; florescent lighting avoided
- ☐ The classroom has controlled temperature (heating and cooling)
- ☐ Background noises are minimal, including sounds from fans, music, chatter
- ☐ Noise reduction headphones/personal headphones are permitted
- ☐ Quiet spaces are close by (i.e., do not require long transitions to access)
- ☑ Transitions are flexible, allowing students to use wide corridors or avoid loud/busy/chaotic spaces
- ☐ Closed captioning is used alongside verbal instructions/lectures
- ☐ Technology is charged and readily accessible (i.e., laptops, iPads)

Additional Information:
Charlie will have the choice of which PE units he will participate in the gym and for those that he declines participation in, he will have the opportunity to earn credit by engaging in preferred physical activity outside of the gymnasium, after school, or during community recreation. The school occupational therapist will be consulted as an additional resource to assess and provide sensory support.

Learning and Inclusionary Benefits

The anticipated learning and inclusionary benefits of using the Classroom Environment framework are:

- The framework is adapted to support Charlie in gym class, which highlights staff flexibility in using a tool to support students in learning environments out side of the classroom.
- Teachers develop a shared understanding of Charlie's sensory preferences and identify a gap, where a consultation with the school occupational therapist is needed to learn more about Charlie's sensory profile and investigate add-itional ways to support Charlie's participation in gym class.

- Teachers acknowledge Charlie's interpretations of his sensory experiences, and an action plan is clearly defined to support Charlie's concerns.
- Accommodations are flexible, allowing for Charlie's self-determination in when, how, and where he participates in physical activity.
- Charlie's voice and choice (autonomy) are included in the programming and the selection of supports and accommodations to ensure they are responsive to his changing sensory and regulatory states and social preferences.
- Charlie actively evaluates selected supports and accommodations, providing him with real-world opportunities to practice and develop his self-advocacy and problem-solving skills.

Vignette 2: Inattention or Distraction?

Parent

Musa is in grade eight and has enjoyed attending school up until recently. Thankfully, he has a good group of friends with whom he has gone to school since grade one, which helps him stay motivated. Our biggest challenge this year is the number of different teachers he has had to get to know, which is much different than when he was in elementary school. Each teacher has different rules and approaches, which means that Musa does well in some classes and not others. As we are nearing the end of the school year, I am concerned about his grades slipping and how this will impact the courses he chooses in high school and his chances of getting into university. Class sizes are much larger, too, and Musa seems to need help understanding what he has to do to complete homework. Thankfully most of his teachers post lesson notes online so that I can help him, but it feels like we are doing night school after daytime school—which to be honest is frustrating for both Musa and me. This term, Musa complains a lot about having headaches at school and dislikes the lab's smell where they do science experiments. We have had his vision checked, so know that's not the problem. Having 15 minutes to meet with each teacher during parent-teacher interviews is difficult to really get at the root of the problem, and everyone seems to have a different opinion and solution. I have tried to talk with Musa, but he says he doesn't know why he is getting headaches and gets irritated if I talk about his grades or university too much. He never really likes to talk a lot. He generally is an easygoing kid and doesn't complain too much, which is also concerning because if he doesn't tell me what's happening, it's hard for me to help.

Child

Yea, my grades aren't as good as they used to be, which kinda sucks, but I'm not too worried about it because they are okay. At the end of the day, I am so tired, I like my teachers, but they talk so much sometimes, which makes my brain hurt. There is always so much talking and less time for breaks in junior high. Also, it's a bit hard to concentrate on what the teachers are saying when I have to sit at the back of the classroom, especially when the kids are moving around a lot and making little tapping sounds with their feet or pencil, even whispering. I started to get headaches by the third period, especially if I had science. In elementary I really liked science class, but now the smell in the lab makes me want to gag, it's so strong some days. But I don't really say anything to my friends or teachers because it doesn't seem to bother anyone else, and what else am I supposed to do, it's not like I will wear my nose plugs or do experiments in the library, but I am starting to dread going there. Sometimes I go late to class just so I don't have to be in there as long, but then I hate walking in front of everyone, so it's another double whammy. I don't really like to talk about it too much, it's more talking and it's kinda embarrassing. I just try and cope and get through the day.

Research Connections

Autistic students repeatedly share how noisy, busy, and chaotic classrooms negatively impact their ability to attend to information and concentrate on completing their schoolwork (Goodall, 2018; Hummerstone & Parsons, 2021; Lebenhagen, 2022; Saggers et al., 2011; Williams et al., 2019), which provokes the question of inattention or distractibility (Mallory & Keehn, 2021). Inattention is often framed as a skill deficit, whereas distractions are commonly viewed as originating from a person's surroundings. Attention is the act of conscious observation, whereas distractibility refers to a person's ability to maintain attention (APA, 2023). Studies show that autistic students have difficulty ignoring sensory information that is irrelevant to the task they are attending to (Smith & Sharp, 2013), which may be a result of their increased perceptual capacity or sensitivity to environmental stimuli (Ben-Sasson et al., 2023; Smith & Sharp, 2013; Tillmann & Swettenham, 2017).

Specifically, autistic students may struggle with one or several aspects of attention, including divided attention (i.e., listening to the teacher talk while taking notes), sustained attention (i.e., reading long passages of text), selective attention (i.e., listening to a friend tell a story in a noisy cafeteria), and spatial attention (i.e., moving around desks to get to the pencil sharpener (Parmar et al., 2021; Smith, 2014; Gonçalves & Monterio, 2022). Avoidance is a strategy many autistic students use to prevent feelings of embarrassment and failure associated with distractibility and sensory processing, which includes cafeterias, gymnasiums, busy corridors, and loud classrooms (Mallory & Keegn, 2021; Rouvali & Riga, 2021). Autistic students report that the stress caused by unpredictable environmental stimuli can increase feelings of anxiousness because they are uncertain how their bodies will respond, making them feel unprepared and ill-equipped to cope

(Mallory & Keegn, 2021). Often, adults are unaware of the inner tension autistic students feel and the self-talk they use to help them prepare for uncertainty. For example, as one autistic student shares, "And I heard the buzzer and I started to have panic, like, 'Ahh!,' like the panic that my brain is going in, like 'what should I do, what should I do? Ahh!' It's kind of like bouncing off the walls in, um, my head, like 'what should I do?'" (Kirby et al., 2015, p. 9). These events highlight the importance of proactively incorporating student voice into information-gathering practices used by stakeholders to be better positioned to identify effective and ethically responsive support for autistic students.

Regularly, autistic students describe their sensory preferences in phrases of likes and dislikes (Kirby et al., 2015; Rouvali & Riga, 2021). For example, they may share that they don't like wearing denim or long-sleeved shirts or, concerning Musa, he expresses his dislike for science class because of the strong odour in the lab. While expressing sensory preferences in terms of likes and dislikes is helpful, when a distinction between activity preference and sensory preference is not made, there is the potential for autistic students to unnecessarily restrict their interests, leading to reduced participation in school activities that they are both interested and skillful in engaging with. Research finds that the sensory reactions and preferences of autistic children change over time; explanations for these alterations vary and may be a result of maturation, the effectiveness of interventions, student choice in supports, and masking reactions to their sensory aversions (Costley et al., 2021; Miller et al., 2021; Unwin et al., 2021). For example, a young child may dislike showers, brushing their hair, or eating foods with soft textures, but over time, more readily engage in these activities with little to no protest. The heterogeneity of sensory preferences in autistic children, the timing of interventions, and the different ways autistic students utilise coping responses also help to explain variability in the effectiveness of interventions in autistic students in school settings (Kirby et al., 2015; Scheerer et al., 2021). Therefore, understanding and supporting autistic students' unique sensory profiles in different classroom environments is a necessary step. Negating the provision of appropriate environmental accommodations for autistic students leads to increased distractibility, reduced perceptions of ability, poor academic performance, anxiousness, frustration, embarrassment, and even physical pain (Kirby et al., 2015); they should strongly be considered alongside the provision of other universal student supports.

Section Highlights

- Autistic students' attention and concentration are highly affected by sensory stimuli from school environments.
- Many autistic students express their sensory preferences in the form of likes and dislikes; however, with the help of teachers, practitioners, and parents,

they can learn to differentiate between their interest in activities and sensory experiences associated with the activity.

- While autistic students want access to sensory supports and accommodations, they do not want to stand out from their peers when receiving them.

Responsive Framework

Classroom Environment			
Student Name: Musa **Grade:** Eight	**Initial Date:** February **Review Dates:** Monthly (email)		**Team Members:** Musa, parents, humanity teacher, science teacher
	Sensory Seeks	**Sensory Avoids**	**Accommodations**
Auditory		Tapping noises when the teacher is speaking (i.e., feet, pens). People talking for extended periods of time.	Musa will have a choice in seating at the front of the room to minimise distractions and to be closer to the teacher
Visual			
Tactile			
Taste/Smell		Odours in the science lab	All chemicals will be stored in the back room and an air purifier will be requested. On days when the smell is too strong, Musa will have the option to participate online, with 1-2 peers from the library

Universal Supports
☑ Students have a choice of seating
☐ Learning tools, resources, supplies, and activities are minimal and well organised
☐ Desks/tables are organised with spaces for sitting, standing, and moving
☑ Classroom walls, shelves, and desks are free from clutter
☐ Walls are a neutral background, and displays use soft colours and low sheen
☐ Space is provided for visual information (i.e., daily schedule and announcements)
☐ Lighting is natural and diffused; florescent lighting avoided
☐ The classroom has controlled temperature (heating and cooling)
☑ Background noises are minimal, including sounds from fans, music, chatter
☐ Noise reduction headphones/personal headphones are permitted
☑ Quiet spaces are close by (i.e., do not require long transitions to access)
☑ Transitions are flexible, allowing students to use wide corridors or avoid loud/busy/chaotic spaces
☐ Closed captioning is used alongside verbal instructions/lectures
☐ Technology is charged and readily accessible (i.e., laptops, iPads)

Additional Information:
Teachers will connect monthly with Musa and parents via email to share the effectiveness of classroom accommodations to support Musa's sensory needs and make adjustments as necessary. A list of accommodations and supports will be compiled to develop a clear transition plan into grade 9.

Learning and Inclusionary Benefits

The anticipated learning and inclusionary benefits of using the Classroom Environment framework are:

- The framework allows Musa, his parents, and multiple teachers to develop a shared understanding of Musa's sensory needs in a junior high setting that requires him to adapt to various classroom environments.
- Musa's preference for minimal talking is accounted for by setting up regular check-ins using email among team members.
- Musa has a voice and choice (autonomy) in which supports and accommodations he will use in different classroom and social environments and the context of the learning tasks being presented to him.
- Through collaboration and shared problem-solving, Musa learns to select, use, and evaluate the effectiveness of his chosen supports and accommodations,

which helps Musa increase his self-awareness, develop problem-solving skills, and improve his confidence as an integral partner in his education.

SECTION TWO

Inclusionary Framework to Support Student Connection

		Classroom Environment		
Student Name: **Grade:**	**Initial Date:** **Review Dates:**		**Team Members:**	
	Sensory Seeks	**Sensory Avoids**	**Accommodations**	
Auditory				
Visual				
Tactile				
Taste/Smell				
Universal Supports				

- ☐ Students have choice of seating
- ☐ Learning tools, resources, supplies, and activities are minimal and well organised
- ☐ Desks/tables are organised with spaces for sitting, standing, and moving
- ☐ Classroom walls, shelves, and desks are free from clutter
- ☐ Walls are a neutral background, and displays use soft colours and low sheen
- ☐ Space is provided for visual information (i.e., daily schedule and announcements)
- ☐ Lighting is natural and diffused; florescent lighting avoided
- ☐ The classroom has controlled temperature (heating and cooling)
- ☐ Background noises are minimal, including sounds from fans, music, chatter

Universal Supports
☐ Noise reduction headphones/personal headphones are permitted
☐ Quiet spaces are close by (i.e., do not require long transitions to access)
☐ Transitions are flexible, allowing students to use wide corridors or avoid loud/busy/chaotic spaces
☐ Closed captioning is used alongside verbal instructions/lectures
☐ Technology is charged and readily accessible (i.e., laptops, iPads)

Additional Information:

Reflective Questions for Teachers, Parents, and Practitioners

1. In what ways is the knowledge and expertise of an occupational therapist integrated into the physical set-up of the classroom?
2. What exploratory activities do you use to learn about the sensory preferences of your students?
3. Which learning spaces, activities, and people do autistic students move towards (seek) or away from (avoid)?
4. Do your students have a choice in seating? What opportunities are provided to students to flexibly participate in learning from sensory-friendly people and spaces?
5. What school-wide processes encourage stakeholders to develop a shared understanding of how Universal Design for Learning principles can be used to create sensory-friendly and inclusive school spaces?

Additional Readings and Resources

1. Alcott, A. (2022). *When things get too loud: A story about sensory overload.* Tiny Horse Books.
2. Acevedo, S. M., & Nusbaum, E. A. (2020). *Autism, neurodiversity, and inclusive education.* Oxford University Press. https://doi.org/10.1093/acrefore/978019 0264093.013.1260
3. Williams, Z. J., Failla, M. D., Gotham, K. O., Woynaroski, T. G., & Cascio, C. (2018). Psychometric evaluation of the short sensory profile in youth with autism spectrum disorder. *Journal of Autism and Developmental Disorders,* 48(12), 4231–4249. https://doi.org/10.1007/s10803-018-3678-7

Chapter Summary

A major theme identified by autistic students is that sensory aspects of the classroom and the school environment significantly impact their educational success and psychological and physical well-being. To avoid stigmatisation and to promote feelings of inclusion, autistic students' first preference is to have their individual sensory needs supported through universal school-wide approaches. For students who are not yet able to define, articulate, or feel comfortable expressing their sensory preferences, teachers and practitioners can gather informative data by observing school environments, activities, and people students gravitate towards or away from or ask simple yes/no questions related to activities, objects, spaces, and people they like or dislike, which is beneficial in helping students strengthen their self-awareness and develop a personalised toolkit of effective strategies to support their academic and well-being success.

Notes & Reflections

References

American Psychological Association. (2023). *APA dictionary of psychology*. https://diction ary.apa.org/distractibility

Ashburner, J., Ziviani, J., & Rodger, S. (2008). Sensory processing and classroom emotional, behavioral, and educational outcomes in children with autism spectrum disorder. *The American Journal of Occupational Therapy: Official Publication of the American Occupational Therapy Association, 62*(5), 564–573. https://doi.org/10.5014/ajot.62.5.564

Asperger, H. (1944). Autistic psychopathy in childhood. *Archiv fur Psychiatrie und Nervenkrankheiten, 117,* 76–136.

Aubineau, M., & Blicharska, T. (2020). High-functioning Autistic students speak about their experience of inclusion in mainstream secondary schools. *School Mental Health, 12*(3). https://doi.org/10.1007/s12310-020-09364-z

Bal V. H., Kim S. H., Cheong D., & Lord C. (2015). Daily living skills in individuals with autism spectrum disorder from 2 to 21 years of age. *Autism,* 19, 774–784. https://dpi. org/10.1177/1362361315575840

Baranek, G. T. (2002). Efficacy of sensory and motor interventions for children with autism. *Journal of Autism and Developmental Disorders, 32*(5), 397–422. https://doi.org/ 10.1023/a:1020541906063

Beker, S., Foxe, J. J., & Molholm, S. (2018). Ripe for solution: Delayed development of multisensory processing in autism and its remediation. *Neuroscience & Biobehavioral Review, 84,* 182–192. https://doi:10.1016/j.neubiorev.2017.11.008

Ben-Sasson, A., Gal, E., Fluss, R., Katz-Zetler, N., & Cermak, S. A. (2019). Update of a meta-analysis of sensory symptoms in ASD: A new decade of research. *Journal of Autism and Developmental Disorders, 49*(12), 4974–4996. https://doi.org/10.1007/s10 803-019-04180-0

Cascio, C. J., Woynaroski, T., Baranek, G. T., & Wallace, M. T. (2016). Toward an interdisciplinary approach to understanding sensory function in autism spectrum disorder. *Autism Research, 9,* 920–925. https://doi:10.1002/aur.1612

Chan, J. S., Langer, A., & Kaiser, J. (2016). Temporal integration of multisensory stimuli in autism spectrum disorder: A predictive coding perspective. *Journal of Neural Transmission, 123,* 917–923. https://doi:10.1007/s00702-016-1587-5

Costley, D., Emerson, A., Ropar, D., & Sheppard, E. (2021). The anxiety caused by secondary schools for autistic adolescents: In their own words. *Education Sciences.* https:// doi:11.726.10.3390/educsci11110726

Crosse, M. J., Foxe, J. J., Tarrit, K., Freedman, E. G., & Molholm, S. (2022). Resolution of impaired multisensory processing in autism and the cost of switching sensory modality. *Communications Biology, 5*(1), 1–17. https://doi.org/10.1038/s42003-022-03519-1

Dynia, J. M., Walton, K. M., Sagester, G. M., Schmidt, E. K., & Tanner, K. J. (2022). Addressing sensory needs for children with autism spectrum disorder in the classroom. *Intervention in School and Clinic.* https://doi.org/10.1177/10534512221093786

Feldman, J. I., Dunham, K., Cassidy, M., Wallace, M.T., Liu, Y., & Woynaroski, T.G. (2018). Audiovisual multisensory integration in individuals with autism spectrum disorder: A systematic review and meta-analysis, *Neuroscience and Biobehavioral Reviews.* https:// doi.org/10.1016/j.neubiorev.2018.09.020

Foley, G. M., & Baz, T. (2021). "Aggression" in young children on the autistic spectrum: The dysregulation–"aggression" hypothesis. *Emerging Programs for Autism Spectrum Disorder*, 141–160. https://doi.org/10.1016/B978-0-323-85031-5.00031-1

Gonçalves, A. M., & Monteiro, P. (2022). Autism Spectrum Disorder and auditory sensory alterations: A systematic review on the integrity of cognitive and neuronal functions related to auditory processing. *Journal of Neural Transmission, 130*(3), 325-408. https://doi.org/10.1007/s00702-023-02595-9

Goodall, C. (2018). 'I felt closed in and like I couldn't breathe': A qualitative study exploring the mainstream educational experiences of autistic young people. *Autism & Developmental Language Impairments, 3*. https://doi.org/10.1177/2396941518804407

Kanner, L. (1943). Autistic disturbances of affective contact, *Nervous Child, 2*, 217–250.

Kirby, A. V., Dickie, V. A., & Baranek, G. T. (2015). Sensory experiences of children with autism spectrum disorder: in their own words. *Autism: The International Journal of Research and Practice, 19*(3), 316–326. https://doi.org/10.1177/1362361314520756

Lebenhagen, C. (2022). Autistic students' views on meaningful inclusion: A Canadian perspective. *Journal of Education*. https://doi.org/10.1177_00220574221101378

Mallory, C., & Keehn, B. (2021). Implications of sensory processing and attentional differences associated with autism in academic settings: An integrative review. *Frontiers in Psychiatry, 12*, 695825. https://doi.org/10.3389/fpsyt.2021.695825

Marco, E. J., Hinkley, L. B., Hill, S. S., & Nagarajan, S. S. (2011). Sensory processing in autism: A review of neurophysiologic findings. *Pediatric Research, 69*(8), 48–54. https://doi.org/10.1203/PDR.0b013e3182130c54

Miller, D., Rees, J., & Pearson, A. (2021). "Masking is life": Experiences of masking in autistic and nonautistic adults. *Autism in Adulthood*, 330–338. http://doi.org/10.1089/aut.2020.0083

Moore, K. M., Cividini-Motta, C., Clark, K. M., & Ahearn, W.H. (2015). Sensory integration as a treatment for automatically maintained stereotypy. *Behavioral Interventions, 30*(2), 95–111. https://doi.org/10.1002/bin.1405

Nagib, W., & Williams, A. (2017) Toward an autism-friendly home environment, *Housing Studies, 32*(2), 140–167. https://doi/10.1080/02673037.2016.1181719

Neal, S., & Frederickson, N. (2016). ASD transition to mainstream secondary: A positive experience? *Educational Psychology in Practice*, 32(4), 355–373. http://doi.org/10.1080/02667363.2016.1193478

O'Donnell, S., Deitz, J., Kartin, D., Nalty, T., & Dawson, G. (2012). Sensory processing, problem behavior, adaptive behavior, and cognition in preschool children with autism spectrum disorders. *The American Journal of Occupational Therapy, 66*(5), 586–594. https://doi.org/10.5014/ajot.2012.004168

Parmar, K. R., Porter, C. S., Dickinson, C. M., Pelham, J., Baimbridge, P., & Gowen, E. (2021). Visual sensory experiences from the viewpoint of autistic adults. *Frontiers in Psychology*. https://doi.org/10.3389/fpsyg.2021.633037

Pfeiffer, B. A., Koenig, K., Kinnealey, M., Sheppard, M., & Henderson, L. (2013) Effectiveness of sensory integration interventions in children with autism spectrum disorders: A pilot study. *The American Journal of Occupational Therapy, 65*(1), 76. https://doi.org/10.5014/ajot.2011.09205

Reichow, B., Barton, E. E., Sewell, J. N., Good, L., & Wolery, M. (2010). Effects of weighted vests on the engagement of children with developmental delays and autism. *Focus on*

Autism and Other Developmental Disabilities, 25(1), 3–11. https://doi.org/10.1177/10883 57609353751

Roberts, J. E., King-Thomas, L., & Boccia, M. L. (2007). Behavioral indexes of the efficacy of sensory integration therapy. *The American Journal of Occupational Therapy, 61*(5), 555–562. https://doi.org/10.5014/ajot.61.5.555

Roberts, J., & Webster, A. (2022). Including students with autism in schools: A whole school approach to improve outcomes for students with autism, *International Journal of Inclusive Education, 26*(7), 701–718. https:/doi.org/10.1080/13603116.2020.1712622

Robertson, A. E., & Simmons, D. R. (2015). The sensory experiences of adults with autism spectrum disorder: A qualitative analysis. *Perception, 44*, 569–586.

Rouvali, A., & Riga, V. (2021) Listening to the voice of a pupil with autism spectrum condition in the educational design of a mainstream early years setting, *Education, 49*(4), 464–480. https://doi.org/10.1080/03004279.2020.1734042

Saggers, B., Hwang, Y. S., & Mercer, K.L. (2011). Your voice counts: Listening to the voice of high school students with autism spectrum disorder. *Australasian Journal of Special Education, 35*(2), 173–190. https://doi.org/10.1375/ajse.35.2.173

Scheerer, N. E., Curcin, K., Stojanoski, B., Anagnostou, E., Nicolson, R., Kelley, E.... & Stevenson, R. A. (2021). Exploring sensory phenotypes in autism spectrum disorder. *Molecular Autism, 12*(1), 67. https://doi.org/10.1186/s13229-021-00471-5

Siemann, J. K., Veenstra-VanderWeele, J., & Wallace, M. T. (2020). Approaches to understanding multisensory dysfunction in autism spectrum disorder. *Autism Research: Official Journal of the International Society for Autism Research, 13*(9), 1430. https://doi.org/10.1002/aur.2375

Simmons, D., Robertson, A., McKay, L., Toal E., McAleer, P., & Pollick, F. (2009). Vision in autism spectrum disorders. *Vision Research, 49*, 2705–2739. https://doi/10.1016/j.vis res.2009.08.005

Skafle, I., Nordahl-Hansen, A., & Øien, R. A. (2020). Short report: Social perception of high school students with ASD in Norway. *Journal of Autism and Developmental Disorders, 50*(2), 670–675. https://doi.org/10.1007/s10803-019-04281-w

Smith, A. D. (2014). Spatial navigation in autism spectrum disorders: A critical review. *Frontiers in Psychology, 6*. https://doi.org/10.3389/fpsyg.2015.00031

Smith, R. S., & Sharp, J. (2013). Fascination and isolation: A grounded theory exploration of unusual sensory experiences in adults with Asperger syndrome. *Journal of Autism and Developmental Disorders, 43*(4), 891–910. https://doi.org/10.1007/s10803-012-1633-6

Stein, B. E., & Stanford, T. R. (2008). Multisensory integration: Current issues from the perspective of the single neuron. *Nature Reviews, Neuroscience, 9*(4), 255–266. https://doi.org/10.1038/nrn2331

StEvens, C. (2022). The lived experience of autistic teachers: A review of the literature. *International Journal of Inclusive Education.* https://doi.org/10.1080/13603 116.2022.2041738

Stevenson, R. A., Segers, M., Ferber, S., Barense, M. D., Camarata, S. M., & Wallace, M. T. (2016). Keeping time in the brain: Autism spectrum disorder and audiovisual temporal processing. *Autism Research, 9*, 720–738. https://doi/10.1002/aur.1566

Tillmann, J., & Swettenham, J. (2017). Visual perceptual load reduces auditory detection in typically developing individuals but not in individuals with autism spectrum disorders. *Neuropsychology, 31*(2), 181–190. https://doi.org/10.1037/neu0000329

Turi, M., Karaminis, T., Pellicano, E., & Burr, D. (2016). No rapid audiovisual recalibration in adults on the autism spectrum. *Scientific Reports, 6,* 21756–21763. https://doi/10.1038/srep21756

Unwin, K. L., Powell, G., & Jones, C. R. (2021). The use of multi-sensory environments with autistic children: Exploring the effect of having control of sensory changes. *Autism.* https://doi.org/10.1177/13623613211050176

Williams, E. I., Gleeson, K., & Jones, B. E. (2019). How pupils on the autism spectrum make sense of themselves in the context of their experiences in a mainstream school setting: A qualitative metasynthesis. *Autism: The International Journal of Research and Practice, 23*(1), 8–28. https://doi.org/10.1177/1362361317723836

Zanuttini, J. Z. (2023). Capturing the perspectives of students with autism on their educational experiences: A systematic review. *International Journal of Educational Research, 117,* 102115. https://doi.org/10.1016/j.ijer.2022.102115

Chapter 7

Curriculum

CHAPTER OVERVIEW

SECTION ONE

1. The 5Cs of Inclusion | Curriculum
2. Vignette 1: Structured Work Systems and Student Motivation
3. Vignette 2: Arousal Regulation and Student Engagement
4. Vignette 3: Functional Life Skills and Self-Monitoring

SECTION TWO

5. Inclusionary Framework to Support Curriculum Adaptions and Modifications
6. Reflective Questions for Teachers, Practitioners, and Parents
7. Additional Readings and Resources
8. Chapter Summary

DOI: 10.4324/9781032687926-7

SECTION ONE

The 5Cs of Inclusion | *Curriculum*

Review of the Research	• Keeping up with curriculum demands and increased workloads is stressful for autistic students, especially as they advance into higher grades. • Fatigue, frustration, and a lack of motivation negatively affect autistic students' academic achievement. • Autistic students appreciate when teachers provide clear and consistent feedback and are open to providing adaptions and modifications. • Autistic students benefit from technology-aided support to help with written output.

Research finds that there is significant variability in autistic students' academic achievement (Keen et al., 2016; Kim et al., 2018), and despite high or low achievement, their graduation rates remain consistently poor (Griffith et al., 2012; Anderson et al., 2017; Humphrey & Lewis, 2008; Mason et al., 2018; McDougal et al., 2020; van Heijst & Geurts, 2015). This discrepancy suggests that intelligence scores (Ashburner et al., 2008) and academic achievement (McLaughlin & Rafferty, 2014) are not the only factors to be considered when preparing autistic students for school success, including graduation.

Approximately one-quarter to one-third of autistic students with average to above-average intelligence demonstrates below to low-average achievement in at least one academic area (Kim et al., 2018). Co-occurring learning disorders may partly explain lower-than-expected achievement (Hendren et al., 2018), estimated to occur in between 50–70% of autistic children (Mayes & Calhoun, 2006; McIntyre et al., 2017), with reading disorders the most common (Ibrahim, 2019), followed by writing and math disorders (Chung & Patel, 2015; May et al., 2015). Hence, many interventions used to support autistic students in inclusionary settings focus on improving academic achievement primarily in reading and mathematics (Macmillian et al., 2023; Ollson & Nilholm, 2023); although a weakness in one area (i.e., reading) does not mean a student will struggle in the other (i.e., math) (Kim et al., 2018). For example, many autistic children have trouble with phonetic-based reading and spelling programs, potentially because of challenges associated with processing verbal language, preference for visual learning, and responding to sensory stimuli involved with phonetic instruction (i.e., whole-class read-aloud while sitting on the carpet) (Wood, 2019).

Math achievement for autistic students is also inconsistent and has been found to change over time (Solari et al., 2019). Some autistic students demonstrate gifted abilities, while others find the subject difficult because of visual perception issues and seeing numbers (Woods, 2019). Which may be a reason why some students prefer and are more successful with virtual manipulatives over three-dimensional ones (Root et al., 2016). While most research finds that non-verbal cognitive ability and expressive language are the main factors affecting math achievement for autistic students, another important factor to consider is class-based math anxiety, which helps to explain up to 15% variability in math performance for autistic students (Howard, 2020). However, despite variability in math achievement, some autistic students report themselves as their favourite subject that they excel at (Clark & Adams, 2020).

Long-term academic outcomes are more favourable for autistic students who do not struggle with working memory or processing speed (Assouline et al., 2012) and when they meet grade-level reading targets (Whalon et al., 2009). However, the dilemma with meeting grade-level targets greatly depends on their development of emergent literacy skills, including alphabet knowledge, book knowledge, vocabulary, and phonological awareness (Dynia et al., 2014). Researchers also recommend that reading interventions should help autistic students develop nonverbal thinking, expressive language, and social skills, as these areas are accurate predictors of long-term reading ability (Davidson & Weismer, 2014; Ricketts et al., 2013).

When adaptions are made to learning environments to ensure that demands do not exceed ability, research finds student competency in written expression, including handwriting and essay writing, improves (Blakeley-Smith et al., 2009). Achievement in math also depends on ability to divide their attention between auditory and visual tasks, where autistic students with poor attention score lower than autistic students with average to above-average attention (McDouget et al., 2020), thus emphasising the need for teachers to consider environmental factors impacting students' attention and achievement. The relationship between attention, concentration, and academic achievement (McDougal, 2020) suggests that adaptions should primarily focus on removing environmental barriers while also providing support that enables autistic students to more easily and consistently access parts of their brain required for higher-order thinking (Theoharides & Kavalioti, 2019). Therefore, when designing learning tasks for autistic students (see Figure 1), it is important to find the sweet spot between the learning environment (i.e., attention and regulation) and the cognitive demand of the task (i.e., interesting and achievable) to optimise student engagement (i.e., time on task and independence) and achievement (i.e., learning and confidence). The uniqueness of this learning task design process means that environmental and cognitive factors *specific to the student* are considered the first step to success-based learning. If the learning environment and cognitive factors are unaligned or metaphorically too far apart, the likelihood of student disengagement increases, as does the perceived need for more support (or ineffective support), resulting in decreased

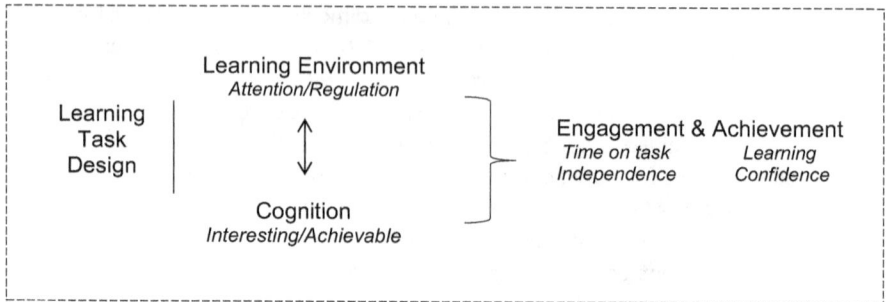

```
Learning Environment
     Attention/Regulation
Learning
  Task              ↕            Engagement & Achievement
 Design                          Time on task      Learning
                                 Independence      Confidence
             Cognition
        Interesting/Achievable
```

Figure 1 Learning Task Design

student confidence and achievement. Figure 1: Learning Task Design illustrates the effects of learning environment and cognitive engagement on student engagement and achievement.

Adaptions and Modifications

Due to the heterogeneity of the sensory and cognitive profiles of autistic students, a challenge for many teachers is finding ways to effectively adapt instructional pedagogies and modify curriculum to maximise student engagement and achievement. Adding to the issue is that teachers need to clearly understand the definition and purpose of adaptions and modifications, which often are misused with autistic students (Humphrey & Lewis, 2008; Lee et al., 2010). Adaptions are changes made to the learning environment and the methods used to assess student knowledge, they involve accommodations, including extended time and access support such as a scribe or technology (McGlynn & Kelly, 2019). Adaptions are used to make learning more accessible and, therefore, equitable for students, and despite misconceptions, do not give students an unfair advantage over other students. Modifications involve changing the learning objectives and skills students require to achieve the learning objectives (McGlynn & Kelly, 2019). Some students benefit from adaptions or modifications, while others benefit from both adaptations and modifications depending on the subject matter and their abilities. Simply put, adaptions are changes to the *how* of learning, and modifications are changes to the *what* of learning.

Universal Approaches to Support Learning

Universal approaches to enhance autistic students' engagement and success in learning incorporate autistic students' special interests and passions (Bond & Hebron, 2016). From the viewpoint of autistic students, this means that lessons and activities are interesting, fun, rewarding, and taught by passionate teachers

(Lebenhagen, 2022; Saggers et al., 2011). Incorporating student interests and passions to enhance learning provides an instructional "hook," it signals to students that their interests are important and promotes peer recognition and connection based on shared interests.

Peer-based learning is an instructional method used to help students solidify their knowledge and skills by teaching others, which has also been shown to decrease off-task behaviours in autistic students (McCurdy & Cole, 2014). **Game-based learning** is another evidence-based approach (Yi et al., 2021) designed to enhance student motivation, attention, and reward for learning while encouraging social interactions between students (Strickroth et al., 2020). Research finds that when autistic students use video games for educational purposes, there are positive effects on language development, math (Del Moral Pérez et al., 2018) and science skills (Lester et al., 2014). Video games are **technology-aided instruction,** defined as electronics, applications, online, and virtual networks used to teach skills or increase independence and productivity for learning, work, daily living, and leisure or recreation (Odom, Thompson et al., 2015).

Online games that teach spelling or story-based math problems are examples of game-based technology-aided instruction that incorporates principles of **task analysis**, **direct instruction**, **modeling**, **prompting**, and **reinforcement**. Task analysis involves breaking down a large and more complex task into smaller parts to make it more manageable and, therefore, likely the student will successfully learn the skill and use it independently in the future (Anderson et al., 1996). Direct instruction is the process of teaching smaller skills identified in task analysis and incorporates modeling, prompting, and reinforcement to promote student motivation, skill mastery, and generalisation before introducing the next step of the learning sequence (Strickroth et al., 2020). For online games, instructional components are pre-programmed according to standardised criteria. For example, in a game that teaches addition, a character moves three jelly beans into a basket holding four jelly beans (modeling) and then each jelly bean sparkles as they are counted out loud by the game character (verbal and visual prompt), when the number seven is selected as the answer balloons are released (reinforcement), which after a series of correct responses (mastery), the student moves on to addition to the value of ten (next step in the task-analysis sequence). In addition to improving academic skills, technology-aided instruction, such as tablets with timers, visual schedules, and lists, are also used to support skill development at home and community settings in areas of daily living (i.e., toileting and handwashing) and independent living (i.e., purchasing groceries, meal preparation, banking) (Shic & Goodwin, 2015). To highlight ways teachers and practitioners use adaptions and modifications to support autistic students, the framework titled *Curriculum Adaptations and Modifications* is used following the presentation of vignettes. The third vignette demonstrates how task analysis can be used as a self-monitoring strategy to develop functional living skills in the home environment; therefore, it does not include the *Curriculum Adaptations and Modifications* framework.

Section Highlights

- Despite having average to above-average intelligence, many autistic students show below-average to low-average school achievement and have poorer graduation rates compared to neurotypical students.
- The provision of adaptions and modifications alongside universal approaches to support learning strengthens autistic students' learning and motivation.
- Peer-based learning, game-based learning, and technology-aided instruction are evidence-based interventions to teach autistic students' academic, social, and adaptive functioning skills.

Vignette 1: Structured Work Systems and Student Motivation

Teacher

Emily started grade 1 by attending mornings only. At that time, trying to get her into the classroom was a huge challenge. Ms. Amanda, our education assistant, was instrumental in supporting Emily's transition, which some days took up to 45 minutes. Most days, Ms. Amanda also supported Emily with learning her basic numeracy and literacy skills. I think having an extra set of hands and eyes was beneficial to begin the year because we really got to know Emily's likes and dislikes and her pockets of strength, which also provided an opportunity for me and Ms. Amanda to grow our connection with Emily. Looking back, taking the time to get to know Emily to create fun learning activities at her level and to develop trust increased her motivation to take up her personalized work systems. I worked with our school's inclusive education consultant for September, and they helped me develop a personalised work system for Emily that focused on very short, low-demand, success-focused tasks that included pictures of Disney princess characters.

1As we approach the mid-way part of the school year, Emily is now attending full days of school but has been leaving the classroom unexpectedly in the afternoons and showing resistance and refusal at times to engage in her work system. Emily's communication challenges sometimes make it difficult for adults to understand her wants and needs. When Emily exits the classroom, she usually goes to the gym equipment and creates elaborate and imaginative narratives using the equipment as characters in her imaginative storylines. As a school team, we are exploring potential reasons why Emily is leaving the classroom. We plan to introduce more challenging learning tasks, as we think she is getting bored and seeking novelty. We also continue to balance keeping the bar high for Emily and providing unstructured free time for imaginative play when she is tired.

Student

I have fun playing with Ms. Amanda after I finish my work. We play princess board games and sometimes hide and seek in the hallway. My work bins are my very own centres. I take out the direction card, and after I finish, I stamp the card with my Little Mermaid stamp, Ariel. The other kids work in groups at centres. Sometimes Ms. Amanda tells me I can have a friend to play the game with us. Today, my teacher put me and Ms. Amanda in a math group with Cameron and Adam. I used the whiteboard to draw the numbers. I didn't want to do my work bins again in the afternoon. Sometimes I feel sleepy. I like going to the gym, laying on the cool mats, and playing princesses with the different coloured bean bags.

Research Connections

A major factor affecting the successful inclusion and achievement of autistic students is the teacher's ability to adapt learning environments and modify learning objectives (Petersson-Bloom & Holmqvist, 2022). Teachers' confidence in their ability to provide effective adaptations and modifications is based on how well they know their students (Howell et al., 2022). Teachers who have an in-depth understanding of their autistic student's report being able to "read" them (Howell et al., 2022); however, teachers admit that relationship building can take a long time, sometimes the entire school year, which can result in delays in programming and implementation of needed supports (Howell et al., 2022). Emily's teacher and education assistant recognise the benefits of getting to know Emily and how this has led to the development of positive relationships and insight into ways to provide Emily with meaningful adaptions and modifications. Taking the time to develop relationships with students and incorporate their interests into "just right" learning activities increases student motivation, which is considered a non-cognitive enabler for achievement (Aubineau & Blicharska, 2020; Keen et al., 2023). Teaching autistic students *how* to learn is as important as teaching *what* to learn and involves providing instructional experiences that not only challenge students cognitively, but also build their self-confidence, risk-taking, problem-solving, and independence (Howell et al., 2022).

Work systems are visually structured learning activities that teach students how and what to learn by systematically organising learning objectives to clarify what is required to complete the task (Hume & Odom, 2007). The design of work systems is typically based on four student-focused questions: 1) What activity am I expected to complete? 2) How many steps are involved? 3) How do I know when I am finished? and 4) What do I do when I am finished? (Mesibov et al., 2005). By using highly organised visual prompts such as trays, bins, and folders, the steps of the activity are sequenced to guide students from beginning to end, including a clearly marked "finished" basket or bin for the student to place the activity in once completed, followed by a visual prompt informing students what activity they can do once finished (Carnahan et al., 2009), such as jump on the trampoline or listen to music. More commonly used in elementary classrooms, the use of structured work systems at any age requires careful consideration and input from all stakeholders, including students, so that they are purposeful and practical, including the availability of resources needed to develop, monitor and evaluate their effectiveness concerning skill development, generalisation, and risk for stigmatisation (Howley, 2015). Work systems may be a worthwhile bridging strategy for students who require additional time to develop foundational learner skills and confidence in their abilities, as many autistic students' developmental path is delayed or different, not necessarily deficient (Keen et al., 2023).

Also affecting engagement and achievement are autistic students' reports of fatigue and how this negatively affects their attention, concentration, regulation, and behaviour (Howell et al., 2022; McCrae et al., 2020; Smith et al., 2016). Understanding factors contributing to autistic fatigue and burnout is gaining more interest in research, with autistic people reporting sensory overload (Phung et al., 2021), completing daily tasks, and constantly having to act normal (Welch et al., 2021) as primary causes. Therefore, when investigating explanations for students' inconsistent or underperformance, even disengagement, it is advantageous to seek parent and student perspectives on potential reasons for fatigue to identify proactive solutions to prevent or minimise contributing factors in the school environment, and to prevent misdirected behavioural-based interventions.

Section Highlights

- Successfully adaptions and modifications depend on how well teachers feel they know students.
- Structured work systems are useful tools to teach autistic students *how* and *what* to learn by providing structure and predictability.
- Fatigue and burnout are barriers to school motivation, participation, and achievement for autistic students.

Responsive Framework

Curriculum Adaptations and Modifications		
Student Name: Emily **Grade:** One	**Initial Date:** September **Review Dates:** Mid-year and End Year	**Team Members:** Emily, Mrs. B, Ms. Amanda (EA), Mom
Adaptions	**Notes**	
☐ Extended time for exams and assignments ☑ Separate learning spaces for independent work/exams ☐ Low/high arousal activity prior to learning ☐ Online/virtual attendance and participation ☑ Flexible timetable ☐ Assistive technology (specify type) ☐ Access to presentation notes/slides ☐ Flexible assessment (oral, written, visual) ☐ Access to a reader or scribe ☐ Graphic organisers	Emily will complete her work systems in a quiet area of the classroom alongside two other students who also use work systems. Over time, we would like to transition her bins and file folders to her desk. Emily will occasionally arrive later to school on days that she has had interrupted sleep and has slept in.	
Modifications	**Notes**	
☑ Altered learning objectives ☑ Altered tests/exams ☑ Altered grading criteria ☑ Significantly modified or no homework	Grade-level curriculum outcomes, tests, and grading criteria will be modified for the first term of grade 1 to the pre-K level so that Emily continues to develop her foundational learning skills (motivation, organisation, sequencing, problem-solving, independence) and stamina for attending full days. Homework will be modified to accommodate Emily's fatigue.	

> **Additional Information:**
> Emily's foundational learner skills and pre-academic skills will be assessed at mid-year to determine which subject areas will continue to be modified for the remainder of the year and which grade 1 learner outcomes will be introduced.

Summary of Learning and Inclusionary Benefits

The learning and inclusionary benefits of using the Curriculum Adaptations and Modifications framework are:

- Adaptions and modifications are clearly identified and implemented to support Emily's development of foundational learner skills and to support her during periods of fatigue.
- Selected adaptions and modifications support Emily's current needs and abilities and will be re-assessed as she transitions into full-day grade one.
- Assessing Emily's skills at mid-year allows stakeholders to reflect on her achievements, set new learning goals, and re-evaluate required adaptions and modifications based on acquiring new skills.
- Emily's social inclusion is accounted for by working alongside peers who use work systems.
- Emily is encouraged to generalise her skills by transitioning her work systems to her desk to engage in learning parallel to her classmates.

Vignette 2: Arousal Regulation and Student Engagement

Physical Therapist

Sara is an energetic and vibrant grade 4 elementary student, but many challenges prevent her success in school. Sara experiences challenges with staying regulated in the classroom and engaging in activities. Math, in particular, is a difficult subject for Sara to pay attention to and to complete her assignments, even though the teacher uses a lot of great visuals and objects to support Sara. Other strategies include allowing Sara to take walking breaks and use sensory tools in class, but these strategies help only slightly. I met with the teacher and principal for a planning meeting, which revealed more details about Sara's background and current situation. We all agreed Sara is very capable and has many strengths, she is also very responsible. When she independently leaves the classroom, she returns without any support or reminders. This led to the idea of creating a movement break strategy using floor tape, outside the classroom in the common area of the school that would be good for Sara, but also for many other students in the school who needed movement breaks throughout the day. Before we began, I talked with Sara about the idea, and based on a fairly open and flexible discussion of ideas, Sara said she thought the ocean theme sounded like a pretty good idea. Over the next few days, Sara and I worked on a floor tape pattern in the central common area of the school. The final design ended up including an ocean, air, and land theme. To introduce the idea and purpose, as well as the different ways students could use the visual prompts to guide movement, I created a short instructional video. I also worked one-to-one with Sara, and I modeled different ways she could move through the floor theme. Both Sara and her teacher were very excited, and Sara began using the floor theme for her movement breaks that same day. Months later, Sara continues to use the floor tape and seems to access it just prior to math class as a way to calm her body and mind. Sara was one of many students who accessed the floor tape strategy in the school, but it was very powerful to learn why it worked for her. It was like the floor tape and visual theme sparked Sara's, and other students, creativity, but also served as a purposeful movement break. An inspirational takeaway for me, from this inclusive strategy, was the importance of soliciting student voice in the design and use of the movement strategy.

Student

I like the fish and whale! When I need a break, I go to the whale [floor tape] and imagine being by the ocean. This helps me forget about things I worry about, and it helps my mind feel clear. When my mind and body feel good, I learn better. I like that I can do different things with the fish. Sometimes I walk, sometimes I jump. Sometimes I imagine I am in the ocean like a fish or a whale. I like to see the different ways other kids use it too. Before math I come out to the [whale] for a movement break and then I feel better and I can get through math better. Sometimes, doing math makes my brain feel stuck, like I can't start and I just sit there.

Research Connections

Arousal regulation refers to a person's ability to manage their mental and physical activation levels for daily functioning (Welch et al., 2021). Autistic students' ability to maintain ideal states of arousal affects their perception, concentration, decision-making skills, and, ultimately, their ability to engage in learning tasks with changing environmental demands (Arora et al., 2021). When students are in a state of high arousal, they may experience headaches, nausea, stomach aches, increased heart rate, confusion, excessive concern, and narrow attention (Arora et al., 2021; Orekhava & Stroganova, 2014). Narrow attention and fixed or obsessive interests are also called monotropism (Lawson, 2011) by autistic theorists (Woods & Waltz, 2019). The theory of monotropism describes the sensory and cognitive experiences of an autistic person (Chown, 2017) that create narrow tunnels of focus, resulting in a harmonious state of cognition and regulation; however, when unexpectedly or suddenly interrupted, it can cause high levels of distress for the autistic individual (Woods & Waltz, 2019).

Autistic adolescents with co-occurring anxiety are found to be in a hyper-aroused state more frequently than autistic adolescents without anxiety (Keith et al., 2019). Approximately 50–70% of autistic children are also diagnosed with attention-deficit/hyperactivity disorder (McIntyre et al., 2017), further impacting their ability to achieve optimal sensory processing (Ben-Sasson et al., 2009). Low arousal is often affected by a lack of sleep or fatigue (Souders et al., 2017), and autistic students with lower baseline arousal levels may seek sensory experiences (i.e., jumping, chewing, or rocking) and cognitive activities (i.e., novel objects and learning) to increase their arousal states. In addition to navigating high and low states of arousal, autistic students report that their ability to participate in learning reliably is sometimes affected by what is referred to as a brain-body disconnect (Buckle et al., 2021), including when a student has difficulty starting and stopping actions or mixes up their response, such as when a student's actions don't match their intentions despite having full understanding and awareness (Higashida, 2016; Welch et al., 2021).

Experiencing a disconnect between intention is sometimes called autistic inertia, which significantly affects the day-to-day functioning and well-being of autistic people (Buckle et al., 2021; Welch et al., 2021). The reasons for autistic inertia are not well understood; however, possible explanations include difficulties with motor functioning, unpredictability, undesired outcomes, fear, executive functioning, and mental health (Buckle et al., 2021; Paterson, 2016; Phung et al., 2021). Instances of bind-body disconnect can be mistakenly interpreted as laziness, avoidance, non-compliance, and even skill regression by those with little understanding of the difficulties autistic people face in completing familiar, simple tasks.

Proprioception, which is the ability to sense one's body in space (Blanche et al., 2012), is also known to impact autistic students' ability to move their bodies in desired ways and can also impact regulation and behaviour (Izawa et al., 2012; Mukhopadhyay, 2003; Riquelme et al., 2016). Research shows that because of poor motor anticipation (Schmitz et al., 2003) and reduced ability to match proprioception with vision when reaching for things (Glazebrook et al., 2009), autistic students may struggle with fine motor skills, including printing and handwriting (Costa et al., 2016), which combined with executive functioning difficulties may lead to a diagnosis of dysgraphia (Chung & Patel, 2015). Therefore, to gain a more comprehensive picture of factors impacting student engagement and achievement, it is worthwhile to incorporate the lens of occupational and physical therapists into assessment practices to determine the impact of arousal regulation, inertia, and proprioception alongside cognitive factors. A collaborative assessment would benefit Sara in determining additional ways she can use **exercise and movement** breaks to support her regulatory and cognitive needs, as evident in her sharing, "When my mind and body feel good, I learn better."

Section Highlights

- Arousal regulation is a student's ability to maintain an ideal mental and physical state for learning and well-being.
- Autistic inertia is described by autistic people as the inability to start and stop desired and intended actions.
- Proprioception is the ability to sense one's body in space and affects gross and fine motor movements.
- It's important for teachers to consult with occupational therapists and physical therapists to explore how arousal regulation, inertia, and proprioception affect autistic students school engagement and achievement.

Responsive Framework

Curriculum Adaptations and Modifications

Student Name: Sara **Grade:** Four	**Initial Date:** February **Review Dates:** At parent-teacher conferences	**Team Members:** Sara, homeroom teacher, Physical Therapist, principal
Adaptions	**Notes**	
☐ Extended time for exams and assignments ☐ Separate learning spaces for independent work/exams ☑ Low/high arousal activity prior to learning ☐ Online/virtual attendance and participation ☐ Flexible timetable ☐ Assistive technology (specify type)	Sara will be invited to access the ocean-themed floor activity in the main foyer of the school prior to math class (and other self-identified times). Typically, Sara spends up to 10 minutes jumping, hopping, and walking as she follows different coloured floor objects and then she returns to class and seems more relaxed and engaged in math.	

Adaptions	Notes
☐ Access to presentation notes/slides ☐ Flexible assessment (oral, written, visual) ☐ Access to a reader or scribe ☐ Graphic organisers	
Modifications	**Notes**
☐ Altered learning objectives ☐ Altered tests/exams ☐ Altered grading criteria ☐ Significantly modified or no homework	
Additional Information: Sara's use of the ocean-themed floor activity will be monitored to understand how often and long (frequency and duration) she is requiring regulation breaks. This information will help the school team program for her next year, as the curriculum becomes more demanding, but also to explore ways this need can be met in the future, in a junior high setting.	

Learning and Inclusionary Benefits

The learning and inclusionary benefits of using the Curriculum Adaptations and Modifications framework are:

- A school-wide regulation strategy is developed based on Sara's arousal regulation needs, therefore normalising regulation activities for the benefit of many students.
- The ocean-themed gross motor activity is co-developed with Sara based on her interests, increasing student motivation, and engagement.
- Sara is developing an increased awareness of the positive impact regulation breaks have on her ability to concentrate and is encouraged to self-identify the timing of breaks based on her states of regulation.
- While Sara's regulation needs are being supported, team members are aware that collecting data on how often and long she accesses the ocean-themed activity will be beneficial to inform support as she progresses throughout the grades.
- Adapting school environments based on the lived experiences and self-reports of autistic students helps to reduce ableist practices.

Vignette 3: Functional Life Skills and Self-Monitoring

Parent

I was recently diagnosed with autism and ADHD, which helps explain a lot of things I have struggled with personally and as a parent. One positive is that some of the strategies I have learned I am using with my son, who is now in high school. He was diagnosed just before grade 1, and then in grade 4 he was diagnosed with ADHD and a learning disorder in reading, he is dyslexic, which also explains why we struggled so much during the first few years of school. Oliver would have really big, explosive meltdowns at school, and I would have to go and pick him up, but with the help of the school occupational therapist, psychologist, and resource teacher we learned that Oliver really struggled with managing his feelings because he couldn't cope with unpredictability and all the sensory stuff that came along with that. This was also confusing because of his ADHD, he seemed to always want to be moving and couldn't focus on learning for very long, which, combined with his dyslexia, was really complicated to unravel! Now we have a really good system in place, which has helped Oliver get ready for school and to the bus on time, and with a lot less friction between the both of us. We have a morning checklist with times entered beside each item on the checklist. This helps Oliver not only follow the sequence of steps needed to get out of bed and ready for school, but it helps take the pressure off if he gets stuck in a small ritual, is feeling anxious, or when he called being "frozen." Telling him to hurry up was a big trigger for Oliver, I have learned that his not completing easy things like brushing his teeth wasn't because he didn't know how to but that something inside him (thinking, emotion, or physical) was preventing him from doing it and by me putting pressure on him made it worse. The checklist helps him get in the flow better, and allowing for chunks of time to complete each step helps Oliver mentally because he is less hard on himself if he needs to take more time to complete each step, depending on how he feels that day. Overall, I think out of five days a week, we have four that go smoothly and one day (usually the end of the week) where we use the backup checklist that is much shorter, and I drive him to school.

Child

Yea, I don't always love using the checklists, but I know that they really help me get out the door. They have changed quite a bit since we first started using them in grade 6, I don't really have the same things on the checklist because now those things I seem to do automatically and I don't need pictures beside the words. My biggest struggle is actually just getting out of bed.

Some mornings I feel so tired and some days, my body just has a dull ache all over. Then I start to think of all the things I need to do in the day and it can feel pretty overwhelming, especially if I don't feel good. It's better for me if I just focus on sections of my day. I have my morning section, school section, and evening section. I also have a checklist that I use at school, that I make the night before. I put the classes that I have on it and the assignments that I have to hand in. My evening checklist I do on the bus ride home or when I get home and has the homework I have to do that night and the time I am going to play soccer or online gaming, depending on the night. I also schedule buffer time so that I have extra time somewhere else if I don't get something done. I just put it all on my phone in notes. It's easy that way because I can either dictate my list or copy and paste from previous days. I can also set timed reminders, which helps if I forget to look at my checklist.

Research Connections

Functional living skills are the actions people take to complete daily tasks such as dressing, toileting, washing, and eating. The continuum of functional living skills is broad. It becomes more complex with age, where young adults are expected to learn to wash and fold laundry, help prepare meals, take public transportation, and become employed as independent and contributing members of society (Sparrow, 2005). There is a relationship between functional living skills, independent living, and employment for autistic people (Ayres et al., 2011), which may help explain why a majority (80–90%) of autistic adults live at home or in community-supported housing (Howlin et al., 2004; Skinner et al., 2021; Shattuck et al., 2012) and only up to 10% of young autistic adults are competitively employed (Austin & Pisano, 2017; Wehman et al., 2014; Wilczynski et al., 2013), which is lower than any other reported disability group (Barnhill, 2016). As discussed in Chapter 2, autistic students who regularly acclimatise to their sensory environment have the strongest adaptive functioning skills, and students with generalised sensory differences have the lowest adaptive functioning skills; however, despite misconceptions, they are not the most cognitively impaired students (Scheerer et al., 2021).

Visual supports (Ninci et al., 2015), **video modeling** (Hong et al., 2017), and **task analysis** with **self-monitoring** (Parker & Kamps, 2010) are effective strategies for teaching functional living skills to autistic children and youth because they have been found to improve engagement, independence, and generalisation of skills (Parker & Kamps, 2010). Since task analysis breaks down larger, more complex skills into smaller steps when paired with visual cues, such as photographic schedules and checklists, the individual can more easily self-manage the completion of each step by following a sequence, which in the case of check-lists, mark off each step until completion. Video modeling is an evidence-based practice that provides a visual example of each task step being completed in sequence (Rosenbloom et al., 2019). To complete a laundry task, the following steps might be included: 1) bring laundry to the washing machine, 2) sort laundry into piles of light and dark colours, 3) put the light pile in the washing machine, 4) put laundry soap in the washing machine, 5) close washing machine, 6) turn on washing machine, 7) set timer for 45 minutes, 8) when the timer rings transfer washed clothes into the dryer, 9) turn on the dryer, 9) set timer for 60 minutes, 10) when timer rings take out dry clothes and fold, and 11) put away folded clothes (repeat steps for dark coloured clothing). Task analysis paired with visual cues can be used to support skill development and independence in a variety of daily living routines, including personal hygiene, preparing food, setting the table, and household chores, and is especially beneficial as it models desired actions in contextually relevant ways, including home and culture. Research has found that when autistic individuals are familiar with the routine of following schedules with the support of visuals, they are more engaged, are more able to undertake longer and more complex activities, and are better able to adapt to changes because they are familiar with the process and confident in their skills (Parker & Kamps, 2010).

Cognitive behavioural instructional strategies also use a step-by-step process to teach individuals strategies to become more self-aware of their thoughts, feelings, and behaviours. They are most used to reduce feelings of anxiety in autistic individuals (Sharma et al., 2021). The efficacy of cognitive behavioural strategies is mixed, dependent on the ratings of symptoms by parents, clinicians, or children (Sharma et al., 2021); however, because a reported 20% of autistic people meet the criteria for an anxiety disorder (Lai et al., 2019), it is a common approach used by clinicians to improve education and quality of life outcomes for autistic individuals (Wang et al., 2017). **Parent-implemented instruction** is when parents are taught to use evidence-based techniques from professionals in home and community environments, which have shown effectiveness in improving language, communication, attention, behaviour, and adaptive functioning in autistic children (Althoff et al., 2019). Combining interventions into a multi-modal approach to support autistic children and youth in the context of education, home, and community allows stakeholders to build on the communication, sensory, and adaptive functioning strengths of the individual while at the same time using a holistic viewpoint to ensure collaborative implementation of interventions that promote student achievement, independence, and confidence in a variety of settings.

Section Summary:

- The development of functional living skills improves life outcomes for autistic people, including increased opportunities for independent living and employment.
- Combining task analysis with visual supports and video modeling helps support the development of self-monitoring and independence skills.
- Cognitive behavioural instruction and parent-implemented instruction are evidence-based interventions to support communication, regulation, and functional living skills.

SECTION TWO

Inclusionary Framework to Support Curriculum

Curriculum Adaptations and Modifications		
Student Name: **Grade:**	**Initial Date:** **Review Dates:**	**Team Members:**
Adaptions (Equity)	**Notes**	
☐ Extended time for exams and assignments ☐ Separate learning spaces for independent work/exams ☐ Low/high arousal activity prior to learning ☐ Online/virtual attendance and participation ☐ Flexible timetable ☐ Assistive technology (specify type) ☐ Access to presentation notes/ slides ☐ Flexible assessment (oral, written, visual) ☐ Access to a reader or scribe ☐ Graphic organisers		

Modifications	Notes
☐ Altered learning objectives ☐ Altered tests/exams ☐ Altered grading criteria ☐ Significantly modified or no homework	
Additional Information:	

Reflective Questions for Teachers, Practitioners, and Parents

1. What adaptions and modifications are co-selected with autistic students?
2. What information-gathering activities do you use to get to know students before adapting or modifying learning environments and curriculum objectives?
3. How often do you evaluate the effectiveness of adaptions and modifications alongside the perspectives of autistic students?
4. List the non-cognitive enablers you use to promote student motivation and achievement.
5. How are co-occurring diagnoses (i.e., learning disorder, attention deficit hyperactive disorder, anxiety) accounted for in adaptions?
6. How often are autistic students' interests and passions incorporated into lessons and projects?
7. In what ways are game-based learning and technology-aided instruction incorporated into pedagogical practices?
8. What activities do you use to promote optimal arousal regulation for students?
9. What tools and visual supports do you use to develop students' self-monitoring and independence in learning and daily living skills?

Additional Readings and Resources

1. Hayes, M. (2022). *Being twice exceptional.* Jessica Kingsley Publishers.
2. Jacobs, P., Beamish, W., & McKay, L. (2020). Please listen to us: Adolescent autistic girls speak about learning and academic success. *Improving Schools.* https://doi.org/10.1177/1365480220973112

3. Zajic, M. C., & Brown, H. M. (2022). Measuring autistic writing skills: Combining perspectives from neurodiversity advocates, autism researchers, and writing theories. *Human Development, 66*(2), 128–148. https://doi.org/10.1159/000524015

Chapter Summary

Autistic students share that keeping up with the demands of the curriculum and increased workloads is stressful, especially in higher grades. Barriers to achievement include frustration and a need for more motivation, which can be addressed by incorporating student interests into lessons and assignments. Enablers of student achievement include teachers' mindsets, getting to know students personally, provision of arousal regulation strategies, and effective adaptations and modifications. Technology-aided instructions, game-based learning, and combining task analysis with visual cues to develop self-monitoring strategies teach students *what* and *how* to learn. Incorporating exercise and movement throughout the school day helps students regulate their brains, bodies, and emotions, leading to increased engagement in learning. Cognitive behavioural strategies and parent-implement instruction are also evidence-based interventions that use step-by-step processes to develop self-awareness and adaptive functioning skills. Using a multi-pronged collaborative approach may lessen gaps between student ability and achievement and improve graduation rates for autistic students.

Notes & Reflections

References

Althoff, C. E., Dammann, C. P., Hope, S. J., & Ausderau, K. K. (2019). Parent-mediated interventions for children with autism spectrum disorder: A systematic review. *The American Journal of Occupational Therapy, 73*(3), 1–13. https://doi.org/10.5014/ajot.2019.030015

Ambrose, K., Simpson, K., & Adams, D. (2021). The relationship between social and academic outcomes and anxiety for children and adolescents on the autism spectrum: A systematic review. *Clinical Psychology Review, 90*, 102086. https://doi.org/10.1016/j.cpr.2021.102086

Anderson, S. R., Taras, M., & Cannon, B. O. (1996). Teaching new skills to young children with autism. In C. Maurice, G. Green, & S. C. Luce (Eds.), *Behavioral intervention for young children with autism* (pp. 181–194). Austin, TX: Pro-Ed.

Arora, I., Bellato, A., Ropar, D., Hollis, C., & Groom, M. J. (2021). Is autonomic function during resting-state atypical in autism: A systematic review of evidence. *Neuroscience & Biobehavioral Reviews, 125*, 417–441. https://doi.org/10.1016/j.neubiorev.2021.02.041

Ashburner, J., Ziviani, J., & Rodger, S. (2008). Sensory processing and classroom emotional, behavioral, and educational outcomes in children with autism spectrum disorder. *The American Journal of Occupational Therapy, 62*(5), 564–573. https://doi.org/10.5014/ajot.62.5.564

Assouline, S. G., Foley Nicpon, M., & Dockery, L. (2012). Predicting the academic achievement of gifted students with autism spectrum disorder. *Journal of Autism and Developmental Disorders, 42*(9), 1781–1789. https://doi.org/10.1007/s10803-011-1403-x

Aubineau, M., & Blicharska, T. (2020). High-functioning autistic students speak about their experience of inclusion in mainstream secondary schools. *School Mental Health, 12*, 537–555. https://doi.org/10.1007/s12310-020-09364-z

Barnhill, G. P. (2016). Supporting students with Asperger syndrome on college campuses: current practices. *Focus on Autism and Other Developmental Disabilities, 31*(1), 3–15. https://doi.org/10.1177/1088357614523121.

Ben-Sasson, A., Carter, A. S., & Briggs-Gowan, M. J. (2009). Sensory over-responsivity in elementary school: Prevalence and social-emotional correlates. *Journal of Abnormal Child Psychology, 37*(5), 705–716. https://doi.org/10.1007/s10802-008-9295-8

Blakeley-Smith, A., Carr, E. G., Cale, S. I., & Owen-DeSchryver, J. S. (2009). Environmental fit: A model for assessing and treating problem behavior associated with curricular difficulties in children with autism spectrum disorders. *Focus on Autism and Other Developmental Disabilities, 24*(3), 131–145. https://doi.org/10.1177/1088357609339032

Blanche, E. I., Reinoso, G., Chang, M. C., & Bodison, S. (2012). Proprioceptive processing difficulties among children with autism spectrum disorders and developmental disabilities. *The American Journal of Occupational Therapy, 66*(5), 621. https://doi.org/10.5014/ajot.2012.004234

Buckle, K. L., Leadbitter, K., Poliakoff, E., & Gowen, E. (2021). "No way out except from external intervention": First-hand accounts of autistic inertia. *Frontiers in Psychology, 12*, 631596. https://doi.org/10.3389/fpsyg.2021.631596

Carnahan, C. R., Hume, K., Clarke, L., & Borders, C. (2009). Using structured work systems to promote independence and engagement for students with autism spectrum disorders. *TEACHING Exceptional Children, 41*(4), 6–14. https://doi.org/10.1177/004005990904100401

Chung, P., & Patel, D. R. (2015). Dysgraphia. *International Journal of Child and Adolescent Health, 8*(1), 27.

Clark, M., & Adams, D. (2020). The self-identified positive attributes and favourite activities of children on the autism spectrum. *Research in Autism Spectrum Disorders, 72*, 101512. https://doi.org/10.1016/j.rasd.2020.101512

Costa, L. J., Edwards, C., & Hooper, S. (2015). Writing disabilities and reading disabilities in elementary school students: Rates of co-occurrence and cognitive burden. *Learning Disability Quarterly, 39*. https://doi.org/10.1177/0731948714565461

Davidson, M. M., & Weismer, S. E. (2014). Characterization and prediction of early reading abilities in children on the autism spectrum. *Journal of Autism and Developmental Disorders, 44*(4), 828. https://doi.org/10.1007/s10803-013-1936-2

Del Moral Pérez, M. E., Guzmán Duque, A. P. & Fernández García, L. C. (2018). Game-based learning: Increasing the logical-mathematical, naturalistic, and linguistic learning levels of primary school students. *New Approaches in Educational Research, 7*(1). https://doi.org/10.7821/naer.2018.1.248

Dynia, J. M., Lawton, K., R. Logan, J. A., & Justice, L. M. (2014). Comparing emergent-literacy skills and home-literacy environment of children with autism and their peers. *Topics in Early Childhood Special Education*. https://doi.org/10.1177/0271121414536784

Dynia, J. M., & Lebenhagen, C. (2024, January). Associations among literacy ability, autism traits, and quality of life. [Poster Presentation]. Pacific Coast Research Conference, San Diego, CA.

Griffith, G. M., Totsika, V., Nash, S., & Hastings, R. P. (2012). 'I just don't fit anywhere': support experiences and future support needs of individuals with Asperger syndrome in middle adulthood. *Autism: The International Journal of Research and Practice, 16*(5), 532–546. https://doi.org/10.1177/1362361311405223

Higashida, N. (2016). *The reason I jump: The inner voice of a thirteen-year-old boy with autism*. Random House Trade Paperbacks.

Hong, E., Davis, J., Neely, L., Ganz, J., Morin, K., Ninci, J. & Boles, M. B. (2017). Functional living skills and adolescents and adults with autism spectrum disorder: A meta-analysis. *Education and Training in Autism and Developmental Disabilities, 52*, 268–279.

Howard, K. (2020). The role of achievement emotions in math performance outcomes of students with autism spectrum disorder. [Master's Thesis, University of Alberta]. https://doi.org/10.7939/r3-aee0-c674

Howell, M., Bradshaw, J., & Langdon, P. E. (2022). 'There isn't a checklist in the world that's got that on it': Special needs teachers' opinions on the assessment and teaching priorities of pupils on the autism spectrum. *Journal of Intellectual Disabilities, 26*(1), 211–226. https://doi.org/10.1177/1744629520972901

Howley, M. (2015). Outcomes of structured teaching for children on the autism spectrum: Does the research evidence neglect the bigger picture? *Journal of Research in Special Educational Needs, 15*(2), 106–119. https://doi.org/10.1111/1471-3802.12040

Howlin, P., Goode, S., Hutton, J., & Rutter, M. (2004). Adult outcome for children with autism. *Journal of Child Psychology and Psychiatry, and Allied Disciplines, 45*(2), 212–229. https://doi.org/10.1111/j.1469-7610.2004.00215.x

Humphrey, N., & Lewis, S. (2008). What does 'inclusion' mean for pupils on the autistic spectrum in mainstream secondary schools? *Journal of Research in Special Educational Needs, 8*(3), 132–140. https://doi.org/10.1111/j.1471-3802.2008.00115.x

Ibrahim, I. (2020). Specific learning disorder in children with autism spectrum dis-order: Current issues and future implications. *Advances in Neurodevelopmental Disorders, 4*. https://doi.org/10.1007/s41252-019-00141-x

Izawa, J., Pekny, S. E., Marko, M. K., Haswell, C. C., Shadmehr, R., & Mostofsky, S. H. (2012). Motor learning relies on integrated sensory inputs in ADHD, but over-selectively on proprioception in autism spectrum conditions. *Autism Research, 5*(2), 124. https://doi.org/10.1002/aur.1222

Keen, D., Adams, D., & Simpson, K. (2023) Teacher ratings of academic skills and academic enablers of children on the autism spectrum. *International Journal of Inclusive Education, 27*(10), 1085–1101. https://doi.org/ 10.1080/13603116.2021.1881626

Keen, D., Webster, A., & Ridley, G. (2016). How well are children with autism spec-trum disorder doing academically at school? An overview of the literature. *Autism: The International Journal of Research and Practice, 20*(3), 276–294. https://doi.org/10.1177/1362361315580962

Keith, J. M., Jamieson, J. P., & Bennetto, L. (2019). The Importance of adolescent self-report in autism spectrum disorder: Integration of questionnaire and autonomic meas-ures. *Journal of Abnormal Child Psychology, 47*(4), 741–754. https://doi.org/10.1007/s10802-018-0455-1

Kim, S. H., Bal, V. H., & Lord, C. (2018). Longitudinal follow-up of academic achievement in children with autism from age 2 to 18. *Journal of Child Psychology and Psychiatry, and Allied Disciplines, 59*(3), 258–267. https://doi.org/10.1111/jcpp.12808

Lai, M. C., Kassee, C., Besney, R., Bonato, S., Hull, L., Mandy, W.... & Ameis, S. H. (2019). Prevalence of co-occurring mental health diagnoses in the autism population: A system-atic review and meta-analysis. *The Lancet. Psychiatry, 6*(10), 819–829. https://doi.org/10.1016/S2215-0366(19)30289-5

Lawson, W. (2011). *The passionate mind: How people with autism learn.* London: Jessica Kingsley Publishers

Lester, J. C., Spires, H. A., Nietfeld, J. L., Minogue, J., Mott, B. W., & Lobene, E. V. (2014). Designing game-based learning environments for elementary science education: A narrative-centered learning perspective. *Information Sciences, 264*, 4–18. https://doi.org/10.1016/j.ins.2013.09.005

Li, Y., Sutedjo, A., Ramos, S. J., Garcimartin, H. R., & Thomas, A. (2021). A naturalistic inquiry into digital game-based learning in stem classes from the instructors' perspective. In C. Aprea & D. Ifenthaler (Eds.). *Game-based learning across the disciplines. Advances in game-based learning.* Springer, Cham. https://doi.org/10.1007/978-3-030-75142-5_10

Love, A. M., Findley, J. A., Ruble, L. A., & McGrew, J. H. (2019). Teacher self-efficacy for teaching students with autism spectrum disorder: Associations with stress, teacher engagement, and student IEP outcomes following COMPASS consultation. *Focus on Autism and Other Developmental Disabilities.* https://doi.org/10.1177/1088357619836767

McCrae, C. S., Chan, W. S., Curtis, A. F., Deroche, C. B., Munoz, M., Takamatsu, S.... & Mazurek, M. O. (2020). Cognitive behavioral treatment of insomnia in school-aged chil-dren with autism spectrum disorder: A pilot feasibility study. *Autism Research: Official Journal of the International Society for Autism Research, 13*(1), 167–176. https://doi.org/10.1002/aur.2204

McCurdy, E. E., & Cole, C. L. (2014). Use of a peer support intervention for promoting academic engagement of students with autism in general education settings. *Journal of Autism and Developmental Disorders, 44*(4), 883–893. https://doi.org/10.1007/s10 803-013-1941-5

McDougal, E., Riby, D. M., & Hanley, M. (2020). Profiles of academic achievement and attention in children with and without autism spectrum disorder. *Research in Developmental Disabilities, 106*, 103749. https://doi.org/10.1016/j.ridd.2020.103749

McDougal, E., Riby, D. M., & Hanley, M. (2020). Teacher insights into the barriers and facilitators of learning in autism. *Research in Autism Spectrum Disorders, 79*, 101674. https://doi.org/10.1016/j.rasd.2020.101674

McGlynn, K., & Kelly, J. (2019). Adaptations, modifications, and accommodations. *Science Scope, 43*(3), 36–41. https://www.jstor.org/stable/26899082

McIntyre, N. S., Solari, E. J., Gonzales, J. E., Solomon, M., Lerro, L. E., Novotny, S.... & Mundy, P. C. (2017). The scope and nature of reading comprehension impairments in school-aged children with higher-functioning autism spectrum disorder. *Journal of Autism and Developmental Disorders, 47*(9), 2838–2860. https://doi.org/10.1007/s10 803-017-3209-y

McLaughlin, S., & Rafferty, H. (2014). Me and 'it': Seven young people given a diagnosis of Asperger's Syndrome. *Educational and Child Psychology, 31*, 63–78. https://doi.org/ 10.53841/bpsecp.2014.31.1.63

Macmillan, C. M., Pecora, L. A., Ridgway, K., Hooley, M., Thomson, M., Dymond, S.... & Stokes, M. A. (2021). An evaluation of education-based interventions for students with autism spectrum disorders without intellectual disability: A systematic review. *Review Journal of Autism and Developmental Disorders.* https://doi.org/10.1007/s40 489-021-00289-0

May, T., Rinehart, N., Wilding, J., & Cornish, K. (2014). Attention and basic literacy and numeracy in children with autism spectrum disorder: A one-year follow-up study. *Research in Autism Spectrum Disorders, 9*. https://doi.org/10.1016/ j.rasd.2014.10.010

Mesibov, G., Shea, V., & Schopler, E. (2005). *The TEACCH approach to autism spectrum disorders.* New York: Kluwer Academic/Plenum.

Ninci, J., Neely, L. C., Hong, E. R., Boles, M. B., Gilliland, W. D., Ganz, J.B.... & Vannest, K. J. (2015). Meta-analysis of single-case research on teaching functional living skills to individuals with ASD. *Journal of Autism and Developmental Disorders, 2*, 184–198 (2015). https://doi.org/10.1007/s40489-014-0046-1

Odom, S.L., Thompson, J.L., Hedges, S., Boyd, B.A., Dykstra, J.R., Duda, M.A.... & Bord, A. (2015). Technology-aided interventions and instruction for adolescents with autism spectrum disorder. *Journal of Autism and Developmental Disorders, 45*(12), 3805–3019. https://doi.org/10.1007/s10803-014-2320-6

Olsson, I., & Nilholm, C. (2023). Inclusion of pupils with autism– A research overview. *European Journal of Special Needs Education, 38*(1), 126–140. http://doi.org/10.1080/ 08856257.2022.2037823

Orekhova, E. V., & Stroganova, T. A. (2014). Arousal and attention re-orienting in autism spectrum disorders: Evidence from auditory event-related potentials. *Frontiers in Human Neuroscience, 8*. https://doi.org/10.3389/fnhum.2014.00034

Parker, D., & Kamps, D. (2010). Effects of task analysis and self-monitoring for children with autism in multiple social settings. *Focus on Autism and Other Developmental Disabilities.* https://doi.org/10.1177/1088357610376945

Petersson-Bloom, L., & Holmqvist, M. (2022). Strategies in supporting inclusive education for autistic students-A systematic review of qualitative research results. *Autism & Developmental Language Impairments, 7.* https://doi.org/10.1177/23969415221123429

Phung, J., Penner, M., Pirlot, C., & Welch, C. (2021). What I wish you knew: Insights on burnout, inertia, meltdown, and shutdown from autistic youth. *Frontiers in Psychology, 12,* 741421. https://doi.org/10.3389/fpsyg.2021.741421

Riquelme, I., Hatem, S. M., & Montoya, P. (2016). Abnormal pressure pain, touch sensitivity, proprioception, and manual dexterity in children with autism spectrum disorders. *Neural Plasticity.* https://doi.org/10.1155/2016/1723401

Root, J. R., Browder, D. M., & Saunders, A. F. (2016). Schema-based instruction with concrete and virtual manipulatives to teach problem solving to students with autism. *Remedial and Special Education.* https://doi.org/10.1177/0741932516643592

Rosenbloom, R., Wills, H. P., Mason, R., Huffman, J. M., & Mason, B. A. (2019). The effects of a technology-based self-monitoring intervention on on-task, disruptive, and task-completion behaviors for adolescents with autism. *Journal of Autism and Developmental Disorders, 49*(12), 5047–5062. https://doi.org/10.1007/s10803-019-04209-4

Saggers, B., Hwang, Y. S., & Mercer, L. (2011). Your voice counts: Listening to the voice of high school students with autism spectrum disorder. *Australasian Journal of Special Education, 35,* 173–190. https://doi.org/10.1375/ajse.35.2.173

Scheerer, N. E., Curcin, K., Stojanoski, B., Anagnostou, E., Nicolson, R., Kelley, E.... & Stevenson, R. A. (2021). Exploring sensory phenotypes in autism spectrum disorder. *Molecular Autism, 12*(1), 67. https://doi.org/10.1186/s13229-021-00471-5

Sharma, S., Hucker, A., Matthews, T., Grohmann, D., & Laws, K. R. (2021). Cognitive behavioural therapy for anxiety in children and young people on the autism spectrum: A systematic review and meta-analysis. *BMC Psychology, 9*(1), 151. https://doi.org/10.1186/s40359-021-00658-8

Shattuck, P. T., Narendorf, S. C., Cooper, B., Sterzing, P. R., Wagner, M., & Taylor, J. L. (2012). Postsecondary education and employment among youth with an autism spectrum disorder. *Pediatrics, 129*(6), 1042–1049. https://doi.org/10.1542/peds.2011-2864

Simpson, K., Adams, D., Bruck, S., & Keen. D. (2019). Investigating the participation of children on the autism spectrum across home, school and community: A longitudinal study. *Child: Care, Health and Development, 45,* 681–687. https://doi.org/10.111/cch.12679

Shic, F., & Goodwin, M. (2015). Introduction to technologies in the daily lives of individuals with autism. *Journal of Autism and Developmental Disorders, 45,* 3773–3776. https://doi.org/10.1007/s10803-015-2640-1

Solari, E. J., Grimm, R. P., McIntyre, N. S., Zajic, M., & Mundy, P. C. (2019). Longitudinal stability of reading profiles in individuals with higher functioning autism. *Autism.* https://doi.org/10.1177/1362361318812423

Souders, M. C., Zavodny, S., Eriksen, W., Sinko, R., Connell, J., Kerns, C.... & Pinto-Martin, J. (2017). Sleep in children with autism spectrum disorder. *Current Psychiatry Reports, 19*(6), 34. https://doi.org/10.1007/s11920-017-0782-x

Sparrow, S. S., Cicchetti, D. V., & Balla, D. A. (2005). *Vineland adaptive behavior scales* (2nd ed.). Circle Pines, MN: AGS Publishing.

Strickroth, S., Zoerner, D., Moebert, T., Morgiel, A. & Lucke, U. (2020). Game-based promotion of motivation and attention for socio-emotional training in autism: Exploring the secrets of facial expressions by combining Minecraft and a mobile App. *i-com, 19*(1), 17–30. https://doi.org/10.1515/icom-2020-0003

Van der Wurff, I., Meijs, C., Hurks, P., Resch, C., & De Groot, R. (2021). The influence of sensory processing tools on attention and arithmetic performance in Dutch primary school children. *Journal of Experimental Child Psychology, 209*, 105143. https://doi.org/10.1016/j.jecp.2021.105143

Wang, Z., Whiteside, S. P. H., Sim, L., Farah, W., Morrow, A. S., Alsawas, M.... & Murad, M. H. (2017). Comparative effectiveness and safety of cognitive behavioral therapy and pharmacotherapy for childhood anxiety disorders: A systematic review and meta-analysis. *JAMA Pediatrics, 171*(11), 1049–1056. https://doi.org/10.1001/jamapediatrics.2017.3036

Wehman, P. H., Schall, C. M., McDonough, J., Kregel, J., Brooke, V., Molinelli, A.... & Thiss, W. (2014). Competitive employment for youth with autism spectrum disorders: Early results from a randomized clinical trial. *Journal of Autism and Developmental Disorders, 44*(3), 487–500. https://doi.org/10.1007/s10803-013-1892-x

Welch, C., Cameron, D., Fitch, M., & Polatajko, H. (2021) Living in autistic bodies: Bloggers discuss movement control and arousal regulation. *Disability and Rehabilitation, 43*(22), 3159–3167. https://doi.org/10.1080/09638288.2020.1729872

Whalon, K. J., Otaiba, S. A., & Delano, M. E. (2009). Evidence-based reading instruction for individuals with autism spectrum disorders. *Focus on Autism and Other Developmental Disabilities, 24*(1), 3. https://doi.org/10.1177/1088357608328515

Wilczynski, S., Trammell, B., & Clarke, L. (2013). Improving employment outcomes among adolescents and adults on the autism spectrum. *Psychology in the Schools, 50*. https://doi.org/10.1002/pits.21718

Wong, C., Odom, S. L., Hume, K. A., Cox, A. W., Fettig, A., Kucharczyk, S...., & Schultz, T. R. (2015). Evidence-based practices for children, youth, and young adults with autism spectrum disorder: A comprehensive review. *Journal of Autism and Developmental Disorders, 45*(7), 1951–1966. https://doi.org/10.1007/s10803-014-2351-z

Woods, R., & Waltz, M. (2019). The strength of autistic expertise and its implications for autism knowledge production: A response to Damian Milton. *Autonomy, the Critical Journal of Interdisciplinary Autism Studies, 1*(6). http://shura.shu.ac.uk/24752/

Chapter 8

Collaboration

CHAPTER OVERVIEW

SECTION ONE

1. The 5Cs of Inclusion | Collaboration
2. Vignette 1: Parents as Allies
3. Vignette 2: Transition Planning

SECTION TWO

4. Inclusionary Framework to Support Collaboration
5. Reflective Questions for Teachers, Practitioners, and Parents
6. Additional Readings and Resources
7. Chapter Summary

DOI: 10.4324/9781032687926-8

SECTION ONE

The 5Cs of Inclusion | *Collaboration*

Review of the
Research

- Autistic students often feel misunderstood and underestimated by teachers because of deficit-based views of ability.
- Autistic students want to be able to share with teachers what works best for them in learning, communication, regulation, and socialisation.
- Autistic students want to be involved in decisions about goal setting, assessment practices, and the provision of support.

Intersectional collaboration involves multiple people coming together to share knowledge and approaches (Cheng & Levey, 2019), enabling stakeholders to develop a common understanding to inform decision-making (An et al., 2016), which is considered fundamental for achieving equity in education (Kwak, 2021). Students, teachers, practitioners, and parents agree that a high degree of coordination and collaboration is necessary to overcome barriers to inclusion (Howell et al., 2020; Shahidullah et al., 2020). However, often lacking are clearly defined collaborative processes that promote partnerships while at the same time valuing diverse, sometimes conflicting perspectives and priorities. Research finds that a lack of collaboration between professionals is a main barrier to supporting autistic students in inclusive classrooms (Al Jaffal, 2022) and prioritising open communication between parents and teachers is more productive than finding agreement (Azad & Mandell, 2015). The benefits of research on the school priorities of autistic students are not only useful in improving awareness in ways that neurotypical professionals cannot fully appreciate on their own (Pellicano & den Houting, 2022), they can also be used to inform essential aspects of collaborative frameworks that are responsive to the heterogeneous needs of autistic students. For instance, autistic students identify that communication, connection, classroom environments, and curriculum are primary factors impacting their school success; therefore, these elements should be at the core of any collaborative agenda and inclusive framework to support positive school outcomes for autistic learners.

Conversely, if a collaborative agenda or framework overlooks one or several of these core student-identified factors, the risk of misunderstanding increases, resulting in misdirected programming and support for autistic students, including the use of one-size-fits-all approaches (Chandroo et al., 2018; Hummerstone & Parsons, 2021). Researchers have found that when autistic students are left out of collaborative discussions and planning, staff priorities tend to overshadow student priorities (Esqueda Villegas et al., 2022), and educational decisions are based on deficit-based medical models of disability (Hummerstone & Parsons, 2021). Therefore, developing student-centred collaborative frameworks founded on research on the school priorities of autistic students provides relevant points of entry for professionals while promoting student agency in the context of their identities, abilities, interests, and aspirations. Allowing for student agency enables students to set goals, reflect on their progress and factors affecting achievement, and act responsibly and confidently to create change (OCED, 2019). Therefore, commitments to using student-centred collaborative frameworks are another positive strategy to reform outdated and ableist educational processes, including "experts" narrating the educational experiences and priorities of autistic students.

The collaborative framework presented in this chapter integrates the school priorities of autistic students presented in the previous four chapters (Communication, Connection, Classroom Environment, and Curriculum) to highlight that autistic students' educational, social, and well-being success does not solely rely on understanding and supporting symptomatic features of their autism, but also strongly dependent on the inter-reliance of community, culminating as the 5Cs of Meaningful Inclusion. The framework titled Collaboration for Inclusion is applied following two vignettes showcasing the perspectives of two autistic students—one just beginning school and the other preparing for graduation—alongside the perspectives of an occupational therapist, teachers, autism consultant, and parents.

Section Highlights

- Intersectional collaboration is needed to improve learning, social, and well-being outcomes for autistic students.
- Collaborative frameworks founded on the school priorities of autistic students provide clarity for stakeholder input and promote student agency.
- Viewing student abilities and needs through the 5Cs of Meaningful Inclusion (Communication, Connection, Classroom Environment, Curriculum, Collaboration) helps reduce ineffective programming and support.

Vignette 1: Parents as Allies

Occupational Therapist

I was called in to support Amira, a 5-year-old student in her new kindergarten classroom last week. As the school occupational therapist, I provide consultation to teachers and administrators regarding supports that can benefit a student's self-care, play and leisure, and social and academic participation. Occupational therapists are real-life detectives that go into different school environments and figure out what barriers are hindering students' optimal performance in those particular spaces. I was able to connect with Amira's mom by phone call for consent purposes and to gather more information about Amira. I then observed Amira's participation in classroom activities and self-help tasks, transitions, sensory processing skills, co-regulation skills, fine motor participation, movement of her body in space, play, and social skills. Amira was able to participate in fine motor tasks, she enjoyed using jumbo crayons and writing alphabets and numbers. Amira moved quickly between classroom centers and tasks, exploring and touching toys and materials as she moved around the class. She absolutely loved playing with water, soap, and bubbles at the water table and stayed for a longer amount of time at that station. She was interested in watching a peer paint on an easel, but when given the opportunity to paint she began to cry. A peer saw her crying and ran over and gave her a big hug, and this helped her calm down and feel better.

During group instruction, Amira had difficulty staying seated with her peers at the table and on the carpet. On a few occasions, I observed Amira cover her ears and crouch down when the classroom was louder and busier. To increase Amira's participation in her day-to-day classroom activities, I made the following suggestions for her teacher to incorporate into classroom routines. First, we provided a small rocking chair during group activities along with a weighted turtle for her lap. The combination of vestibular movement and deep pressure helped her to feel more snug and secure. We observed that she was able to stay seated for most of the group instruction with these tools and initiated an occasional walk around classroom when she needed to be moving. Second, we created a small space in the classroom for Amira to go to when she wanted time away from the chaos and noise. We provided preferred activities such as writing alphabets, colouring, interactive books, water play, kinetic sand, and fidget toys. Third, we created a visual choice board, which included the rocking chair, vibrating cushion, fidget toys, headphones, sunglasses, and weighted lap pad. The teacher or educational assistant would assist Amira's autonomy in decision-making by providing her with access to chosen activities once she indicated what she wanted them. For all sensory tools, children must be the primary decision-makers for which sensory tool they want to use and for how long.

During my visit, I also assisted Amira with trialling noise-cancelling headphones so that she could gauge if she liked them or not. She was very happy to wear them for short periods, and we could see her body relax as soon as she put them on. I explained to her teacher that Amira would need to be the one deciding when she wanted to wear the headphones and when she wanted them taken off.

I also met with the school speech-language therapist, who is working with the teacher to support Amira's communication needs. Together we encouraged the teacher to set up a visual schedule for Amira's day, along with a first-then visual that can be supported by the educational assistant. The purpose of these visual supports is to help with Amira's regulation during transitions. After my observations and gathering information from Amira's mother, teacher, education assistant, speech therapists, I worked with the teacher and educational assistant to set up a sensory diet for Amira which included beneficial *sensory-motor tasks that would help her body feel calm and ready to learn based on her unique sensory profile. A schedule was set so that Amira could be taken on these breaks at regular intervals during her day to participate in sensory-motor tasks. Over future visits, I plan to take a closer look at Amira's participation in self-help routines at school such as dressing, feeding and toileting and will provide consultation to her teacher with strategies to enhance her independence in these areas. Following these visits, a consultation report will be put together and shared with Amira's teacher and parents. I will continue to follow Amira's progress through meetings with her teacher and classroom observations, as required by the team throughout the school year.*

Parent

It was nice to receive a phone call from both Amira's teacher and occupational therapist at the beginning of the school year. It really helps reduce some of the worry and stress I feel with Amira moving from an early intervention preschool to our community school. It also helps that some of the neighborhood children are in Amira's class, so she knows some familiar faces. The teacher seems to have a lot of experience working with children with special needs and talked about how the different therapists will be involved in supporting Amira. Although she is still really young, I like that they are setting things up for her to choose what works best for her-everyone seems so knowledgeable and caring! Amira is our first child, and navigating her autism diagnosis and all the therapies has been overwhelming at times. Sometimes, I also receive conflicting advice on what priorities for Amira should be. We haven't all met together yet, but I have talked to everyone on Amira's school team, and the teacher has said that priority recommendations from all reports will be recorded and updated in one document, which will be nice to refer to as Amira moves into full-day grade 1 next year.

Student

I like school. I go with Taylor. The lady brought me headphones and sunglasses, and I like all the toys I can play with. I have the same sand and crayons at home.

Research Connections

Collaborating with parents in the education of their children is considered best practice (National Research Council, 2001) and supported by laws such as the *Individuals with Disabilities Education Improvement Act* in the United States (US Department of Education, 2004), and the *Children and Families Act 2014* in the United Kingdom (UK Government, 2014). Commonly referred to as school-family partnerships (Azad & Mandell, 2016) in education and family centered-care (Klatte et al., 2023) in health, collaboration between educational professionals and parents results in more positive outcomes for autistic students (Gabovitch & Curtin, 2009; Al Jaffal, 2019) and is a major predictor of parent satisfaction with their child's school experiences (Kurth et al., 2019). Teachers report that when they work with parents and practitioners, they feel more confident and equipped to support student needs and can better assess student progress and manage workloads (Danker et al., 2019; Howell et al., 2022). Successful collaborative service delivery relies on four elements: mutually agreed-upon goals, shared planning, shared implementation, and shared evaluation (An & Palisano, 2014).

Purposeful collaboration provides opportunities for shared problem-solving among stakeholders, and teachers appreciate receiving advice on which strategy best fits the situation in question (Van der Steen et al., 2019). Parents also value open and consistent communication with teachers willing to listen to their ideas and concerns (Gabovitch & Curtin, 2009; Roberts & Webster, 2020), which is especially helpful for parents with younger children just beginning their school careers. Research finds that although parent's first preference is for their child to be placed in inclusive classrooms (Simon et al., 2023), these decisions are not easy ones to make, as they are concerned about staff knowledge, availability of support, and equitable opportunities for their children (Clark & Adams, 2020; Roberts & Webster, 2020). Without well-coordinated communication and collaboration, parents report feeling disempowered, especially when educational decisions are made without input and are merely invited to meetings to agree with school recommendations (Kurth et al., 2019).

Parents have a long history of advocating for their children in various contexts and people. They know their children and know what works (Danker et al., 2019; Reichow et al., 2018); therefore, they can offer nuanced information and advice about their children to school-based staff. However, year-over-year advocacy is difficult for families of autistic children (Kurth et al., 2019; Roberts & Webster, 2020) and often results in unwanted and unnecessary stress for parents and their children. Adults are not the only ones who benefit from consistency in communication, autistic students feel less confused and frustrated when they receive similar messages given to them at school as at home (Danker et al., 2019). Research finds that teachers and parents rarely discuss their primary and secondary concerns with each other, even though when asked individually, their concerns are similar (Azad & Mandell, 2016).

Factors preventing open and clear communication between adult stakeholders may be due to a lack of teacher training in pre-service programs (Al Jaffal, 2022), practical strategies for therapists (Klatte et al., 2023), and parents preferring to avoid conflict (Azad & Mandell, 2016). Adding to potential barriers to collaboration, without the support of a practical and unifying framework, the likelihood of achieving clear communication and consistent expectations among stakeholders may be challenging when working within standard reporting processes such as those typically used during individualised education planning and report card meetings. Proactive, strength-based approaches that enable collaboration between stakeholders may also present positive opportunities to change inclusive mindsets and, in turn, inspire autistic students to view themselves as capable and contributing members of school communities (Brown et al., 2021).

Section Summary:

- Collaboration is considered best practice in inclusive education, leading to long-term positive outcomes for autistic students.
- Parents value open and consistent communication with school staff and want input in their child's educational decisions.
- Engaging autistic students in collaborative processes supports self-advocacy, autonomy in decision-making, and shared problem-solving and promotes equity in education.

Responsive Framework

Collaboration for Inclusion			
Student Name: Amira **Grade:** Kindergarten (AM)	**Initial Date:** September **Review Dates:** IEP Meetings	**Team Members:** Amira, Mr. T Parents, Occupational Therapist, Speech-Language Therapist	
Communication			
Preferred Method ☑ Speaking ☐ Non-Speaking ☐ Speaking & Non-Speaking ☐ Other		**Preferred Mode** ☑ Verbal ☐ Typing ☐ Email ☐ AAC ☐ Text ☐ Other	
Connection			
Student Priorities Prefers to sit with and play with Taylor (neighbour). Enjoys observing peers and accepts physical touch.	**Parent Input** Partnering with Taylor helps Amira prepare for the school day and share events with her parents.	**Teacher Input** Amira and Taylor will be class buddies to support the transition to school.	**Practitioner Input** OT-Regular access to sensory supports will enable Amira to more successfully interact with peers.

Supports and Accommodations:
The teacher will send home pictures of two new peers to assist Amira's recall and sharing of related social interactions.

Classroom Environment			
Student Priorities	**Parent Input**	**Teacher Input**	**Practitioner Input**
Covers ears and crouches when the classroom is loud/busy.	At home will cover her ears and leave the room when it's too loud.	Will work with the speech therapist to identify strategies for Amira to express when she needs a break.	OT- Access to sensory-motor activities at regular intervals and when Amira self-identifies need for.

Supports and Accommodations:
Noise-cancelling headphones, rocking chair, weighted lap turtle, separate regulation space.

Curriculum			
Student Priorities	**Parent Input**	**Teacher Input**	**Practitioner Input**
Curious and interested in centres likes exploratory play, cause and effect activities.	Amira does better if she has "something to do." She is busy, we would like her to spend more time on one-task.	Focus on developing foundational learner skills (following instructions, asking for help).	SLP/OT-visual schedule to support regulation transitions.

Supports and Accommodations:
Space for walking or rocking during instruction to promote regulation and attention.

Additional Information:
Self-help routings (dressing, feeding, toileting) will be assessed next visit from OT.

Learning and Inclusionary Benefits

The learning and inclusionary benefits of using the Collaboration for Inclusion framework are:

- Identified themes (Communication, Connection, Classroom Environment) draw attention to key inclusionary aspects (identified by autistic students in research) that stakeholders should focus on to support Amira's transition to full-day school.
- It emphasises the importance of including Amira's perspective alongside team members to inform programming priorities and identify effective supports.
- Integrating perspectives allows team members to better understand Amira's strengths and abilities; therefore, there is more alignment between goals and supports and consistency in program implementation.
- It creates predictability and purpose for team meetings, including information sharing, co-assessment, and future goal setting.

Vignette 2: Transition Planning

Teacher

As a teaching team, we have noticed Jennifer either shutting down or become highly frustrated when asked to complete a written assignment, especially in Social Studies or English. Jennifer either refuses to engage with those who are trying to help her or will slam her books or fists on the desk, vocalise loudly or, in some cases, leave the classroom slamming the door as she exits. Her choices are extremely disruptive to her peers and, lately, have impacted her social connections.

Academically, Jennifer struggles with organising her thoughts, articulating her ideas, and ensuring her finished product aligns with the assignment's expectations. She can get stuck in the never-ending loop of writing and rewriting her paragraphs, which inhibits her from completing and handing in her projects on time. We implemented some of the supportive strategies that we thought would be helpful—chunking the task, highlighting the important concepts, and giving her extra time to complete the assignment. These were minimally successful, and we still see a high level of frustration from Jennifer.

In talking to a learning strategist, we were encouraged to engage in a conversation with Jennifer to better understand her point of view, what she felt she needed from our team and come up with some strategies that could be used to support both Jennifer and the entire class. She pointed out that, very likely, many other students in our class were also struggling with the application of knowledge, organising their thoughts, engaging in the initial stages of writing and feeling confident in their completed project,

In talking to Jennifer, she clearly expressed her discomfort with being singled out in front of her peers. She did not want to be the only one who had to be "babied." We changed our teaching style to include supportive strategies for all learners. As a class, everyone began highlighting key concepts and requirements, mind mapping to organize their ideas, noting important information that needed to be included in each paragraph prior to writing the essay, and the adults in the classroom began helping all students to elevate their writing.

With the help of our district autism consultant, we also implemented individual strategies for Jennifer, including access to a scribe when Jennifer felt it was necessary. Clear, concise timelines have also been implemented to complete each paragraph to reduce perseveration and perfectionism. After consultation with Jennifer and her parents, we have planned for Jennifer to complete high school in four years to help reduce the pace and minimise time pressures on completing academic courses.

Autism Consultant

Mr. Kim, Jennifer's teacher, called me to brainstorm some ways he could support Jennifer in high school. I have worked with many of Jennifer's teachers over the years as I have known Jennifer since she was in elementary school. She is a very bright student and wants to do well in school and can get quite down on herself if she isn't meeting the high standards, she has for herself. Last I spoke with Jennifer, she wanted to be a teacher and attend university while living at home. When students enter high school, my focus for finding ways to support students shifts a bit, and I begin to have conversations with teachers and students on finding strategies to support their goals after graduation and discuss priorities to help their transition to adulthood. So basically, I try to view things from a post-high school perspective and think of which are the best stepping stones we should lay out for students to help prepare them for adulthood. In high school there is a lot of talk from teachers and among students about their future, what they are going to be, where they are going to live, etc. and I know that Jennifer wants these things too. So, when I talked with Mr. Kim about some of the strategies that have worked and not worked in the past to support Jennifer's learning and her feelings of frustration when she perseverates or is really focused on her writing being perfect, we tried to think of skills and strategies she would need in university that would help change her mindset, but also support her executive functioning needs. As a first step, we decided to focus on providing universal support in the classroom so that Jennifer doesn't feel singled out, but also we agreed with Jennifer's point that many students need assistance and to encourage them seeking help, we needed to increase self-awareness and respect for individual differences and to emphasise that in high school, they need to focus on identifying what works best for them, and less on what other students are doing, so that they learn to self-advocate for supports and accommodations now and in the future—whether it's for high school, post-secondary, or in their jobs.

Student

I am so tired of always being the one who stands out in my English and Social Studies classes. When we have to hand in a written assignment, my friends all get what they are supposed to do right as soon as the teacher hands out the instructions. They start writing right away, and I just sit there, trying to figure out what I am supposed to be doing or I have so many ideas, I don't know where to start. If I do actually get anything written down, it is never good enough. I go back and re-write it over and over again. I feel so stupid and get so frustrated all the time. Everything goes so fast. I can't keep up. I sit in my desk trying to get even one sentence down when all my classmates have full pages completed. That puts even more pressure on me. I have good ideas, but I can't always get them on to the paper. Then, to make it even worse, Mr. Kim will ask, in front of the whole class, if I want to go work in the resource room. Thanks, like I needed more attention on me! That doesn't help me to feel part of the class, get my work done—because now I can't think because I am even more frustrated AND I still don't either understand what to do or how to start.

What I need my teachers to understand is I want to be stand out. I want to be there learning what the other kids are learning, not walking in front of everyone to go to the resource room. I also know that sometimes being in the classroom can be hard. The noise distracts me, and I have a hard time concentrating. The resource room can be helpful, but I want it to be my choice. Which to be honest, I am not going to choose very much, unless my friends can come. Talking through my ideas with a teacher and have them write them down for me helps eliminate that pressure, but I don't like everyone listening in.

Parent

Everyone has been so committed to helping Jennifer over the years, which I really appreciate. She has come a long way with everyone's support and it's so nice when previous teachers take the time to talk to each other, then we don't have to waste so much of the beginning of the school year sharing, sometimes convincing people what works best for Jennifer to get the grades

I know she can achieve. Jennifer and one of her best friends have wanted to be teachers together since they were little. They always talked about it. I think Jennifer would make an excellent teacher, she loves school and learning. I am most concerned about her outbursts in school and how she will deal with the added pressure and frustration in university. The other kids are so familiar with her at school that sometimes I think that she gets away with too much because she isn't always thinking about how her frustration affects other people. She's too old to be slamming doors, which we don't tolerate at home. I think the added stress of completing all her high school courses in three years slowly adds pressure on Jeniffer. We talked about summer school, but I also want her to be a kid and not be so focused on meeting deadlines, she compares herself a lot to what other students are doing. I think she is open to the idea of taking three and a half to four years to complete high school, which I also think will give her just a little bit more time to mature.

Research Connections

Student-centred planning is known to be an important factor influencing student success following graduation from secondary school for autistic students (Chandroo et al., 2020); however, like other instances where the perspectives of autistic students are absent or inadequate, their involvement in planning for their future is poor (Chandroo et al., 2020; Griffin et al., 2013). While autistic students report feeling overwhelmed when thinking about major life transitions, including attending post-secondary, gaining employment, and living independently, they desire active involvement in decisions impacting their adult lives (Webster et al., 2022) and, when given the opportunity, clearly articulate their goals and desires for their future (Chandroo et al., 2020).

Autistic students need frequent and supported opportunities to learn and practice autonomy and self-determination and skills to confidently identify their strengths, needs, priorities, and interests, set realistic goals, and advocate for support (Van Laarhoven-Myers et al., 2016). A high level of intentional and well-coordinated support from teachers, practitioners, and parents is required to prepare autistic students for their transition to adulthood; however, research finds that although mandated in federal and district policies, such as individual education program planning, collaboration during transition planning with autistic students is inadequate (Chandroo et al., 2018; Brock et al., 2020). Many autistic students also report that their contributions during transition planning meetings are minimal due to unclear expectations and primarily being asked closed-ended or yes/no questions, sometimes causing students to be fearful, shy, and nervous (Chandroo et al., 2018). Therefore, a clear understanding of the functionality of processes used to support transition planning must be established to improve coordination, communication, and collaboration among educators, practitioners, parents, and students. Furthermore, in preparation for adulthood, collaborative frameworks used for students in high school must encourage the development and maturation of self-determination and self-efficacy skills.

Originating in the professional context of therapists collaborating with parents of children with disabilities, researchers Klatte et al. (2023) systematically reviewed therapists' effective strategies for collaborating with parents. Their findings are relevant to educators seeking ways to improve collaborative processes with parents and other education partners who experience difficulties with communication and coordination. Klatte et al. (2023) found that collaboration's most positive and productive outcomes involved mindsets, communication styles, tailored approaches, and empowered parents. Collaborative mindsets are defined as respecting diversity such as cultural factors, open-mindedness, being non-judgemental, and refraining from making assumptions; communication style includes using open-ended questions (i.e., What is important to you? What do you want to work on together?), focusing on strengths, providing equal opportunity for stakeholder input, active listening, and remaining solution-focused; tailored approaches means that professionals flex to the individual priorities and circumstances of students and families as they change over time; and lastly, empowering parents to be equal partners meant that they were provided timely information and were offered frequent opportunities to ask questions and provide input (Klatte et al., 2023). Schools that utilise student-centred collaborative frameworks alongside inclusionary mindsets, open and non-judgemental communication, and tailored approaches that empower students and parents have the cultural characteristics of inclusive schools (Zollers, 2010) and when autistic are provided with opportunities to have agency (i.e., voice and choice) in decisions, it leads to increased achievement (Josilowski & Morris, 2019) and long-term positive outcomes into adulthood (Lai et al., 2020).

Section Highlights

- Student-centered collaborative planning improves student achievement and long-term life outcomes for autistic students.
- Autistic students want to be involved in decisions about their future, including post-secondary, employment, and independent living.
- Positive mindsets, open and non-judgemental communication styles, tailored approaches, and empowered parents are characteristics of effective and efficient collaborative teams.

Responsive Framework

Collaboration for Inclusion		

| **Student Name:** Jennifer
Grade: Ten | **Initial Date:** September
Review Dates: Term 2 | **Team Members:** Jennifer, Mom, Mr. Kim (and Social Studies teacher), Autism Consultant |

Communication

Preferred Method ☑ Speaking ☐ Non-Speaking ☐ Speaking & Non-Speaking ☐ Other	**Preferred Mode** ☑ Verbal ☐ Typing ☑ Email ☐ AAC ☐ Text ☐ Other

Connection

Student Priorities	**Parent Input**	**Teacher Input**	**Practitioner Input**
To not be singled out in class.	For Jennifer to make goals that work best for her and make fewer comparisons to peers. To not slam doors.	To communicate her frustrations and requests for help before becoming overwhelmed.	Consultant-continue to develop self-advocacy skills.

Supports and Accommodations:
Teachers will integrate universal approaches to students to provide multiple entry points for students to begin written assignments and explicit teaching of ways students can respond to situations where they feel "stuck" while at the same time not feeling embarrassed for needing help.

Classroom Environment

Student Priorities	**Parent Input**	**Teacher Input**	**Practitioner Input**
To work in class alongside peers and not be pulled out to work in the resource room (noise is not distracting).	Jennifer isn't affected by sensory input, it's more mental/social stress that affects her ability to stay in class.	Resource room is always available as a second space for extra 1-1 help.	For Jennifer to have a common signal she can use to tell the teacher she needs to take a break from the classroom to re-set.

Supports and Accommodations:
Jennifer will continue to have the option to work in the classroom or resource room and may invite another peer to work within the resource room and will communicate a need for a break by closing her binder and walking to the door.

Curriculum			
Student Priorities	**Parent Input**	**Teacher Input**	**Practitioner Input**
Not feeling stuck with written assignments, extra time for revisions so Jennifer is satisfied with final product.	To complete assignments on-time and to have consistent expectations between home and school.	For Jennifer to more independently start/complete assignments and to use the strategies we provide to help her.	To encourage Jennifer to develop a personal library of strategies she can proactively refer to before starting written assignments.

Supports and Accommodations:
Teachers will provide a rubric for students so that they have a clear understanding of specific content to include in written assignments. Once Jennifer marks off each box in the rubric, this will indicate her assignment is complete and meets teacher expectations.

Additional Information:
Prior to completing written assignments, Jennifer will self-select strategies she thinks will help her (i.e., type assignment, chunking, highlighting, extra time, resource room) and will email her response to her teachers. Overtime, we will evaluate the effectiveness of strategies to see what Jennifer thinks works best for her in different contexts, which will help her understand herself better as a learner.

Learning and Inclusionary Benefits

The learning and inclusionary benefits of using the Collaboration for Inclusion framework are:

- Stakeholders can investigate why previous strategies have been ineffective, use this information to co-select new strategies, and develop a clear and consistent plan to support Jennifer.
- The selection of new supports and strategies are considered in the context of Jennifer's social preferences in a high school environment.

- Opportunities for the implementation of universal approaches to support all students are recognised.
- Selected strategies address short-term needs and promote skill development for Jennifer's long-term success, including post-secondary and adulthood.
- Information gathered can inform the development of a transition plan to support Jennifer in a post-secondary setting.

SECTION TWO

Inclusionary Framework to Support Collaboration

Collaboration for Inclusion			
Student Name: **Grade:**	**Initial Date:** **Review Dates:**	**Team Members:**	
Communication			
Preferred Method ☐ Speaking ☐ Non-Speaking ☐ Speaking & Non-Speaking ☐ Other		**Preferred Mode** ☐ Verbal ☐ Typing ☐ Email ☐ AAC ☐ Text ☐ Other	
Connection			
Student Priorities	**Parent Input**	**Teacher Input**	**Practitioner Input**
Supports and Accommodations:			
Classroom Environment			
Student Priorities	**Parent Input**	**Teacher Input**	**Practitioner Input**

Supports and Accommodations:			
Curriculum			
Student Priorities	**Parent Input**	**Teacher Input**	**Practitioner Input**
Supports and Accommodations:			
Additional Information:			

Reflective Questions for Teachers, Practitioners, and Parents

1. In what ways do you collaborate with autistic students to inform the selection, use, and evaluation of evidence-based practices?
2. How do you gather feedback from parents to know they view themselves as equal partners in their child's education?
3. Do jurisdictional processes support collaboration between stakeholders in clear, consistent, efficient, and productive ways?
4. How is collaborative problem-solving encouraged among all students?
5. Is collaboration considered a pillar of inclusive best practice among the people you work with?

Additional Readings and Resources

1. Sanders, J. (2022). *Included: A book for all children about inclusion, diversity, disability, equality and empathy*. Educate2Empower Publishing.
2. Perryman, T., Ricks, L., & Cash-Baskett, L. (2020). Meaningful transitions: Enhancing clinician roles in transition planning for adolescents with autism spectrum disorders. *Language, Speech, and Hearing Services in Schools, 51*(4), 899–913. https://doi.org/10.1044/2020_LSHSS-19-00048
3. Women and Non-Binary Network. (2021). *Sincerely, your autistic child: What people on the autism spectrum wish their parents knew about growing up, acceptance, and identity*. Beacon Press

Chapter Summary

When autistic students' voices are included alongside the perspectives of teachers, practitioners, and parents, they feel more understood because their interests, abilities and priorities are accounted for in decisions about their education. A lack of collaboration between stakeholders is a barrier to the meaningful and successful inclusion of autistic students and is often overlooked as educators and practitioners prioritise using evidence-based interventions focused on remediating the perceived deficits of autistic students. To promote effective collaboration between stakeholders, openness to autistic students' rights for self-determination, and the development of sustainable processes, frameworks should centre on the identified priorities of autistic students, including communication, connection, classroom environments, and curriculum, which together highlight the 5Cs of Meaningful Inclusion. While each of the 5Cs of Meaningful Inclusion provides an over-arching framework to enhance the inclusionary and well-being success of autistic students, ongoing input from autistic students helps to ensure that knowledge continues to be co-constructed based on the lived experiences of students and that the selection of goals and supports are responsive to the individual abilities, needs, and contexts over time, including autistic students transition to adulthood.

Notes & Reflections

References

Able, H., Sreckovic, M. A., Schultz, T. R., Garwood, J. D., & Sherman, J. (2014). Views from the trenches. *Teacher Education and Special Education.* https://doi.org/10.1177/08884 06414558096

Al Jaffal, M. (2022). Barriers general education teachers face regarding the inclusion of students with autism. *Frontiers in Psychology, 13,* 873248. https://doi.org/10.3389/fpsyg.2022.873248

An, M., & Palisano, R. J. (2014). Family-professional collaboration in pediatric rehabilitation: A practice model. *Disability and Rehabilitation, 36*(5), 434–440. https://doi.org/10.3109/09638288.2013.797510

An, M., Palisano, R. J., Dunst, C. J., Chiarello, L. A., Yi, C.-H., & Gracely, E. J. (2016). Strategies to promote family-professional collaboration: Two case reports. *Disability and Rehabilitation, 38*(18), 1844–1858. https://doi.org/10.3109/09638288.2015.1107763

Azad, G., & Mandell, D. S. (2016). Concerns of parents and teachers of children with autism in elementary school. *Autism: The International Journal of Research and Practice, 20*(4), 435. https://doi.org/10.1177/1362361315588199

Brock, M. E., Dynia, J. M., Dueker, S. A., & Barczak, M. A. (2020). Teacher-reported priorities and practices for students with autism: Characterizing the research-to-practice gap. *Focus on Autism and Other Developmental Disabilities, 35*(2), 67–78. https://doi.org/10.1177/1088357619881217

Brown, H. M., Stahmer, A. C., Dwyer, P., & Rivera, S. (2021). Changing the story: How diagnosticians can support a neurodiversity perspective from the start. *Autism, 25*(5), 1171–1174. https://doi.org/10.1177/13623613211001012

Chandroo, R., Strnadová, I., & Cumming, T. M. (2018). A systematic review of the involvement of students with autism spectrum disorder in the transition planning process: Need for voice and empowerment. *Research in Developmental Disabilities, 83,* 8–17. https://doi.org/10.1016/j.ridd.2018.07.011

Chandroo, R., Strnadová, I., & Cumming, T. M. (2020). Is it really student-focused planning? Perspectives of students with autism. *Research in Developmental Disabilities, 107,* 103783. https://doi.org/10.1016/j.ridd.2020.103783

Cheng, L. L., & Levey, S. (2019). Collaborative approaches to the support of people with disabilities: The underserved and unserved. *Folia Phoniatrica et Logopaedica: Official Organ of the International Association of Logopedics and Phoniatrics (IALP), 71*(2–3), 62–70. https://doi.org/10.1159/000492530

Clark, M., & Adams, D. (2020). Listening to parents to understand their priorities for autism research. *PLoS ONE, 15.* https://doi.org/10.1371/journal.pone.0237376

Danker, J., Strnadová, I., & Cumming, T. M. (2019). "They don't have a good life if we keep thinking that they're doing it on purpose!": Teachers' perspectives on the well-being of students with Autism. *Journal of Autism and Developmental Disorders, 49*(7), 2923–2934. https://doi.org/10.1007/s10803-019-04025-w

Gabovitch, E., & Curtin, C. (2009). Family-centered care for children with autism spectrum disorders: A review. *Marriage and Family Review, 45,* 469–498. https://doi.org/10.1080/01494920903050755

Griffin, M. M., Taylor, J. L., Urbano, R. C., & Hodapp, R. M. (2013). Involvement in transition planning meetings among high school students with autism spectrum disorders. *The Journal of Special Education.* https://doi.org/10.1177/0022466913475668

Howell, M., Bradshaw, J., & Langdon, P. E. (2022). 'There isn't a checklist in the world that's got that on it': Special needs teachers' opinions on the assessment and teaching priorities of pupils on the autism spectrum. *Journal of Intellectual Disabilities, 26*(1), 211–226. https://doi.org/10.1177/1744629520972901

Hummerstone, H., & Parsons, S. (2021) What makes a good teacher? Comparing the perspectives of students on the autism spectrum and staff, *European Journal of Special Needs Education, 36*(4), 610–624. https://doi.org/10.1080/08856257.2020.1783800

Josilowski, C., & Morris, W. (2019). A qualitative exploration of teachers' experiences with students with autism spectrum disorder transitioning and adjusting to inclusion: Impacts of the home and school collaboration. *The Qualitative Report.* https://doi.org/10.46743/2160-3715/2019.3757

Klatte, I., Ketelaar, M., Groot, A., Bloemen, M., & Gerrits, E. (2023). Collaboration: How does it work according to therapists and parents of young children? A systematic review. *Child: Care, Health and Development.* https://doi.org/10.1111/cch.13167

Kurth, J. A., Love, H., & Pirtle, J. (2019). Parent perspectives of their involvement in IEP development for children with autism. *Focus on Autism and Other Developmental Disabilities.* https://doi.org/10.1177/1088357619842858

Kwak, J. (2021). Promoting equity in the classroom with intersectional pedagogy. https://www.everylearnereverywhere.org/blog/promoting-equity-in-the-classroom-with-intersectional-pedagogy/

Lai, M. C., Anagnostou, E., Wiznitzer, M., Allison, C., & Baron-Cohen, S. (2020). Evidence-based support for autistic people across the lifespan: maximising potential, minimising barriers, and optimising the person-environment fit. *The Lancet. Neurology, 19*(5), 434–451. https://doi.org/10.1016/S1474-4422(20)30034-X

National Research Council. (2001). *Educating children with autism.* Washington, DC: National Academy Press.

OCED (2019). *OCED Future of Education and Skills 2030: Conceptual Learning Framework, Student Agenda for 2030.* https://www.oecd.org/education/2030-project/teaching-and-learning/learning/student-agency/Student_Agency_for_2030_concept_note.pdf

Pellicano, E., & den Houting, J. (2022). Annual research review: Shifting from 'normal science' to neurodiversity in autism science. *Journal of Child Psychology and Psychiatry, and Allied Disciplines, 63*(4), 381–396. https://doi.org/10.1111/jcpp.13534

Reichow, B., Hume, K., Barton, E. E., & Boyd, B. A. (2018). Early intensive behavioral intervention (EIBI) for young children with autism spectrum disorders (ASD). *The Cochrane Database of Systematic Reviews, 5*(5), CD009260. https://doi.org/10.1002/14651858.CD009260.pub3

Roberts, J., & Webster, A. (2022) Including students with autism in schools: A whole school approach to improve outcomes for students with autism, *International Journal of Inclusive Education, 26*(7), 701–718.https://doi.ork/10.1080/13603116.2020.1712622

Shahidullah, J. D., McClain, M. B., Azad, G., Mezher, K. R., & McIntyre, L. L. (2020). Coordinating autism care across schools and medical settings: Considerations for school psychologists. *Intervention in School and Clinic.* https://doi.org/10.1177/10534 51220914891

Simón, C., Martínez-Rico, G., McWilliam, R. A., & Cañadas, M. (2023). Attitudes toward Inclusion and benefits perceived by families in schools with students with autism spectrum disorders. *Journal of Autism and Developmental Disorders, 53*(7), 2689–2702. https://doi.org/10.1007/s10803-022-05491-5

United Kingdom Government, (2014). *Children and Families Act 2014.* https://www.legislation.gov.uk/ukpga/2014/6/contents/enacted

US Department of Education. (2004). *Individuals with Disabilities Education Improvement Act.* http://idea.ed.gov/

van der Steen, S., Steenbeek, H. W., Den Hartigh, R. J. R., & van Geert, P. L. C. (2019). The link between microdevelopment and long-term learning trajectories in science learning. *Human Development, 63*(1), 4–32. https://doi.org/10.1159/000501431

Van Laarhoven-Myers, T. E., Van Laarhoven, T. R., Smith, T. J., Johnson, H., & Olson, J. (2014). Promoting self-determination and transition planning using technology. *Career Development and Transition for Exceptional Individuals, 9.* https://doi.org/10.1177/2165143414552518

Webster, A., Bruck, S., & Saggers, B. (2022). Supporting self-determination of autistic students in transitions. *Research in Developmental Disabilities, 128*, 104301. https://doi.org/10.1016/j.ridd.2022.104301

Zollers, N., Arun K. R., & Moonset, Y. (1999) The relationship between school culture and inclusion: How an inclusive culture supports inclusive education, *International Journal of Qualitative Studies in Education, 12*(2), 157–174. https://doi.org/10.1080/095183999236231

Chapter 9

Re-Conceptualising Problem Behaviour

CHAPTER OVERVIEW

SECTION ONE:

1. Student Perspectives on Behaviour and Inclusion
2. Vignette 1: Looking at the Bigger Picture, the Importance of Setting Events
3. Vignette 2: Too Much of a Good Thing

SECTION TWO:

4. Framework to Support Autistic Students in Inclusive Settings
5. Reflective Questions for Teachers, Practitioners, and Parents
6. Additional Readings and Resources
7. Chapter Summary

DOI: 10.4324/9781032687926-9

SECTION ONE

Student Perspectives on Behaviour and Inclusion

The previous five chapters discuss the 5Cs of Meaningful Inclusion based on the perspectives of autistic students, which are Communication, Connection, Classroom Environment, Curriculum, and Collaboration. Interestingly, autistic students do not identify behaviour as an area where they desire additional support to improve their inclusive school experiences, highlighting the disparity between student priorities and those of researchers, teachers, practitioners, and parents who identify positive behaviour support as a main priority (Azad & Mandell; 2016; Brock et al., 2020; Howell, 2022; Roberts & Simpson, 2016). Discourse on opposing perspectives between autistic and non-autistic people is becoming more prevalent due to technological advancements where autistic people face fewer restrictions to share their views, including through blogs and social media platforms. Most autistic people share that they require and value supports that improve their quality of life, whereas non-autistic people tend to focus on interventions that reduce autistic traits (Schuck et al., 2022).

Applied behaviour analysis is a teaching methodology based on principles of learning theory that promotes behavioural change in autistic children and youth in areas related to language, cognition, behaviour, and social and daily living skills (Gitimoghaddam et al., 2022; Reichow et al., 2018). Since its early use in the 1980s by Ivar Lovaas, whose research defended that 47% of autistic children who participated in 40-hour-per-week intensive behavioural therapy would demonstrate abilities required for placement in mainstream education (Lovaas, 1987), applied behaviour analysis continues to be the most used intervention to teach autistic students communication, learning, social, and adaptive behaviour skills (Xu et al., 2019). Over the last 50 years, the effectiveness of other forms of behavioural-based interventions has been explored, including **antecedent-based interventions**, **behavioural momentum interventions**, **cognitive-behavioural strategies**, and **functional communication training**, which all use principles of applied behaviour analysis, which include phases of **prompting, modeling**, and **reinforcement** (Wong et al., 2015). Prompting is a teaching procedure that uses a least-to-most physical hierarchy of physical, verbal, and gestural prompts to teach skill acquisition and generalisation (Sheplay et al., 2018); modeling is consciously exhibiting, sometimes in sequential exaggerated form, behaviours that students are to imitate through observational learning (Wright et al., 2020); and reinforcement is the actions occurring following a behaviour that increase or decrease the likelihood of the behaviour occurring again and is used to promote skill development through motivation (Scheutze et al., 2017).

While behavioural-based interventions are the most common interventions used with autistic children and youth, they have been highly criticised by neurodiversity advocates who defend that repeated exposure to such interventions causes long-term harm and even trauma because they force recipients to suppress their autistic traits through rewards and aversives (Cumming et al., 2020; Kedar, 2012; Kupferstein, 2018; Sequenzia, 2016). Also, variability exists in research on the positive effects of behaviour interventions, where some researchers find little to no observed effects in adaptive behaviour, restricted and receptive behaviour, daily living skills, receptive language, and intelligence (Yu et al., 2020), where other research finds moderate to strong improvements in adaptive behaviour, problem behaviour, emotion, cognition, language, social-communication, but not quality of life (Gitimoghaddam et al., 2022).

Adding to the discord are concerns about research validity, including researcher bias, conflict of interest, such as a lack of transparency in funding sources, over-reporting positive findings and little to no reporting of adverse outcomes, and not enough studies replicating original findings (Bottema-Beutel & Crowley, 2021; Dawson & Fletcher-Watson, 2022; Yeung et al., 2022). Furthermore, most, if not all, research on behavioural interventions is not conducted alongside autistic people and, therefore, is predominantly based on medical models of disability that seek to reduce or eliminate autistic traits (Ollson & Niholm, 2023; Pellicano & den Houting, 2022; Schuck et al., 2022; Yeung et al., 2023). Autistic and non-autistic scholars working together to lessen the division for and against behaviour-based interventions (Schuck et al., 2022) propose that a middle ground might be found in **naturalistic developmental behavioural interventions** (Schreibman et al., 2015). Naturalistic developmental behavioural interventions are approaches used in a child's natural environment that centre on shared decision-making between the adult and child, contingencies, and desired outcomes (Vivanti & Zhong, 2020); also, the child's personal interests, abilities, motivations, and natural reinforcers are strongly considered and accounted for in pedagogical methods (Schuck et al., 2022). With continued collaboration among stakeholders and further research, supporters of the neurodiversity movement are hopeful that traditional behavioural interventions can be transformed into strength-based respectful approaches that lead to practical skill development and improved quality of life for autistic individuals (Chapman & Bovell, 2020; den Houting, 2019; Fletcher-Watson et al., 2019). Additional advantages of naturalistic developmental behavioural interventions are that since they are created and implemented alongside the perspectives of the child, family, and professionals, they are more likely to be culturally respectful and functional within family units (Gengoux et al., 2019), leading to an increased sense of empowerment and confidence among parents (Minjarez et al., 2020).

While autistic students do not prioritise behaviour support, teachers and parents believe that problem behaviours are the most significant barrier to school inclusion for autistic students (Cassady, 2011; Roberts & Simpson, 2016; Watkins et al., 2019). School behaviours can be divided into three main areas: adaptive behaviours (i.e., following routines, sitting at a desk, standing in line, cooperative learning, etc.) (Mouga et al., 2015), challenging behaviours (i.e., aggression, tantrums, inappropriate vocalisations, and self-injury) (Machalicek et al., 2007), and restricted or repetitive behaviour (i.e., hand-flapping, finger-flipping, rocking, jumping, finger-flicking, etc.) (Leekham et al., 2011).

Functional behaviour assessment is a tool used by teachers and practitioners to gather information to identify factors and contingencies affecting autistic students' academic, social, emotional, and behavioural success (Wong et al., 2015). Although time-consuming and highly dependent on the expertise and experience of implementors, functional behavioural analysis has evolved from its original use in therapeutic settings to consider more broad-based school factors enabling or preventing student success and, thus, is considered an effective approach to identifying specialised supports for autistic students (Roberts & Webster, 2020). To promote understanding and effectiveness of functional behaviour assessments among stakeholders, this chapter discusses their use in response to two vignettes from the perspectives of teachers, consultants, and autistic students.

Section Highlights

- Although a main priority for researchers, teachers, practitioners, and parents, autistic students do not identify behaviour and behaviour interventions as a school priority.
- Many forms of behavioural-based interventions are used to teach autistic students skills, including **antecedent-based interventions, behavioural momentum interventions, cognitive-behavioural strategies,** and **functional communication training**.
- Supporters of the neurodiversity movement encourage caregivers and educators to use **naturalistic developmental behavioural interventions** because they reduce deficit-based and harmful approaches that do not account for student voice and choice.
- **Functional behaviour assessment** is an evidence-based practice to investigate factors enabling or preventing student achievement, safety, and well-being.

Vignette 1: Looking at the Bigger Picture, the Importance of Setting Events

Teacher

Smith is having an off day today; he is extra wiggly. His mom wrote in his communication book that he did not sleep well and complained of a headache at breakfast. This morning, I went to give his other teacher a heads-up that Smith might be off today, I encountered some frustration. It has been challenging to support Smith's homeroom teacher to understand that allowing Smith to move and have breaks are necessary accommodations, not rewards for disengagement. Smith is always moving; it helps him stay focused. I understand it can be challenging to manage the classroom with other kids sitting at their desks while Smith moves around the room, making noises, jumping, and flapping. I reached out to our school OT for support, and they suggested that I give him headphones and a bouncy band for his desk. This way, we can meet his need to move at the same while he can still be seated at his desk. We tried it for a few weeks, but I could not get him to sit for the duration of instructions, and in the end, it became more disruptive and dysregulating for him and us. I decided to let Smith move around and observe what happened. I realised that although he did not have verbal language to tell me what was going on for him, his nonverbal cues provided a lot of information. For instance, when he enjoys a learning task like math, he becomes louder and jumps more frequently. When he does not like something or becomes frustrated, he turns away or leaves the space. Additionally, I noticed that Smith needs to approach and spend time around novel objects or tasks before we integrate them into his learning activities; he also enjoys watching his peers engage with them before he does. Everything is a balancing act, Smith can become more easily overwhelmed when he is tired, hungry, or overwhelmed by sensory stimuli—which we are still trying to figure out. We are working hard to find the best way to handle moments of disruptive behaviour. Recently, we learned that Smith seems to become even more dysregulated when we leave the classroom, so we have tried to provide helpful strategies within the classroom. He sure does love learning new things.

Student

For a while, Mrs. Matheson would try to make me sit at my desk all day, but sometimes, it feels like my body will burst if I sit too long. I was frustrated because she didn't understand that I wanted to do what the other kids were doing, but my body really needs to run and jump. When I try to control it, it makes it worse, like I am going to explode. It makes me not think straight, my body gets hot, and I cry. Now she lets me move around the class and even has different learning stations where me and Ashley can go when we need a body break. New things are hard for me sometimes. Sometimes I don't like the way things feel and so I want to touch them first. Mrs. Matheson always changes the stations on Tuesdays, so at least I know that is coming. She also knows I am really good at math. Sometimes I feel really tired and can't understand my work, though, and Mrs. Matheson asks if I need a break in the dark den. I like the dark den because it is quiet and dark, but I don't like leaving the classroom; it's like stop-start-stop-start-stop-start.

Research Connections: The A-B-Cs of Behaviour

Understanding the function of behaviour, or the underlying reasons why a student responds the way they do to specific requests, activities, people, and environments, requires an investigation of what happens immediately prior (i.e., antecedent) and following (i.e., consequence) to the student's behaviour. There are two types of antecedents—triggers and setting events—where triggers occur just before a behaviour occurs, and setting events can occur hours, even days before a behaviour and are intermittent, meaning they occur sometimes but not consistently all the time (Iovannone et al., 2017). For example, Smith having poorly slept and having a headache is a setting event and being told to leave the classroom to go to the dark den is a trigger.

Taking the time to learn about setting events is an essential first step to completing functional behaviour assessments because of their far-reaching impact on the type and power of triggers, behaviours, and consequences (Michael, 1982). Furthermore, if setting events are not identified based on a shared definition and include perspectives from different stakeholders, data collected will be inaccurate because it will narrowly focus on triggers, consequently impacting the observer's judgement and, consequently, the identification of responsive supports and strategies. Setting events are not places or physical locations where behaviour occurs; they are events or actions (Iovannone et al., 2017), such as missing the school bus. The importance of seeking multiple perspectives, including student perspectives, in identifying setting events is that it helps reduce assessment bias, including ableist views on what may or may not be considered a legitimate setting event (Brown & Broido, 2020), such as painful physical experiences because of prolonged overstimulation from noisy classroom environments. Medication changes, missed medication, sleepless nights, diet, and physical symptoms such as headaches and stomach aches are common setting events for students and should be investigated prior to conducting a functional behaviour assessment. When students experience periods of physical discomfort, understanding the intricacies of interoception alongside the expertise of occupational and physical therapists is a valuable and proactive measure teacher, and parents can take to better understand setting events affecting the child.

Interoception is a person's ability to perceive internal bodily sensations such as pain, thirst, and hunger (Sherrington, 1906); and is found to be experienced differently in autistic people, where some may have a high threshold (i.e., under-responsive) or a low threshold (i.e., over-responsive) to internal bodily sensations (Fiene & Brownlow, 2015; Schauder et al., 2015). Additionally, for some autistic students who dependably perceive internal discomfort, they may not be able to precisely locate which part of their body the discomfort is stemming from (Mahler, 2017).

Functional Behaviour Assessments and the 5Cs of Meaningful Inclusion

While no identifiable research exists on the school priorities of autistic students in relation to functional behaviour assessments, it may be worthwhile for stakeholders to consider the ways in which the 5Cs of Meaningful Inclusion affect setting events from a macro psycho-social-physical perspective. For example, how might an autistic student who has no friends at school (Connection) and who has a stomach-ache (setting event) respond to being accidentally bumped in the hallway by a peer, compared to a student with a strong peer group who has a stomach-ache and was accidentally bumped into by a peer? Additionally, when school teams have little control over setting events outside of school that are of a biological nature, contemplating macro-level setting events concerning the 5Cs of Meaningful Inclusion may be more productive.

Therefore, conducting an in-depth functional behaviour assessment would be premature in Smith's situation as more information is needed to develop a shared understanding of setting events. Questions might include: How often does Smith experience sleep disruptions and headaches? How does interrupted sleep affect Smith's morning routine? Does Smith eat breakfast in the mornings when he has not slept well? Does interrupted sleep affect Smith's school attendance, transitions, and bus ride? Does Smith's mother notice increased sensory-seeking behaviours when Smith is tired? What information can Smith provide on why he experiences sleep interruptions and how this affects him throughout the day?

Section Highlights

- Understanding student behaviours requires investigating antecedents and consequences.
- Antecedents include triggers (what happens immediately prior to a behaviour) and settings events (what happens hours, up to days prior to a behaviour).
- Including multiple perspectives, including student perspectives, on setting events helps minimise the effects of ableism in assessment procedures and provides important information on when functional behaviour assessments should be completed to support students.
- Considering setting events from a micro perspective (hours and days prior) and macro perspective (5Cs of Meaningful Inclusion) may provide more relevant broad-based information to better understand student behaviour and inform the selection interventions that are both effective and inclusive.

Vignette 2: Too Much of a Good Thing

Teacher

Kai is new to our school, and based on the transition meeting we had with his parents and his teachers from his previous school, our team decided that it would be a good idea to provide Kai with a part-time education assistant.

Specifically, the role of Ms. Z would be to help Kai become familiar with our school, help with written output, and support Kai with some of the outbursts reported by last year's teacher. Luckily, Ms. Z is very experienced; she has worked with the kinders and grade 1 team for years. Kai is also twice exceptional, and based on previous report cards and assessment information, he has a high full-scale IQ, exceptional memory and verbal comprehension skills, and a low average processing speed. Kai is also hilarious and kind, and has already connected with a few peers who share his sense of humour and interest in aerospace, although he can talk a lot about this topic and requires some re-direction. Sometimes, I wonder if his intense focus will impact his friendships in the long run.

I requested to meet with the autism consultant because Kai's behaviours are escalating. He is increasingly refusing to come into class from recess and lunch break. At first, his behaviour was more playful, but lately, he is really digging in and is becoming more obstinate. More often, Kai yells, "leave me alone," and occasionally curses at his education assistant, who is very knowledgeable and supportive of our students. Ms. Z always gives Kai a lot of verbal praise for his accomplishments and provides immediate feedback when needed, but our typical redirection strategies are not working; sometimes, it can take a long time for Kai to transition from one place or activity to the next. He loves learning and has some great friends, but we must get back on track because he is so capable, and I don't want his behaviours to limit his opportunities.

Student

I like my new school, and James and Vishnu are super cool. We all like to play video games after school and go on NASA's website to test who knows the most about space tech. We are all gonna be aerospace engineers. The best university for aerospace engineering is Stanford, we will probably go there. Sometimes, school can be really annoying though. Well not school, but Ms. B. She is a nice person and I like her, but she is like a space sunshade, but not in a good way. She is not diverting radiation from me, she is blocking the entire sun. I need space...ha ha, get it! She is constantly following me and listening to what my friends and I are talking about. When I am working, she is ALWAYS there telling me how good of a job I am doing, or telling me to stop talking. Both are annoying and embarrassing. I know that I am doing a good job, school is easy. It was okay at first, but sometimes she makes me feel like the SN 2023, which is a supernova that burst on May 19, 2023. I don't even want to go into class anymore with her there all the time. I don't need to take a walk to calm down or take deep breaths. I need her to back off and stop talking to me like a baby and telling me what to do. I get hot just thinking about it. And when I get hot, it's hard to think straight, and I say things I don't mean—like bad words. I just want space. I wish she wasn't always standing behind me, watching me.

Autism Consultant

I initially attended a transition meeting at the end of last school year to help develop a plan for Kai, who would be entering our new school for his grade 6 year. After meeting with Kai's parents and his last year's school team, we decided to request additional education assistant support from the principal to help make sure he started the school year strong and on a positive note. Also, we believed some additional support would help Kai learn new school routines and expectations in a middle school environment. Since Kai is social and has such a way of connecting with peers, we also wanted to make sure nothing got in the way of him making some strong peer connections in his new school. Grade 6 is a pivotal time for students wanting to fit in. The teacher called me in mid-October as she and the education assistant reported some increased behaviours from Kai, including protesting, refusal, avoidance, dys-regulation, frustration, and cursing. We agreed I would spend a morning in the classroom to observe and complete a functional behaviour assessment. Before I began, I decided that in addition to taking A-B-C data on problem behaviour, I also wanted to collect data on positive behaviour so that we could learn more about the A-antecedents and C-consequences that were positive and strength-based and compare this information to data on situ-ations that were not going well for Kai. This is the first year the teacher has taught a student with Kai's learner profile, I am impressed at how eager she is to learn and implement new strategies and advocate for Kai. She and the education assistant seem to have a good connection with Kai, too, they have such a welcoming class and good group of students. The process of completing a functional behaviour assessment is always interesting. It seems to shine a light on things that aren't always noticed, I think just having an outsider perspective from someone who isn't with the students all day, every day, is also helpful. After about 30 minutes of observation, I decided to pause taking more data because I noticed a clear interaction pattern between Ms. Z, the education assistant, and Kai. The number of verbal prompts and feedback given to Kai were good in that they were positive and direct, but they seem to have surpassed what was required and looked to be impacting Kai's ability to process the information independently. Additionally, the verbal prompts were different than what was being used with his peers; they were more frequent and sometimes occurred in a sing-song voice. I noticed that when Kai received feedback from the teacher or education assistant, he would glance around to see who was watching and sometimes physically tried to distance himself from the education assistant. As I said, data collection is always an interesting process in the context of classrooms and people. It's not my intention, but sometimes I go into a classroom to take data on students and observe some well-intentioned but problematic behaviours in the adults!

Research Connections

Kai's school team has many positive qualities, including having a strengths-based lens of Kai, proactive and solution-focused thinking and acting, and a basic knowledge of behavioural principles, including setting events, triggers, prompting, and reinforcement. For instance, the school team is aware of changes in Kai's daily schedule that could impact his school behaviour, including that he did not eat breakfast and has a dentist appointment, which will occur during science class, which he does not want to miss (setting events). Regarding the 5Cs of Meaningful Inclusion, it appears that Kai benefits from universal strategies provided by the teacher as Kai's communication skills do not require additional support or technologies; he has developed strong connections with peers and generally likes his teacher and education assistant; he does not require targeted or specialised accommodations to support his sensory preferences in the classroom environment and is motivated to learn and engage in curricular topics (macro setting event). Kai's team also shows characteristics of a collaborative team in that they have co-developed a transition plan and provided additional support by providing an education assistant. However, based on initial data collected in the functional behaviour assessment shown below, the additional support, while good-intentioned, is causing negative reactions from Kai because it does not align with his preferences and priorities. From his perspective, which arguably is the only missing element in his transition and current support plan, he does not require or appreciate the type and frequency of support the education assistant provides him; therefore, he communicates his voice and choice through escalating behaviours such as refusal and verbal protests.

Education Assistants

Research shows that while most teachers and parents believe that help from education assistants is a positive and essential support to autistic students in inclusive classrooms (Hasson et al., 2022), an inverse relationship exists between the type of support students receive and students' academic and social progress (Blatchford et al., 2009; Breyer et al., 2020; Tews & Lupart, 2008). For example, when the education assistant assumes the primary role of caretaker and instructor, it may lead to decreased academic achievement based on fewer interactions between the student and their teacher (Butt, 2016; Humphrey

& Lewis, 2008; Tews & Lupart, 2008; Webster et al., 2010). Additionally, the qualification of the education assistant may not match the needs of unique needs and abilities of the student (Webster et al., 2010), resulting in the ineffective use of strategies, reduced autonomy and problem-solving abilities, and learned helplessness (Tews & Lupart, 2008). These are essential considerations for all students; however, in Kai's situation, autistic students with high intellectual ability often experience increased levels of anxiety and low self-worth, which frequently is masked by their cognitive abilities (Rubenstein et al., 2015) and poor understanding of splinter skills by adults. Therefore, while Ms. B is qualified and proficient in her role as an education assistant, most of her experience is working with younger children, resulting in over-prompting and frequent verbal feedback that is not age or socially appropriate, resulting in frustration and embarrassment for Kai. Further complicating the role of education assistants supporting students like Kai is research on evidence-based practices to support twice-exceptional autistic students in inclusive classrooms is limited (Gelbar et al., 2021), which may lead to inconsistent and ineffective implementation of strategies.

Extending upon research where autistic students do not identify behaviour support as a school priority, they also do not call for more one-to-one support from education assistants (Aubineau & Blicharska, 2020; Lebenhagen, 2022), which may be due to feeling like they stand out from their peers, and it often means that it increases the number of different people they interact with, also affecting predictability and consistency in their school day (Symes & Humphrey, 2011). These dissatisfactions do not mean that autistic students do not value or require individualised support; they do, however, prefer the provision of support in more naturalistic forms, including consistent and precise feedback, curricular accommodations, access to assistive technology, and flexibility opportunities to demonstrate their knowledge, for class presentations and exams (Goodall, 2018; Lebenhagen, 2022; Saggers et al., 2011), and in ways that don't make them feel different than their peers (Turnock et al., 2022). With technological advancements, researchers are investigating the benefits of artificial intelligence teaching assistants for online and in-person learning to teach students curricula social behaviours, and to provide immediate feedback (Kim et al., 2020). While positive feedback has been received from post-secondary students on using artificial intelligence, as research advances, it would be beneficial to include the perspectives of students with disabilities in K–12 settings. The following framework, *Functional Behaviour Assessment to Support Inclusion,* provides an in-depth example of the importance and benefit of collecting micro-level and macro-level data alongside the perspectives of autistic students.

The framework used in this chapter is titled *Functional Behaviour Assessment to Support Inclusion*. The sections on the left side of the framework provide a space to collect information on common setting events to be investigated by team members, and the sections on the right side of the framework provide a space to collect information relating to macro setting events related to the 5Cs of Meaningful Inclusion: Communication, Connection, Classroom Environment, Curriculum, and Collaboration. Adding another layer of context information related to setting events (5Cs of Meaningful Inclusion) to collaborative discussions and assessment procedures is beneficial for several reasons, including 1) it increases stakeholder awareness of the benefits of universal approaches to support autistic students, 2) it more evenly distributes the responsibility for behaviour change between adults and students, 3) it helps improve the accuracy of data collection and analysis because macro and micro factors are integrated into the viewpoints of the observer/assessor, and 4) it ensures the identification of evidence-based interventions are both responsive to the individual abilities, needs, and contexts of autistic students *and* they promote meaningful inclusion.

Section Highlights

- Autistic students communicate their voice and choice through behaviours. Emphasising the importance of seeking and honouring student perspectives in identifying behaviour-related supports.
- Understanding education assistants' intentional role in supporting autistic students should be based on a shared understanding of priorities and desired outcomes between teachers, parents, and students.
- While autistic students value additional support, they are concerned that they may increase stigma by accentuating their differences.

Responsive Framework

FUNCTIONAL BEHAVIOUR ASSESSMENT TO SUPPORT INCLUSION

Student: Kai	Grade: Six	Teacher(s): Mrs. T	Additional Team Members: Ms. Z, Autism Consultant, parents	Date: October

Part 1: Setting Events	Part 2: 5Cs of Meaningful Inclusion
Medication: None	**Communication Profile and Supports:** Verbal, no expressive communication supports in place, occasional support with writing.
Dietary: Did not eat breakfast today.	**Connection with Peers/Adults:** Very social and has a positive relationship with teacher, EA and two close friends.
Sleep Hygiene: Regular routine	**Classroom Environment (i.e., Sensory Profile/Preferences):** No significant concerns, but may get agitated if there is prolonged talking/background noise.
Attendance: (hrs/day) Normally regular attendance, is being picked up at 1:30 pm today.	**Curriculum Interests and Strengths:** Very motivated to learn in all subjects in school and talk/debate anything related to aerospace.
Transportation (type/ duration): Walked to school today with younger brother, approximately 15 min.	**Collaboration Plan (i.e., Consistency among team members):** The school team met in June to develop a transition plan. The teacher provides weekly updates to mom via email. No additional meetings are scheduled.

Additional Setting Event Info: Kai and his brother are being picked up early for a dentist appointment, which Kai expressed concern because he would miss science class.

Part 3: Data Collection

When	Where	Who		What	
Time	Context	Adults/Peers	A-Antecedent	B-Behaviour	C-Consequence
8:25	Hallway	EA Grade 6 class	Locker routine, Ms. B tells Kai to unpack backpack and change shoes	"I am"	Ms. B "good job Kai, we are off to a great start!"
8:29	Hallway	EA Grade 6 class	Locker routine, Ms. B tells Kai to talk less and to "hippity-hop" into class	Kai roles his eyes and walks into class carrying his shoes	Ms. B follows Kai and briefly touches him on his shoulder
8:31	Classroom-Desk	Teacher/EA Grade 6 class	Welcomes class and instructs students to start reading daily schedule on whiteboard	Kai is looking down putting on his shoes	Ms. B tells Kai that he should have put shoes on in hallway and repeats teacher instructions
8:32	Classroom-Desk	Teacher/EA Grade 6 Class	Kai looks to James	Kai reads daily schedule	Ms. B gives a "thumbs-up"
8:33	Classroom-Desk	Teacher/EA Grade 6 Class	Teacher instructs students to get out their math workbooks and complete pg. 11	Kai gets out his math workbook and pencil and begins working independently	EA paces behind back row of students looking over their work

8:50	Classroom-Desk	Teacher/EA Grade 6 Class	Teacher gives students 1-minute warning before students share their answers	Kai looks to his neighbour to see how far he is in comparison and continues working	Teacher says "eyes on your own work"
8:57	Classroom-Desk	Teacher/EA Grade 6 Class	Teacher asks Kai for his answer to math question #6	Kai uses his pencil to tap down the page to number 6, looks up at peers, then down to page, but loses his place	EA steps beside him and points to question #6
8:57	Classroom-Desk	Teacher/EA Grade 6 Class	EA is leans in and says "here is your answer, can you read it?"	Kai leans pushes his chair back and says "I know" in an agitated tone	Teacher says she will come back to Kai for his answer to question number 10.
8:58	Classroom-Desk	James	Looks at Kai and giggles	Kai says "shut up"	EA puts her hand on Kai's shoulder and whispers "get ready for question 10"

Learning and Inclusionary Benefits

The benefits of using the Functional Behaviour Assessment to Support Inclusion framework are:

- It allows teachers, parents, and practitioners to work alongside autistic students to develop a shared understanding of the setting events and triggers that positively and negatively affect students' behaviour.
- Based on a shared understanding of factors affecting student behaviour, stakeholders distribute responsibility for skill development and behaviour change more appropriately and equally among team members.
- Understanding the function of student behaviour in the context of research on the school priorities of autistic students (5Cs of Meaningful Inclusion) prompts stakeholders to re-consider ableist views on problem behaviour, their underlying causes and responsive interventions.
- The selection of behaviour interventions should consider the knowledge and experiences of adults, the perspectives, abilities, and circumstances of students, and align with international and local policy on inclusive best practices.

SECTION TWO

Framework to Support Autistic Students in Inclusive Settings

FUNCTIONAL BEHAVIOUR ASSESSMENT TO SUPPORT INCLUSION

Student:	Grade:	Teacher(s):	Additional Team Members:	Date:
Part 1: Setting Events				
Medication:				
Dietary:				
Sleep Hygiene:				
Attendance: (hrs/day)				
Transportation (type/ duration):				

Part 2: 5Cs of Meaningful Inclusion

Communication Profile and Supports:	
Connection with Peers/Adults:	
Classroom Environment (i.e., Sensory Profile/Preferences):	
Curriculum Interests and Strengths:	
Collaboration Plan (i.e., Consistency among team members):	

Additional Setting Event Info:

Part 3: Data Collection

When	Where	Who	A-Antecedent	What	C-Consequence
Time	Context	Adults/Peers		B-Behaviour	

Reflective Questions for Teachers, Practitioners, and Parents

1. How are the 5Cs of Meaningful Inclusion: Communication, Connection, Classroom Environment, Curriculum, and Collaboration accounted for when determining factors affecting student behaviour?
2. What universal approaches do you use to support positive behaviour?
3. How do you include the perspectives of autistic students when seeking to understand the function of behaviours and the identification and implementation of supports?
4. How are the perspectives of parents, occupational therapists, physical therapists, speech-language therapists, and psychologists incorporated into the co-development of support plans for autistic students?
5. Does the provision of additional support, including education assistants, draw undesirable and unwanted attention to autistic students?
6. What evaluation methods ensure that behaviour interventions promote skill development, acceptance, and inclusion?
7. What school-wide actions are used to promote understanding and acceptance of behavioural differences?

Additional Readings and Resources

1. Cook, J. (2011). *I just don't like the sound of no! My story about accepting no for an answer and disagreeing the right way!* Boys Town Press.
2. Phung, J., Penner, M., Pirlot, C., & Welch, C. (2021). What I wish you knew: Insights on burnout, inertia, meltdown, and shutdown from autistic youth. *Frontiers in Psychology, 12*, https://doi.org/10.3389/fpsyg.2021.741421
3. Sutton, M. (2011). *The real experts: Readings for parents of autistic children.* Autonomous Press.

Chapter Summary

In research on the self-reported school priorities of autistic students, students do not identify the need for additional behaviour support; however, supporting positive behaviour is a main priority for teachers and parents, and therefore, behavioural-based interventions are the most used interventions with autistic students. Functional behaviour assessments are a tool used by school teams to understand student behaviour in relation to setting events, triggers, and consequences. When used alongside the perspectives of autistic students, functional behaviour assessments provide valuable information to stakeholders on positive actions and interventions to promote skill development and the inclusion of autistic students in ways that align with their learning preferences and social priorities.

Notes & Reflections

References

Aubineau, M., & Blicharska, T. (2020). High-functioning autistic students speak about their experience of inclusion in mainstream secondary schools. *School Mental Health, 12,* 537–555. https://doi.org/10.1007/s12310-020-09364-z

Azad, G., & Mandell, D. S. (2016). Concerns of parents and teachers of children with autism in elementary school. *Autism: The International Journal of Research and Practice, 20*(4), 435–441. https://doi.org/10.1177/1362361315588199

Blatchford, P., Bassett, P., Brown, P., & Webster, R. (2009). The effect of support staff on pupil engagement and individual attention. *British Educational Research Journal, 35*(5), 661–686. https://doi.org/10.1080/01411920902878917

Bottema-Beutel, K., & Crowley, S. (2021). Pervasive undisclosed conflicts of interest in applied behavior analysis autism literature. *Frontiers in Psychology, 12,* 676303. https://doi.org/10.3389/fpsyg.2021.676303

Breyer, C., Lederer, J., & Gasteiger-Klicpera, B. (2021) Learning and support assistants in inclusive education: a transnational analysis of assistance services in Europe, *European Journal of Special Needs Education, 36*(3), 344–357. https://doi.org/10.1080/08856 257.2020.1754546

Brock, M. E., Dynia, J. M., Dueker, S. A., & Barczak, M. A. (2020). Teacher-reported priorities and practices for students with autism: Characterizing the research-to-practice gap. *Focus on Autism and Other Developmental Disabilities, 35*(2), 67–78. https://doi.org/10.1177/1088357619881217

Brown, K. R., & Broido, E. M. (2020). Ableism and assessment: Including students with disabilities. *New Directions for Student Services, 169,* 31–41. https://doi.org/10.1002/ss.20342

Butt, R. (2016). Teacher assistant support and deployment in mainstream schools. *International Journal of Inclusive Education, 20,* 1–13. https://doi/10.1080/13603 116.2016.1145260

Cassady, J. M. (2011). Teachers' attitudes toward the inclusion of students with autism and emotional behavioral disorder, *Electronic Journal for Inclusive Education, 2*(7).

Chapman, R., & Bovell, V. (Forthcoming). Neurodiversity, advocacy, anti-therapy. In P. Sturmey & J. Matson (Eds.), *Handbook of autism and pervasive developmental disorder.* Springer.

Cumming, T., Strnadová, I., Danker, J., & Basckin, C. (2020). I was taught that my being was inherently wrong: Is applied behavioural analysis a socially valid practice? *International Journal of Arts Humanities and Social Sciences, 5*(12), 72–82.

Dawson, M., & Fletcher-Watson, S. (2022). When autism researchers disregard harms: A commentary. *Autism: The International Journal of Research and Practice, 26*(2), 564–566. https://doi.org/10.1177/13623613211031403

den Houting J. (2019). Neurodiversity: An insider's perspective. *Autism: The International Journal of Research and Practice, 23*(2), 271–273. https://doi.org/10.1177/136236131 8820762

Edelson S. M. (2022). Understanding challenging behaviors in autism spectrum disorder: A multi-component, interdisciplinary model. *Journal of Personalized Medicine, 12*(7), 1127. https://doi.org/10.3390/jpm12071127

Fiene, L., & Brownlow, C. (2015). Investigating interoception and body awareness in adults with and without autism spectrum disorder. *Autism Research: Official Journal of the International Society for Autism Research, 8*(6), 709–716. https://doi.org/10.1002/aur.1486

Fletcher-Watson, S., Adams, J., Brook, K., Charman, T., Crane, L., Cusack, J.... & Pellicano, E. (2019). Making the future together: Shaping autism research through meaningful participation. *Autism: The International Journal of Research and Practice, 23*(4), 943–953. https://doi.org/10.1177/1362361318786721

Garfinkel, S. N., Tiley, C., O'Keeffe, S., Harrison, N. A., Seth, A. K., & Critchley, H. D. (2016). Discrepancies between dimensions of interoception in autism: Implications for emotion and anxiety. *Biological Psychology, 114*, 117–126. https://doi.org/10.1016/j.biopsycho.2015.12.003

Gelbar, N. W., Cascio, A. A., Madaus, J. W., & Reis, S. M. (2021). A systematic review of the research on gifted individuals with autism spectrum disorder. *Gifted Child Quarterly.* https://doi.org/10.1177/00169862211061876

Gengoux, G. W., Abrams, D. A., Schuck, R., Millan, M. E., Libove, R., Ardel, C. M.... & Hardan, A. Y. (2019). A pivotal response treatment package for children with autism spectrum disorder: An RCT. *Pediatrics, 144*(3), e20190178. https://doi.org/10.1542/peds.2019-0178

Gitimoghaddam, M., Chichkine, N., McArthur, L., Sangha, S. S., & Symington, V. (2022). Applied behavior analysis in children and youth with autism spectrum disorders: A scoping review. *Perspectives on Behavior Science, 45*(3), 521–557. https://doi.org/10.1007/s40614-022-00338-x

Goodall, C. (2018). 'I felt closed in and like I couldn't breathe': A qualitative study exploring the mainstream educational experiences of autistic young people. *Autism and Developmental Language Impairments, 3.* https://doi.org/10.1177/2396941518804407

Harbin J. (2017). I'm Jacob, I'm 18, and I have autism. *Anchor of Hope Foundation.* https://www.anchorofhopefoundation.org/single-post/2017/09/19/im-jacob-im-18-and-i-have-autism

Hasson, L., Keville, S., Gallagher, J., Onagbesan, D., & Ludlow, A.K. (2022). Inclusivity in education for autism spectrum disorders: Experiences of support from the perspective of parent/carers, school teaching staff and young people on the autism spectrum, *International Journal of Developmental Disabilities.* https://doi.org/10.1080/20473869.2022.2070418

Howell, M., Bradshaw, J., & Langdon, P. E. (2022). 'There isn't a checklist in the world that's got that on it': Special needs teachers' opinions on the assessment and teaching priorities of pupils on the autism spectrum. *Journal of Intellectual Disabilities, 26*(1), 211–226. https://doi.org/10.1177/1744629520972901

Humphrey, N., & Lewis, S. (2008). What does "inclusion" mean for pupils on the autistic spectrum in mainstream secondary schools? *Journal of Research in Special Educational Needs, 8*(3), 132–140. https://doi.org/10.1111/j.1471-3802.2008.00115.x

Iovannone, R., Anderson, C., & Scott, T. (2017). Understanding setting events: What they are and how to identify them. *Beyond Behavior.* https://doi.org/10.1177/1074295617729795

Jaffal, M. A. (2021). Barriers general education teachers face regarding the inclusion of students with autism. *Frontiers in Psychology, 13.* https://doi.org/10.3389/fpsyg.2022.873248

Kedar, I. (2018). *Ido in Autismland: Climbing out of autism's silent prison.* Sharon Kedar.

Kim, J., Merrill, K., Xu, K., & Sellnow, D. D. (2020) My teacher is a machine: Understanding students' perceptions of AI teaching assistants in online education, *International Journal of Human–Computer Interaction, 36*(20), 1902–1911. https://doi/10.1080/10447 318.2020.1801227

Kupferstein, H. (2018). Evidence of increased PTSD symptoms in autistics exposed to applied behavior analysis. *Advances in Autism, 4*(1), 19–29.

Lebenhagen, C. (2022). Autistic students' views on meaningful inclusion: A Canadian perspective. *Journal of Education.* https://doi.org/10.1177/00220574221101378

Leekam, S. R., Prior, M. R., & Uljarevic, M. (2011). Restricted and repetitive behaviors in autism spectrum disorders: A review of research in the last decade. *Psychological Bulletin,* 137, 562–593. http://dx.doi.org/10.1037/a0023341

Lovaas O. I. (1987). Behavioral treatment and normal educational and intellectual functioning in young autistic children. *Journal of Consulting and Clinical Psychology, 55*, 3–9.

Machalicek, W., O'Reilly, M. F., Beretvas, N., Sigafoos, J., & Lancioni, G. E. (2007). A review of interventions to reduce challenging behavior in school settings for students with autism spectrum disorders. *Research in Autism Spectrum Disorders,* 1, 229–246. http://dx.doi.org/10.1016/jrasd.2006.10.005

Mahler, K. (2017). *Interoception: The eighth sensory system.* Lenexa, KS: AAPC Publishing.

Michael, J. (1982). Distinguishing between discriminative and motivational functions of stimuli. *Journal of the Experimental Analysis of Behavior, 37*, 149–155. http://doi.org/ 10.1901/jeab.1982.37-149

Minjarez, M. B., Williams, S. E., Mercier, E. M., & Hardan, A. Y. (2011). Pivotal response group treatment program for parents of children with autism. *Journal of Autism and Developmental Disorders, 41*(1), 92–101. https://doi.org/10.1007/s10803-010-1027-6

Mouga, S., Almeida, J., Café, C., Duque, F., & Oliveira, G. (2015). Adaptive profiles in autism and other neurodevelopmental disorders. *Journal of Autism and Developmental Disorders, 45*, 1001–1012.http://dx.doi.org/10.1007/s10803-014-2256-x

Olsson, I. & Nilholm, C. (2023) Inclusion of pupils with autism – A research overview, *European Journal of Special Needs Education, 38*(1), 126–140. https://doi.org/10.1080/ 08856257.2022.2037823

Pellicano, E., & den Houting, J. (2022). Annual research review: Shifting from 'normal science' to neurodiversity in autism science. *Journal of Child Psychology and Psychiatry, and Allied Disciplines, 63*(4), 381–396. https://doi.org/10.1111/jcpp.13534

Putnam, O. C., Eddy, G., Goldblum, J., Swisher, M., & Harrop, C. (2023). How autistic adults' priorities for autism research differ by gender identity: A mixed-methods study. *Women's Health.* https://doi.org/10.1177/17455057231160342

Reichow, B., Hume, K., Barton, E. E., & Boyd, B. A. (2018). Early intensive behavioral intervention (EIBI) for young children with autism spectrum disorders (ASD). *The Cochrane Database of Systematic Reviews, 5*(5).https://doi.org/10.1002/14651858. CD009260.pub3

Roberts, J., & Simpson, K. (2016). A review of research into stakeholder perspectives on inclusion of students with autism in mainstream schools. *International Journal of Inclusive Education, 20*(10), 1084–1096. https://doi.org/10.1080/13603116.2016.1145267

Roberts, J., & Webster, A. (2022) Including students with autism in schools: A whole school approach to improve outcomes for students with autism, *International Journal of Inclusive Education, 26*(7). https://doi.org/10.1080/13603116.2020.1712622

Rubenstein, L. D., Schelling, N., Wilczynski, S. M., & Hooks, E. N. (2015). Lived experiences of parents of gifted students with autism spectrum disorder. *Gifted Child Quarterly.* https://doi.org/10.1177/0016986215592193

Saggers, B., Hwang, Y. S., & Mercer, K.L. (2011). Your voice counts: Listening to the voice of high school students with autism spectrum disorder. *Australasian Journal of Special Education, 35*(2), 173–190.https://doi.org/10.1375/ajse.35.2.173

Schauder, K. B., Mash, L. E., Bryant, L. K., & Cascio, C. J. (2015). Interoceptive ability and body awareness in autism spectrum disorder. *Journal of Experimental Child Psychology, 131*, 193–200. https://doi.org/10.1016/j.jecp.2014.11.002

Schreibman, L., Dawson, G., Stahmer, A. C., Landa, R., Rogers, S. J., McGee, G. G....& Halladay, A. (2015). Naturalistic developmental behavioral interventions: Empirically validated treatments for autism spectrum disorder. *Journal of Autism and Developmental Disorders, 45*(8), 2411–2428. https://doi.org/10.1007/s10803- 015- 2407-8

Schuck, R. K., Tagavi, D. M., Baiden, K. M. P., Dwyer, P., Williams, Z. J., Osuna, A.... & Vernon, T. W. (2022). Neurodiversity and autism intervention: Reconciling perspectives through a naturalistic developmental behavioral intervention framework. *Journal of Autism and Developmental Disorders, 52*(10), 4625–4645. https://doi.org/10.1007/s10 803-021-05316-x

Schuetze, M., Rohr, C. S., Dewey, D., McCrimmon, A., & Bray, S. (2016). Reinforcement learning in autism spectrum disorder. *Frontiers in Psychology, 8.* https://doi.org/10.3389/fpsyg.2017.02035

Sequenzia, A. (2016, April 27). *Autistic conversion therapy.* https://awnnetwork.org/autis tic-conversion-therapy/?fbclid=IwAR1KVUN-h6qJ6paWxAwX2H22PH8ApGHQJqG9 F4arjzWKrZVNh7Z9cp5GBJ4

Sharma, U., Furlonger, B., & Forlin, C. (2019). The impact of funding models on the education of students with autism spectrum disorder. *Australasian Journal of Special and Inclusive Education, 43*(1), 1–11. doi:10.1017/jsi.2019.1

Shepley, C., Lane, J. D., & Ault, M. J. (2018). A review and critical examination of the system of least prompts. *Remedial and Special Education.* https://doi.org/10.1177/07419 32517751213

Sherrington, C.S. (1906) *The integrative action of the nervous system.* New Haven, CT: Yale University Press.

Symes, W., & Humphrey, N. (2011). The deployment, training and teacher relationships of teaching assistants supporting pupils with autistic spectrum disorders (ASD) in mainstream secondary schools. *British Journal of Special Education, 38.* http://doi.org/10.1111/j.1467-8578.2011.00499.x

Tews, L., & Lupart, J. (2008). Students with disabilities' perspectives of the role and impact of paraprofessionals in inclusive education settings. *Journal of Policy and Practice in Intellectual Disabilities, 5*, 39–46. http://doi.org/10.1111/j.1741-1130.2007.00138.x.

Turnock, A., Langley, K., & Jones, R. G. (2022). Understanding stigma in autism: A narrative review and theoretical model. *Autism in Adulthood: Challenges and Management, 4*(1), 76–91. https://doi.org/10.1089/aut.2021.0005

Vivanti, G., & Zhong, H.N. (2020). Naturalistic developmental behavioral interventions for children with autism. In G. Vivanti, K. Bottema-Beutel, & L.Turner-Brown. (Eds.). *Clinical guide to early interventions for children with autism. Best practices in child and adolescent behavioral health care.* Cham: Springer. https://doi.org/10.1007/978-3-030-41160-2_6

Watkins, L., Ledbetter-Cho, K., O'Reilly, M., Barnard-Brak, L., & Garcia-Grau, P. (2019). Interventions for students with autism in inclusive settings: A best-evidence synthesis and meta-analysis. *Psychological Bulletin, 145*(5), 490–507. https://doi.org/10.1037/bul 0000190

Webster, R., Blatchford, P., Bassett, P., Brown, P., Martin, C., & Russell, A. (2010). Double standards and first principles: Framing teaching assistant support for pupils with special educational needs. *European Journal of Special Needs Education, 25.* 319–336. 10.1080/08856257.2010.513533.

Wong, C., Odom, S. L., Hume, K. A., Cox, A. W., Fettig, A., Kucharczyk, S.... & Schultz, T. R. (2015). Evidence-based practices for children, youth, and young adults with autism spectrum disorder: A comprehensive review. *Journal of Autism and Developmental Disorders, 45*(7), 1951–1966. https://doi.org/10.1007/s10803-014-2351-z

Wright, J., Knight, V., & Barton, E. (2020). A review of video modeling to teach STEM to students with autism and intellectual disability. *Research in Autism Spectrum Disorders.* https://doi.org/70.101476.10.1016/j.rasd.2019.101476

Xu, G., Strathearn, L., Liu, B., O'Brien, M., Kopelman, T. G., Zhu, J....& Bao, W. (2019). Prevalence and treatment patterns of autism spectrum disorder in the United States, 2016. *JAMA Pediatrics, 173*(2), 153–159. https://doi.org/10.1001/jamapediatr ics.2018.4208

Yeung, S. K., Warrington, K., Ramji, A., Elsherif, M., Kapp, S., Azevedo, F., & Shaw, J. (2023). Bridging open scholarship with higher education and postgraduate training in autism: A primer and guide. https://doi.org/10.31234/osf.io/duv42

Yu, Q., Li, E., Li, L., & Liang, W. (2020). Efficacy of interventions based on applied behavior analysis for autism spectrum disorder: A meta-analysis. *Psychiatry Investigation, 17*(5), 432–443. https://doi.org/10.30773/pi.2019.0229

Chapter 10

The Future of Inclusive Education

PRESUMING COMPETENCE

Anantha Krishnamurthy, Grade 8

The teachers treat me the same as my classmates, and I am expected to do the same assignments and participate in group projects. Yet, they do treat me differently, in a good way. I am provided with a communication partner who supports me one-on-one at school. He adapts his support to match my strengths and does not impose outdated and dangerous behaviour therapy on me. Work is adapted so that I can work on them at my pace and from my destination of choice. I am allowed to retreat into a sensory room when the classroom becomes too overwhelming.

I spend only half a day at school. However, my teachers never forget to include me while I am gone. My presentations are played with text-to-speech to the class, and I am allowed to video conference into class discussions. I was asked to write a poem for Remembrance Day, and the poem was recited at the school assembly by my classmate. The school principal wrote a personal note about how proud she was of me. My silence does not deter anyone from including me.

I do have a team of experts to support me. However, for the first time, my voice and vision are respected. I vet every single decision. For example, my time at school gradually increased based on continuous feedback from me, and this helped me adapt much better to sensory overload. The Individualized Program Plan (IPP) lists me as the first member of my core support team!

The halls of my school are filled with the sweet fragrance of presuming competence. I dearly hope to breathe this air wherever my academic journey takes me.

From *Speechless Dream: Narratives on Autism, Inclusion and Hope* (Lebenhagen et al., 2022).

DOI: 10.4324/9781032687926-10

Including Student Voice: A Moral Imperative

When autistic students are given equitable opportunities to share their experiences, perspectives, desires, and hopes, it is evident that they possess many strength-based qualities unrecognised in deficit-based models of disability. While the extent of current research on the self-reported experiences of autistic students is limited, a review of current literature clearly demonstrates that speaking and non-speaking autistic students are reflective, articulate, intelligent, creative, passionate, determined, patient, loving, forgiving, and hopeful about their future. Additionally, autistic students are keenly aware of their challenges and the specific areas they would like support with; however, they want to be involved in decisions that affect them, including learning goals and the type and timing of support received. Fundamentally, like any other student, autistic students desire to be treated with respect and viewed as capable learners belonging in school.

By elevating and listening to the voices of autistic students, stakeholders are better positioned to a) learn about the personhood of autism from an autistic person's point of view, b) value different forms of legitimate speaking and non-speaking forms of communication, c) recognise neuro-similarities alongside neuro-differences, and are more likely to view these differences—not deficits—as variations in the human condition, and d) reduce the use of ineffective, sometimes harmful interventions.

Thus, seeking ways to include student voice is not only a moral imperative backed by international human rights law, but autistic students want to be a part of discussions and decisions affecting them, which is necessary in any collaborative processes that aim to improve the education and well-being outcomes of autistic students. Social justice initiatives founded on "nothing about us, without us" beliefs are relevant to education policy and practice because they empower autistic people to self-represent their views (Chown et al., 2017) and encourage outsiders to view autistic people as essential and equal partners in the co-construction of knowledge (Cascio & Racine, 2018; StEvens, 2022).

What Does Inclusion Mean to Autistic Students?

Viewing inclusion as a state of being, not as a place to be (Goodall, 2020) requires a shift in mindset, policy, and practice, including avoiding hyper-focusing on deficit-based remedial practices that perpetuate neurotypical standards and preferences for "typical," "normal," and "average" ways of thinking, perceiving, communicating, socialising, regulating, and behaving. An insightful illustration of neurodivergence shared by an autistic university student is by comparing brain functioning to computer operating systems, where his brain operates on Windows while everyone else functions as a Mac (Vincent et al., 2017). This example serves as a simple but powerful reminder that autistic students need to be respectfully viewed as different, not less, and that non-autistics and allies are equally responsible for learning and adaptation.

Therefore, in summary, autistic students share that inclusion means:

1) They are provided opportunities to use speaking and non-speaking methods to **communicate** their voice and choice in decisions that affect their communication, learning, sensory, and social experiences.
2) They feel **connected** to teachers, peers, and school communities through words, actions, and spaces that promote acceptance and belonging.
3) **Classroom environments** support their psychological and physical states of well-being and safety in flexible ways.
4) They have equitable opportunities to meaningfully participate in **curriculum learning** alongside their peers, with the provision of flexible support and accommodations.
5) They are considered essential and competent members of **collaborative** teams that co-identify goals and supports based on their strengths and areas needing support.

As described in-depth throughout this guide, these five priorities comprise the **5Cs of Meaningful Inclusion**; thus, they should be considered alongside discussions and implementation of evidence-based practices to ensure suitability and sustainability in educational contexts and, foremost, to ensure respect for autistic students' personhood.

What Is the Future of Inclusive Education for Autistic Students?

Research finds that autistic students are absent from school on average five out of 23 days, and school refusal accounts for 43% of school absences (Totsika et al., 2020). Nine percent of autistic students' school refusals are due to school exclusion initiated by the school, including requests not to attend due to accommodations and support, and questionable disciplinary procedures (Totsika et al., 2020). School absenteeism negatively impacts student achievement (Filippello, 2019) and mental health (Adams, 2022), and may partly explain why less than half of autistic students in the United States enroll in post-secondary school (Jackson et al., 2018).

Although there is philosophical agreement among stakeholders on the obligation and importance of the provision of inclusive education (Simón et al., 2022), how this translates to day-to-day experiences varies (Brock et al., 2020; Watkins et al., 2019), resulting in uncertain futures for autistic students. The misalignment in perspectives and priorities between stakeholders is difficult to untangle but likely stems from several intersecting factors, including inconsistent definitions of inclusion and operationalisations of policy (Leifler et al., 2021; Nilholm, 2021), inadequate training (Gómez-Marí et al., 2022), and less than ideal availability of resources, including funding (Sharma et al., 2017). Researchers suggest that to be able to identify inclusionary barriers more accurately, it may be advantageous to consider student outcomes (i.e., learning and well-being) (Loreman, 2014) alongside school characteristics (i.e., visionary leadership, collaboration, and parent involvement) (Lipsky & Gartner, 1996). This recommendation aligns with research that suggests that more favourable outcomes occur for students and stakeholders when student voice is included to create a unified focus, compared to traditional top-down approaches (Graham, 2020) that are done "to and for" students rather than "with" students.

Creating Certainty Through Student Participation

The benefits of viewing inclusion as a participatory student-led experience are supported by several distinct but complementary viewpoints, including international human rights definitions (i.e., Article 24, UNRCPD), social advocacy (i.e., "nothing about us, without us"), research on evidence-best practice (i.e., Hume et al., 2021), and the views of autistic students who clearly state that they want voice and choice in their education (Goodall, 2020; Lebenhagen et al., 2022).

Teachers, practitioners, and parents are in an advantageous position to establish inclusionary certainty for autistic students by using frameworks, such as those provided in this guide, that integrate stakeholder priorities with current research on evidence-based practices in autism and inclusion. Furthermore, since participatory autism research is still in its infancy and is either inconsistently or inadequately included in post-secondary programs for educators and practitioners, frameworks such as these help close the research-to-practice gap in timely and responsive ways that account for individual student and school factors.

Therefore, as research on self-reported school experiences and priorities continues to advance, autistic students currently share that communication, connection with teachers and peers, access to safe classroom environments, engaging curriculum, and the chance to collaborate with education partners are critically important to them, which notably is not different from the needs and desires of most, if not all, students.

References

Adams, D. (2022). Child and parental mental health as correlates of school non-attendance and school refusal in children on the autism Spectrum. *Journal of Autism and Developmental Disorders*, *52*(8), 3353–3365. https://doi.org/10.1007/s10803-021-05211-5

Brock, M. E., Dynia, J. M., Dueker, S. A., & Barczak, M. A. (2020). Teacher-reported priorities and practices for students with autism: Characterizing the research-to-practice gap. *Focus on Autism and Other Developmental Disabilities, 35*(2), 67–78. https://doi.org/10.1177/1088357619881217

Cascio, M. A., Weiss, J. A., Racine, E., & The Autism Research Ethics Task Force (2020). Person-oriented ethics for autism research: Creating best practices through engagement with autism and autistic communities. *Autism: The International Journal of Research and Practice, 24*(7), 1676–1690. https://doi.org/10.1177/1362361320918763

Chown, N., Robinson, J., Beardon, L., Downing, J., Hughes, L., Leatherland, J.... & MacGregor, D. (2017). Improving research about us, with us: a draft framework for inclusive autism research. *Disability and Society*, 32(5), 720–734. https://doi.org/10.1080/09687599.2017.1320273

Filippello, P., Buzzai, C., Costa, S., & Sorrenti, L. (2019). School refusal and absenteeism: Perception of teacher behaviors, psychological basic needs, and academic achievement. *Frontiers in Psychology, 10*. https://doi.org/10.3389/fpsyg.2019.01471

Gómez-Marí, I., Sanz-Cervera, P., & Tárraga-Mínguez, R. (2022). Teachers' attitudes toward autism spectrum disorder: A systematic review. *Education Sciences, 12*(2), 138. https://doi.org/10.3390/educsci12020138

Goodall, C. (2020). Inclusion is a feeling, not a place: a qualitative study exploring autistic young people's conceptualisations of inclusion. *International Journal of Inclusive Education, 24*(12), 1285–1310. https://doi.org/10.1080/13603116.2018.1523475

Graham, L. J., Medhurst, M., Tancredi, H., Spandagou, I., & Walton, E. (2020). Fundamental concepts of inclusive education. In *Inclusive Education for the 21st Century*. https://doi.org/10.4324/9781003116073-3

Hume, K., Steinbrenner, J. R., Odom, S. L., Morin, K. L., Nowell, S. W., Tomaszewski, B.... & Savage, M. N. (2021). Evidence-based practices for children, youth, and young adults with autism: Third generation review. *Journal of Autism and Developmental Disorders, 51*(11), 4013–4032. https://doi.org/10.1007/s10803-020-04844-2

Jackson, S. L. J., Hart, L., & Volkmar, F. R. (2018). Preface: Special Issue—College experiences for students with autism spectrum disorder. *Journal of Autism and Developmental Disorders, 48*, 639–642. https://doi.org/10.1007/s10803-018-3463-7

Lebenhagen, C., Krishnamurthy, A., Ramanath, J., & Choate, C. (2022). *Speechless dream: Narratives on autism, inclusion and hope*. Friesen Press.

Leifler, E., Carpelan, G., Zakresvska, A., Bölte, S., & Jonsson, U. (2021). Does the learning environment 'make the grade'? A systematic review of accommodations for children on the autism spectrum in mainstream school. *Scandinavian Journal of Occupational Therapy, 28*(8), 582-597. https://doi.org.10.1080/11038128.2020.183214

Lipsky, D. K., & Gartner, A. (1996). Inclusion, school restructuring, and the remaking of American society. *Harvard Educational Review, 66*(4). https://doi.org/10.17763/haer.66.4.3686k7x734246430

Loreman, T. (2014). Measuring inclusive education outcomes in Alberta, Canada. *International Journal of Inclusive Education, 18*(5), 459–483. https://doi.org/10.1080/13603116.2013.788223

Nilholm, C. (2021). Research about inclusive education in 2020: How can we improve our theories in order to change practice? *European Journal of Special Needs Education, 36*(3). https://doi.org/10.1080/08856257.2020.1754547

Sharma, U., Furlonger, B., & Forlin, C. (2019). The impact of funding models on the education of students with autism spectrum disorder. *Australasian Journal of Special and Inclusive Education, 43*(1). https://doi.org/10.1017/jsi.2019.1

Simón, C., Martínez-Rico, G., McWilliam, R. A., & Cañadas, M. (2022). Attitudes toward inclusion and benefits perceived by families in schools with students with autism spectrum disorders. *Journal of Autism and Developmental Disorders*. https://doi.org/10.1007/s10803-022-05491-5

StEvens, C. (2022). The lived experience of autistic teachers: A review of the literature. *International Journal of Inclusive Education*. https://doi.org/10.1080/13603116.2022.2041738

UN Committee on the Rights of Persons with Disabilities (CRPD), *General comment No. 4. (2016), Article 24: Right to inclusive education*, 2 September 2016, CRPD/C/GC/4, https://www.refworld.org/docid/57c977e34.html

Vincent, J., Potts, M., Fletcher, D., Hodges, S., Howells, J., Mitchell, A.... & Ledger, T. (2017). 'I think autism is like running on Windows while everyone else is a Mac': Using a participatory action research approach with students on the autistic spectrum to rearticulate autism and the lived experience of university, *Educational Action Research*, *25*(2), 300–315. https://doi.org/10.1080/09650792.2016.1153978

Watkins, L., Ledbetter-Cho, K., O'Reilly, M., Barnard-Brak, L., & Garcia-Grau, P. (2019). Interventions for students with autism in inclusive settings: A best-evidence synthesis and meta-analysis. *Psychological Bulletin*, *145*(5). https://doi.org/10.1037/bul0000190

Index

For Product Safety Concerns and Information please contact our EU
representative GPSR@taylorandfrancis.com
Taylor & Francis Verlag GmbH, Kaufingerstraße 24, 80331 München, Germany